The Obsidian Mirror

An Adult Healing From Incest

Louise M. Wisechild

SEAL PRESS

Library of Congress Catalog-in-Publication Data

Wisechild, Louise M.
   The obsidian mirror

     1. Incest victims—United States—Case studies.
Adult child abuse victims—United States—Case studies.   I. Title.
HQ72.U53W7   1988   306.7′77′0922   88-18395
ISBN 1-878067-39-7

Cover art by Sarah Teofanov.
Design by Clare Conrad.
Printed in the United States of America.
10   9   8   7   6
Second edition, 1993.

Acknowledgements

Many people helped me as I wrote this book. I am grateful to the wisdom, humor and support of my friends and therapists and their willingness to be included in my life and in my writing.

The women I've seen as clients helped me keep writing by telling me their stories and sharing their pain and their healing.

The work of Hilary Bolles, Nina Petrulis, Ginny NiCarthy, Bonnie Olson, Vickie Sears, Kim Greene, Mary Newbill, Jane Klassen and Alice Miller has contributed enormously to my understanding of healing and growth.

I thank the following women who read early manuscripts: Sharon Doubiago, Diane Hood, Gail Fairfield, Deb Clark, Robyn Johnson, Judith Barrington, Pat Andrus, Cara Newoman, Pat Pederson, Barbara Finn and Marianne Twyman. Pesha Gertler spent innumerable Shabbats giving me energy and advice. Sarah Sarai, who knows when a paragraph is repeating itself, gave me valuable assistance in the later stages of editing. And Ron Porter's ability to diagnose computer problems and translate them into English over the phone saved me from tearing my hair out.

Lastly, I am grateful for the calm and patience of the women who work at Seal Press. My editors, Barbara Wilson and Faith Conlon, consistently offered me wise suggestions and encouragement exactly when I needed it. Their efforts have made this a better book and publishing an empowering experience.

Contents

To
Ginny, Jane, Vickie and Emm

Preface to the 1993 Edition

Ten years ago, when I began writing *The Obsidian Mirror*, there was little written information about incest and few accounts by survivors who were recovering repressed memories. Until recently, psychology assumed that incest was infrequent. This was despite the fact that many of Freud's clients reported accounts of childhood sexual abuse. In the five years since the publication of *The Obsidian Mirror*, many more women and men have questioned their amnesia around matters of their childhood and found experiences of incest.

Freud eventually denied his patients' accounts of their childhood. His patients were the nieces and daughters of his friends. He did not wish to believe that his friends would commit these crimes against children.

I have never met a survivor who wanted to be an incest victim. Healing from incest is hard and takes a long time. It takes us into the cut-off, taboo realms of emotion, sexuality and inner knowing. Finding our stories causes us to ask ourselves honest searching questions about why we are as we are and why we treat other people the ways that we do. We do not set out wanting to find forgotten or minimized experiences of assault and betrayal at the hands and genitals of our families. Rather, we begin this journey of self-knowing because we feel crazy or lost or dead or wrong. Asking "Why?" takes us to the circumstances of our lives, both past and present. We question our beliefs, our postures and our roots. We find incest, just as the women who saw Freud also reported this sexual violence against them.

The Victorians of Freud's time did not talk about the violence occurring behind their closed doors. They did not question the oppressive treatment of women and children. Today this violence is ever more visible. But still, no one is held accountable.

Healing from incest is part of healing violence. In healing, we travel from regarding ourselves as victims to treating ourselves as if we matter. This journey rewards us with a sense of self, a right to our body, the power of having a history and the fearlessness in our voice. With this awareness of ourselves comes the ability and the desire to be respectful of each other, to raise our children non-violently and to exercise our personal power. On this path of healing, we become people who will not rape or allow rape.

Our experiences as incest victims should stimulate a genuine concern for the safety of children within the family. Our stories should encourage research into parental attitudes toward their own sexuality. This emergence of memory should sensitize the larger culture toward issues of sexual abuse. The stories of our journey to heal and to parent and to live with more consciousness and caring should be news.

Instead the media is embracing the "false memory syndrome." Our culture would still rather not believe that people we know are capable of sexual violence, whether they are parents or doctors or ministers or therapists.

For me, knowing about the incest of my childhood was profoundly important for my healing. It made sense of my pain, my fear, my beliefs about my self and my relationship with my parents. This was a truth I found in my cells and my blood.

Those who wish to deny survivors' accounts of their own memories claim that we are talked into it by our therapists or that we have invented it for reasons unrelated to our childhood. Yet for twenty-nine years, my mother told me that she and the men who sexually abused me were good people, family, and that I was crazy and bad because of my depression and anger. No one was in a better position to brainwash me than she. Ultimately my own feelings demanded acknowledgement. Remembering was not an experience I was "talked into." The body sensations, emotions, flashbacks and mental pictures of this sexual abuse were the vivid record of my experience.

We live in a culture that does not exercise its memory. As a child, I learned to forget about the past as those before me had done. I was told that in the Bible, Lot's wife was turned to salt as punishment for looking into the past. And yet salt is an essential element. We need this salt to help us look again, to ask questions of our past individually and collectively. Only from this sort of examination can we learn from what has gone before us. Denial is the opposite of memory. Memory is the key to growth.

Coming to terms with the prevalence of incest demands an examination into the very real behaviors of the patriarchal family. The April 17, 1993, issue of *Newsweek* featured a couple, Ray and Shirley Souza, who were accused by both their children and their grandchildren of sexual abuse. This couple was convicted in a criminal case against them. Yet, unlike its coverage of other crimes, *Newsweek* suggested that the Souza's were the victims of a "witch hunt." Despite the verdict and the fact that people do not bring criminal charges against parents who treated them well, *Newsweek* asked, "When does the fight to protect our kids go too far?" I would answer that the challenge is to listen to what the children and the grown children of abuse are telling us. That's where the protection begins. We have hardly started.

Incest is one part of the widespread sexual violence of our times. Politically, this challenges the institutionalization of crimes against children and women. Incest is one legacy of the patriarchal system which regarded children as the possessions of their fathers. Our culture romanticizes children, but it does not care for them. Instead, to be called "childish" or a "baby" is an insult.

For us to eliminate incest requires each individual to examine his or her own behaviors and attitudes toward sexuality and children. Healing the violence requires that we acknowledge our wounds and examine our behavior so that we are not mindlessly repeating what happened to us. Healing insists that we name the violence we have done to ourselves and to each other and that we take responsibility for our actions.

Knowing my story and committing myself to healing has changed my life. My scars are the tattoos of a powerful woman. I began with terror and found boldness. I started with self-hating and discovered inner knowing. I emerged from my childhood distrustful and afraid to care and now I have loving relationships and passion. When I was twenty-nine, I was quiet. Now, at thirty-nine, I am loud.

Knowing ourselves gives us authority. We are the only experts on our experiences and our feelings. This self-knowing does not come easily in this culture of denial. But it does come as we take courage and time: to honor our feelings, to listen to our bodies and to believe the children that we were.

May 27, 1993

The Story

The Obsidian Mirror is my story of healing from incest. It begins in the time before remembering, when despair felt like a heavy stone inside of me. Like many people, I had been taught to "put the past behind" me, as if the examination of my own herstory would make matters worse. It's not surprising that "forgetting" about painful events is a common form of self-protection. Myths of the perfect family and therapies that hold the child responsible for the quality of her childhood make it especially difficult to break the taboo on examining one's own past. I found that I didn't know how to see myself when I looked into a mirror.

This story begins in 1978 when I was a twenty-four-year-old graduate student at Stanford. I believed then that I was a bad person. I assumed I had been born that way. I didn't understand that I was living with beliefs and decisions formed when I was a child trying to make sense of the world. The self-hating and intense depression I was experiencing were indicators of the sexual abuse in my past. I did not remember this abuse until several years later.

I started writing this book in 1983. Six months before I began writing, I had begun remembering the sexual abuse perpetrated by my stepfather, grandfather and uncle. At the time, I didn't know what I would discover about healing nor what the next steps on my journey were. I wanted to convey the extraordinary experience of reopening the closed doors of my past, of finding form in the darkness. It often felt as though I were reliving the actual experiences of abuse. My body was flooded with kinesthetic memories as my muscles began releasing long-held tension and pain. Nor did these incidents confine themselves to a convenient schedule. I found myself having flashbacks in restaurants, while walking down the sidewalk and with my lover as well as in therapy. I felt the pain, betrayal, fear and rage of my past. It shadowed every event of my adult life. During that time, my past was more vivid than my daily existence.

It's only recently that we've allowed ourselves to talk about "incest." But the word incest does not convey the depth of the violation. For me, telling the secret was not saying, "I am an incest victim." Rather, the secret was gagging on a penis in a five-year-old mouth, cringing when the bedroom doorknob turned and feeling shame at being called a "cunt." It is the details of memory that cause specific fears and tensions. For this reason, I have included what I remembered as well as my process of remembering.

For many of us, reading about child abuse is difficult. Since statistics indicate that one-third of all women experienced some type of sexual abuse as children, reading this story may trigger memories and feelings from your past.* Others may be horrified to consider the cruelty that we are capable of as human beings. I chose to be faithful to the chronology of my healing as a guide to other women who may take similar journeys. If, as the reader, you find yourself feeling overwhelmed by this material, you might want to read the last two chapters first as a reminder that the other side of pain is healing.

The first four chapters speak of the time before remembering, when I first started therapy and began to explore the depth of my feelings. Regardless of the circumstances of my adult life, I was unhappy and afraid. As a child, I'd decided that nothing was safe and that no one could be trusted. I was unable to experience pleasure even when the events in my life were pleasant and non-threatening. It was an awakening to begin to feel the motion of my body when I took a walk. It was like

---

* See Ellen Bass and Laura Davis, *The Courage to Heal: A Guide for Women Survivors of Child Sexual Abuse*, New York, Harper and Row, 1988.

coming alive after a death of the spirit. I broke through numbness to feeling, but I didn't know why I felt so much pain and fear.

Chapters 5 though 12 talk about my journey of remembering and include specific memories of sexual abuse. Incest shaped my child sense of the world so dramatically that I had been unable to sort through what was happening to me, as if the light I needed in order to see had been totally blocked out. Remembering abruptly brought confusion, emotional turmoil and my body's kinesthetic responses to the incest into my adult life. As I remembered, I moved from fear and grief to rage and resolve. I began to celebrate my own sensitivity instead of condemning myself for having been hurt.

Subsequent chapters discuss empowerment, the confrontation of my family and the reclamation of self. As an incest victim I had focused on daily survival. It was hard to realistically imagine the future. Remembering allowed me to heal. I understood, for the first time, why I reacted to life with anxiety and distrust. I learned that my suicidal impulses and chronic depressions were symptoms based on actual events. With this understanding, I began to reclaim my body, safety and creativity. Healing is the journey of bringing life back to the self.

At the same time as I began this book, my work as a massage therapist had shifted from Swedish massage to specialized work with women who had been child victims of sexual abuse. The variety of their experience was both similar and dissimilar to mine. I found that each of us felt that we were the only ones this untold horror had been inflicted upon. Their families, like mine, appeared to be "normal" American families. The depth of injury as well as the enormity of grief and rage expressed by these women left no doubt that my clients had also been deeply affected by the weight of the secrets locked inside of them.

I have been as honest as possible in recounting my experiences. This is a true story which uses the devices of characterization and setting to convey my internal processes. I use the concept of inner voices as a way of illustrating the complex aspects of the personality. The use of inner voices made it possible to express my internal conflicts as well as my varying responses to life situations. The settings of Well, Pit, Dust and Tree provided visual images which matched my kinesthetic awareness. I came to understand healing as the changes in these relationships.

Incest is not separate from other abusive messages in our social culture. I couldn't write about incest apart from what I was told as a girl-child growing up in the 50s and 60s. The religious attitudes of my childhood, the myths surrounding the "normal" family and my experience at school helped keep the incest a secret. These messages reinforced the self-hating images I saw in my internal mirror. In addition, each member of my family had a role in the dynamic of secrecy. Until recently, the responsibility for sexual abuse was placed upon the mother instead of on the offender. Although my mother was complicit, this is not necessarily true for other victims of incest.

Healing is not an event confined to the therapeutic process. My search through memory, the confrontation of my family and my subsequent growth could not be separated from my life as a whole. Instead, healing was woven into my work, into my changing relationship with my lover and my friends and into my search for a new understanding of spirituality.

In order to respect the privacy of others involved in my story, I have changed the names of my friends, lover and therapists. The clients and bodyworkers I refer to are a composite of many different women with whom I have worked. I have also changed the names of family members and fictionalized the places where I grew up.

Despite my positive experience with therapy, the history of therapeutic work with sexually abused women has not been a healing one. The memories of many women have been and continue to be labeled as "fantasy" by therapists while their terror is dismissed as "neurotic." Women are still being committed to mental institutions on the basis of their symptoms as incest victims. In choosing a therapist, it is crucial to distinguish between those who heal and those who invalidate the experience of their clients.

For me, healing required long-term verbal and body therapies. I was extremely fortunate to find feminist therapists who supported my growth and challenged me to move beyond victimization. Their wisdom and support of the integrity of my healing allowed me to celebrate my own inner knowing. In this book, I refer to them as "healers."

Obsidian is formed when lava cools quickly and without crystals, forming a solid black stone. Before remembering the incest, it felt like a black rock weighted my belly, holding secrets and haunting me with a heavy mystery that I couldn't name. As I began to work with stones and explore their healing properties, I learned that obsidian is believed to protect gentle-hearted people from abuse. I realized that "forgetting" about the incest by secreting it within my inner darkness had protected me as a child. But obsidian is also said to develop internal and external vision. As I learned to look into my self, I saw that my despair was not the darkness, but the injuries hidden within it.

When obsidian is polished, it is reflective; a glossy black mirror of volcanic glass. Looking at myself in an obsidian mirror, I see my face circled with black. After several minutes of looking into the obsidian, my eyes turn inward, peering inside myself, meeting the blackness within me. Ancient Mexicans used mirrors of obsidian for visions. Some believe that gazing into polished obsidian brings whatever an individual needs to deal with to the surface of consciousness. Looking into the mirror, I saw buried scenes from my past. As I continued to look, I found new possibilities. I saw that darkness is a sacred part of my woman's body. I learned that I could reclaim this body as my own.

Writing this book challenged me to articulate issues and feelings that were hard to face. At other times, it was only in writing that I came to define and celebrate the changes I was undergoing. Creativity has been a partner to my healing, transforming pain to power. As a child, creativity made it possible to adapt to my situation so that I could survive. As an adult, coming to a new wholeness within myself has been both a healing and a creative journey.

1 THE VOICE

SINCE it is inappropriate to discuss religion, I will begin there.

My mother used to say, "Never talk about religion or sex or politics in front of company." Years later, it's still hard to break the tight bonds of my upbringing. I pretend to have outgrown her words. I tell myself that surely I've become more sophisticated in my approach to the dilemmas of my mid-20s. I am after all, a graduate student at a prestigious university. I came here to study politics and justice. I think a lot about ending poverty and war. I talk about unpleasant truths my family never mentioned. But I don't tell anyone about my suspicion that God is out to get me. I still don't talk about religion. I think that I should have matured enough to stop worrying about God and to start putting my energy into something constructive. But God is a shadow. He even followed me here, to Stanford.

I was excited when I was accepted to graduate school: small town girl from Bryce, Washington, hits academic big-time. For a year I'd had an eight-by-ten postcard of the campus scotch-taped to the wall above my desk. The palm trees fanned a path leading to neatly tiled roofs and trimmed lawns. I imagined that graduate school would be orderly and intellectual. I imagined that I would blissfully inhabit a benevolent world of ideas.

But the first thing I noticed when I got here were the black and white photographs of the 1906 California earthquake mounted beside the main doors to the university. The chapel is shown standing untouched amidst the sandstone rubble of academic buildings. After I registered, the graduate adviser led me to the basement where the first year students shared offices.

3

Partitions of metal shelving surrounded rows of wooden desks, leaving eerie shadows in the artificial light. Now I hold my breath on brief visits to my office, haunted by the specter of God shaking the aging building, burying me and my books in an act of His will.

As it turns out, religion and graduate school have a lot in common. Each has a set of rules and acceptable standards. Like church, the classroom has an aura of solemnity. A hush descends when the elder professor enters the classroom, like a minister taking his place behind a pulpit. If I'm not on my best behavior, I'll get punished, just as my grandfather delivered God's punishment if I played too much when I was a kid. I'm afraid that I still don't know how to be good enough.

In Sunday school, a picture showed little kids sitting on Jesus' knees. I sat in a row of tiny wooden chairs and stared at Jesus' sad brown eyes. I bowed my head and whispered long earnest prayers to that picture. I wanted to feel good. But I knew by then that I wasn't good enough for Him to listen to me. I knew that Jesus only held good children, not children that asked too many questions or talked back to their parents. God sent bad children to hell, that's what my grandfather said. Jesus would know I was bad because He could see inside of me, past my Sunday school clothes and my skin. Inside I was full of darkness and bad smells. Trying to be good didn't make it go away.

I've spent a lot of time trying to leave God behind me. I tried being an atheist in junior high and an agnostic in college. So it's disturbing to admit that I became a graduate student for the same reasons I prayed to Jesus nineteen years ago. I want someone to tell me I'm good enough. I need saving. I lack the nerve to try something else. Some persistent part of my past lives on and I can't seem to shake it.

I'm convinced this is related to an inner voice I hear telling me I'm bad. She is a part of my personality who threatens me with repeating critical thoughts. I've named this judgemental voice Sarah. When I close my eyes and imagine what she looks like, I see a prematurely old woman with a tight mouth and a worried forehead. Sarah has told me that I'm bad and hopeless for as long as I can remember. She often quotes God and my grandfather against me.

After my mother's divorce, my brother Jim and I lived with my mother and my grandparents. I was four years old when I decided that Grandpa was God. He had fierce white hair and stern blue eyes. He quoted the Bible a lot, especially "sow as ye shall reap." If I caught a cold or skinned my knee, Grandpa said that God was punishing me for being disobedient. Like God, my grandfather had an indisputable list of what constituted "bad." Making too much noise, playing at the wrong time, talking back and swearing were a smattering of the forbidden sins. Grandpa dispensed discipline. My mother delivered me to him for judgement when I stole a candy bar from Safeway. He pulled my pants down and spanked me with a hand the size of a catcher's mitt. The sound was like thunder.

When I was growing up I didn't understand that each family had a different God. I thought that all families were the same. My family's God threatened hell like the Fundamentalists, had a lot of rules like the Presbyterians, and was political like the right-wing evangelicals my grandfather listened to on the radio. Although I was surrounded by talk of God, it was considered a sin to debate His existence or to ask questions about where in the sky He actually lived. He had a lot of rules, but only grownups got to know exactly what they were. As a child, I discovered them only after breaking one, like the correct interpretation of an essay question revealed after the test. Like the "founding fathers," the male authority of God was taken for granted. I couldn't imagine God ever laughing at Himself or changing the color of the sky just for fun. I supposed that His forehead was gathered in deep disapproving furrows as he sat on a gold throne watching people commit sins.

I'm afraid of my professors, just as I feared my grandfather. I can't seem to relax around them like other students who engage them in casual conversations. My mouth dries up.

The sentences barely stumble over my tongue when I try to speak. Sarah makes it worse. "You'll flunk out," she says inside my mind. "They'll think you're stupid. They'll take away your fellowship. You won't make it."

I feel Sarah in a tight mound on my right shoulder. I feel tense because of her, as if she were poking my inner muscles with a pointing finger. She says that I'd never get anything done without her. "You better. You should. You'll never. Try harder. You can't," she scolds. Even though she's never nice to me, I can't imagine life without her.

When I was a child, I thought I could make Sarah go away. I tried ignoring my grandfather. I scribbled on offering envelopes during the church service. I pretended that my hair could keep their words out of my ears. But the words leaked inside. Sarah spoke even louder. She had already become a part of me, freely voicing her disparaging opinions at every opportunity.

Sometimes Sarah talks like my mother. My mother believed that parents were God's ambassadors. She also believed that there was something especially wrong with me. When the corners of my mouth sagged, she'd nudge me and say "smile." When I told her I didn't like Uncle Jack, she told me that I wasn't being nice. Then she'd look at me and say, "Where have I failed!" sighing deeply. It was clear that she was referring to my failure, not her own. Sarah keeps telling me that I'm a failure now, even though I'm twenty-four and supposed to be a successful adult.

I suspect that other people have voices inside of them too. That's why people don't act the same all the time. A lot of my friends act one way in class and another when we're having lunch together. My mother acted differently toward me than toward anyone else. When she talked on the phone, she used a pleasant voice to chat about the weather and poor Mrs. Kramer who'd just broken her hip. But my mother had a whole other part of herself that only came out around me. It was a loud, mad voice that told me I dressed wrong and was too fat, that my hair was ugly and that I'd lose all my friends if they knew how awful I was. When I got older she told me that I was "crazy" and threatened to send me to reform school. Sarah says mean things to me too. I wish I didn't believe that they were true.

My mother said that she loved me. She said that God was love. I don't really know what love feels like though. I think that's because something's wrong with me. At least that's what Sarah says. I've decided that love isn't really important.

I had hoped that graduate school might make me feel worthwhile, as long as I'm going to live without love. But I seem to have lost the ideals I came here with. I find myself depending on coffee in place of ambition. Stacks of books on the table demand immediate-before-tomorrow reading. Stacks of books on the floor should be read today too but they will probably merge with assignments to do tomorrow. Shelves of books on voting, crime and war statistics climb the walls of my room. Marx next to Rawls and De Coupeville. At night I am afraid that I am really in a library, asleep and unable to wake up. The doors are locked and I cannot escape.

◊

When I turned twelve, I decided again that I'd had quite enough of Sarah. I wanted her to get out of my personality, which she adamantly refused to do. So a new part of me began to speak. "I don't care, I don't care, I don't care," this voice chanted like a demonstrator shouting slogans. I named this inner voice Fuckit. When she speaks, I defiantly harden my chest and poke out my chin. When I visualize Fuckit, I see her wearing flannel shirts, jeans and loud socks. I like her even though Sarah makes me feel guilty when I listen to her.

Fuckit hates being told what to do. "Fuck you!" she says, "Leave me alone! I won't listen to Sarah! I don't care if I do go to hell!"

Despite the vehemence of Fuckit's protests, Sarah has more authority. Between Fuckit's periodic bouts of adolescent

atheism, I was born again to the call of Billy Graham, saved
during the credits of *The Cross and the Switchblade* and saved a
third time in the kitchen of the local Young Life leaders. I
joined the Pentecostals and spoke in tongues. I kept wanting
God's help. I wanted a divinity that I could talk with. "Dear
God, make it okay. Please make me feel better," I'd pray. My
words tumbled to a foam pillow grave. In the Bible, God
seemed only to talk to people who fasted for forty days or who
sacrificed their first born son. Praying was no more effective
than wishing.

Fuckit wished that my parents would be killed in a car
wreck so that I could be adopted by the kind of family that I saw
on TV. The mother would come in and sit on the edge of the
bed. She'd ask me, "What's wrong?" and wrap a comforting
arm around my shoulder. I'd melt into her sweater. She'd hold
me while I cried.

Sarah said it was silly to want that. I learned not to pray for
a fatal car wreck when I was five. That was when I told my
mother that I wished she was dead.

"Be careful or God will hear you," she said, squinting her
eyes close to my face. "God will kill you for saying that." God
seemed better at punishing than at helping.

Sarah still threatens me from within, citing an endless
string of disasters in His name, "You'll flunk. That car will run
over you. That man will stab you with a knife."

"To hell with God!" Fuckit replies.

"You'll die for saying that," Sarah reiterates. "You're bad
inside."

I can't argue with that. I hate it when Sarah reminds me of
the dark, rotting mass that spreads from the secret recesses of
my stomach into my chest. The heaviness is like dough that
cannot rise. I imagine it smelling like an open sewer. I used to
think that if I ate enough, I could hide it under layers of white
flesh. But the darkness grew even thicker, like a sticky black
asphalt covered with litter. I know it's an evil that lives inside.
It keeps growing bigger, like a curse. I feel trapped and small

inside of it. I don't know when it began because I don't remember when I didn't feel this way. I can't seem to make it go away. I can't ever let anyone know it's inside of me. I try not to notice it. When I do, the darkness makes me feel like dying. I know it's not normal. It keeps me from fitting in. If anyone likes me, it's only because they don't know about the darkness and the smells.

◇

When I converted to academia, I hoped that outside knowledge might drown out the voices and help me forget the darkness. My mind is a gadget, spilling out thoughts like a machine. Sometimes I can pretend that I'm a walking head, without a body to bother with. I try to make myself believe that rational thought is all that matters. I've always been "good" at school, that's how I got in here. But I can't believe I'm good enough to be here. Lately, the doubts have gotten worse.

Fuckit responds with rebellion: "I'm fucking sick of studying," she declares. "I don't give a flying fuck about the definition of a definition. Sarah is a dictator!" But when Sarah threatens me with failure, Fuckit is silenced.

It's getting harder to ignore my body too. My stomach hurts with a dull persistence. It started last week, after the student health doctor diagnosed me as having a pelvic inflammatory disease. The antibiotics she gave me cured that, but my belly squeezes me awake before my alarm in the morning. A persistent dissatisfaction lurks behind my ever-operating Mr. Coffee machine. It follows me through red-eyed visits to the library and into the refuge of the women's bathroom. It feels like a large rock is bouncing around in my stomach, right in the center of the dark rotten feeling.

I decide that the best course is to ignore it.

"I have been here a long time," the weight in my stomach replies.

That's a surprise. My stomach has never talked to me before. "Well, I'll just go back to not noticing you," I tell it. The last thing I need is another voice.

My stomach tightens.

"This is finals week, get the fuck out of here!" Fuckit yells from inside of me. "Leave me alone!" Fuckit thinks that bodies are a nuisance. She'd rather ignore the dark place and the pain and just yell at Sarah.

"Psssss." It's that voice again. It seems to come from under a heaviness around my navel.

"Go away!" I eat an old-fashioned donut, down a cup of coffee and smoke seven cigarettes. "I will drown you out!"

"PSSSSS!" the voice responds, like someone trying to get my attention from a street corner.

Fuckitt hisses back, "Go away!"

"PSSSS PSSSS PSSSS!!"

I feel worse than ever. I begin asking myself questions. Why am I in school? Why do I feel so horrible? My sense of inferiority intensifies. I am unbearably self-conscious about my appearance. "Something's wrong with me," I think. "You're bad," Sarah says. The thoughts and questions repeat themselves over and over like commercials on TV.

I start to think about killing myself. I drive around the hills above Palo Alto instead of working on my term papers. I dream of leaping off the highway into a peaceful death.

Sarah tells me I'm a failure for driving around the hills like this. She also tells me that I "deserve to feel bad." "Just smile," she insists, "everything's fine. You're just making this up. Quit being so selfish and think about other people. You could be blind and homeless, you know."

I consider death anyway. Death is a wonderful place where there are no stomachs and therefore no stomachaches. Nor any schools or conflict or yelling voices. In death I could stop saying, "I can't." I could stop worrying that I was saying the wrong thing to the wrong person. I could stop agonizing over what everyone else thinks about me.

This isn't the first time that I've considered suicide. I spent

a lot of time thinking of dying when I was a child. In my imag-
ination, I have shot myself, drugged myself, leapt from bridges
and carbon monoxided myself. Whenever I've felt hopeless,
I've thought of killing myself. I can't imagine any other solution.

"So suicide is your savior?" the voice asks through the
pounding of my stomach.

"Who said that?" I decide to have it out once and for all.
It's clear that no amount of donuts is going to silence this voice.
I park the car in a viewpoint to indicate my intentions.

A fist beats up and down inside the tight darkness of my
stomach. Closing my eyes feels like drinking too much wine;
everything spins. I'm not sure who this voice is, but she's certainly tenacious.

"Why are you at this school?" the voice inquires. "You do
not seem to like it." The voice enunciates each word carefully.
Coming from her, the question almost sounds reasonable.

"Are you kidding?" I shake my head. "There's nothing
else to do. Being smart isn't exactly a skill you know. It's the
only thing I'm good at doing."

"I thought you had other visions once," the voice says. "I
recall you deciding to pursue a creative path. You were deter-
mined to make a difference."

It hurts to remember old dreams. As the voice speaks,
nearly forgotten longings re-emerge. "I can't do those things,"
I tell the voice. "I'm not good enough."

"Well, as long as you are considering death, you might as
well try listening to me," the voice says dryly. "You certainly
have nothing to lose."

"Well, you just better keep her in line then. . . " Inside of
me, Sarah clears her throat and is about to list my many well-
known faults.

"We will start in a circle," the voice replies.

I begin to feel better about this voice. She reminds me of
the times I've felt intuitive, as if I knew more than I thought I
knew.

"Wait a minute," Fuckit objects. "Who the fuck are you anyway? We don't need any more religion. I don't need anybody else telling me what to do."

"I do not intend to tell you what to do." Now the voice speaks softly. Small cracks sound in the timbre of her speaking, as if she is old and her voice has weathered. "I have been collecting your experiences. It is time to review them. It is time for you to see." She sounds definite.

"It doesn't help to look backwards," I tell her. That's what my mother's always said.

"It's a sin," Sarah adds. "In the Bible, Lot's wife looked back and she was turned to salt."

"You carry your past within your self," the voice says firmly. "You have been in school for a long while now. It is time to start learning something."

As she speaks I see pictures of my experience in graduate school:

♦*Memory*. I am at a meeting. I am the only woman. The professors and male students are talking about the Stanford football team. I am sealed into my chair, looking at the floor, searching my mind for a sentence that will let me in to the conversation. ♦

As I see the memory, my body responds as if I were sitting in the chair again. My neck pushes my head down, my shoulders hunch up, my mind frantically searches for words that have vanished. The right words are missing.

♦*Memory*. I am in the black house with orange trim that I share with two roommates. They are whispering. I'm sure that they've noticed something awful about me. I close my door softly so that they won't know that I'm home. I am afraid to be seen on my way to the bathroom. I search the bathroom mirror for clues to who I am. ♦

My heart beats fast in remembering. The car feels stuffy. "They hate you," I hear Sarah repeating inside my head. I want to hide, my breathing is shallow even though I'm just sitting in the car. The memories make me realize how uncomfortable I've felt here.

I look down into smog obscuring the valley. Sarah and Fuckit are suddenly quiet. Their silence makes my body feel calmer. The immediacy of the ache in my stomach has subsided. My mind is empty as if a breeze swept it clean of thoughts. I feel like crying for something that is lost or missing. But I never cry.

"Do you think I'll make it?" I finally ask. "I've always thought I would die before I turned thirty."

"Sure," the voice says. "I'm sure."

◇

When I quit graduate school, I didn't know that Sure Voice had already arranged for my continuing education.

2 THE BODY

I don't miss graduate school. Deadlines and excessive concern over my academic image gradually fade from Sarah's critical commentary. My textbooks quietly collect dust. I write in my journal again, a practice abandoned to Sarah's schedule in graduate school.

Fuckit's in rebel-heaven. For the first time, that part of me can do anything she wants. Fuckit likes to talk with strangers, especially those who've been labeled as outcasts. I spend late nights in downtown twenty-four hour restaurants talking to strangers seated at the counter. One night, I meet a man with green sequins embedded in his teeth. He carries a tape recorder covered with rocks and novelties from gum machines. He says this is the story of his life; it's about being from outer space. I wonder if he's forgotten his real story. I seem to have forgotten the details of mine. Maybe everyone's past is only a hazy blur.

Fuckit is fascinated with prostitution too. I used to think about being a prostitute. It doesn't seem odd to sell the body. It's only another thing. But I could never get away with dressing like the women on street corners. Instead, I work nightshift downtown. A waitress in a pizza parlor where prostitutes and narcotic dealers buy slices of pepperoni pizza for seventy-five cents. Some nights the cook and I drink gin while we work. Fuckit enjoys accomplices in deviant behavior.

Sure Voice encourages my exploration, sometimes even silencing Sarah's outrage. I still test God for punishment though. Just in case. The experience of excitement is new. I don't know how to trust it. I'm afraid that He will take it away.

14

◇

The only thing that surprises me now is that Sure Voice
and I found each other amidst the clattering circumstances of
my upbringing and the general societal confusion over what
constitutes the divine. She's hard to describe. She may be one
way on Thursday and a different way on Friday. "Life can not
be held in lines," she says. There's something about her that
makes me trust her, at least so far. I guess it's that she doesn't
treat me like I'm bad or crazy.

Sure Voice doesn't pop out of my mouth like Fuckit's
swearing or Sarah's criticism of my behavior. With them it's a
matter of designing muzzles. Some of the time, it's even hard
to hear Sure Voice inside of me. Then I think that she's
deserted me. Or I'm afraid I manufactured her from wishful
thinking. I'm not used to paying quiet attention to my self. She
doesn't make my body heavy like Sarah does. Nor does she
wave my arms around like Fuckit.

At first it was hard to recognize her authority. I was led to
expect burning bushes and stone tablets with rules and regula-
tions on them. Sunday school had established a firm polarity:
God the destroyer, Mary with her arms full of Jesus. No one
mentioned a firm, clear voice from the stomach. No one ever
hinted at a woman's voice in any sort of divine capacity. For a
while I underestimated her. But I find myself feeling strangely
confident when I hear her, as if I'm in tune with myself. She
says she's a part of me, but she's greater than me in some way I
don't understand. She feels old, but somehow without an age.
Sure Voice asks questions I've never thought about before.
Sometimes that makes me uncomfortable because I can't stop
thinking about what she says.

"You do not understand power," she observes.

It's hard to imagine power without thinking of war, football or having the final words in disputes like my grandfather
and stepfather did. Power means that someone is controlling
someone else. Power feels like a bad word. It's never been con-

nected to being a woman.

"Perhaps you are not aware of what it is to be a woman," she answers. There's an echo in back of her words. She's speaking from a hollow space behind my breasts.

I have to make my mind consider what she has said, as if she tossed a smelly sock under my nose, forcing me to examine it. Growing up, I learned that girls were not as worthwhile as boys. The value of a woman was in her training. If she came out all right, she functioned like a good appliance. If it were not for her feeble lapses of emotion, she might even be an adequate machine.

In graduate school, I joined a women's study group. I enjoyed the other women in it, but I was embarrassed to talk about being a woman. I didn't know what to say. All I was sure of was that I wasn't a man. And Fuckit didn't want to be a woman. I decided to be something nameless instead.

"I don't know how to think about this," I tell her. "And I don't understand who you are either," I admit. There simply hasn't been a precedent for Sure Voice.

"If people think they have seen you before, then odds are they will never really see you," she answers.

"So how come you're here talking to us?" Fuckit asks. "It seems like there's more important people than us to talk with."

"I am teaching you about vision," Sure Voice announces.

"Is it my glasses?" I ask, confused.

"The vision I speak of is a way of seeing. The development of vision is an art you will grow into. When vision joins emotion you learn and everything is changed." She pauses, considering Fuckit. "You do not have to memorize anything or act a certain way to learn something. But you must feel it. If you do not feel, then the idea or event dies. Only ideas fueled by passion survive. But some feelings are hidden. These cloud your vision, keeping old ideas alive."

I am walking in the park, obedient to Sarah's command

that I am wasting sunshine unless I am outside. Now that I'm here, Sarah's making lists, long ones. "After we get home, you'll clean the kitchen, then the bathroom. Then you should write a letter, buy stamps, go to the bank and do the laundry." My body is pulled behind Sarah's orders on a leash. Fuckit drags my heels, making scuff marks in the gravel.

"Where are you?" Sure Voice asks. Her voice seems to be coming from the cedar tree to my right.

"How come you can talk from inside a tree?" Fuckit is suspicious.

"I am part of everything. Sometimes it is easier to get your attention if I am in a tree. There are times when you will know me in other forms also."

"Just don't push me around," Fuckit warns, making me feel hesitant. She isn't so sure about this new voice. "I already have my hands full fending off Sarah. So be cool or go live in a tree for good."

"I was just wondering what the experience of walking is for you," Sure Voice comments.

My feet meet grass softly, springing lightly into the next step. Muscles connect to bone. Feet to ground. Head to sky. A breeze caresses my face, pushing out my shirtsleeves, tickling my arms. Lifted, the heaviness leaves my body, traveling up my spine and out the top of my head. I notice the sound of other walkers. The walk becomes a symphony of birch, maple, cedar, spruce. A hundred sounds. The distant airplane. The touch of wind against leaves. A bird joining the unfolding orchestration. Inside of me, like a bass line, my heart beats time.

"That was incredible," I tell Sure Voice as Sarah resumes grumbling. "I never noticed those feelings and sounds before. The voices were silent for five minutes! How come I don't feel like that all the time? Usually I just feel depressed what with Sarah roping my shoulder blades together and Fuckit trying to push away responsibility."

"Sometimes old feelings accumulate, making it difficult to notice fresh ways of feeling. Sarah and Fuckit do not know how to be any other way because they do not understand why they are here. I will teach you a different kind of vision for the past."

I feel uncomfortable, even though I'm not sure what Sure Voice is talking about. I wish she hadn't mentioned old feelings. The uneasiness is already stealing my walk from me.

The pizza restaurant is a favorite stop for street people who were evicted from Western State mental institution during the latest budget crisis. Sally believes that midgets are taking over the world. She looks suspiciously around the restaurant, covering her mouth conspiratorially when she tells me that midgets are stealing the handles from umbrellas. She points to a brass pin shaped like an eagle that's fastened to her worn maroon vest. "The President, he sent this to me after... " She stops mid-sentence and looks warily out the window. I follow Sally's gaze to the empty street. I feel more comfortable with people who have been labeled "odd" or "crazy" than I felt at graduate school. It's as if I fit in.

◆*Memory*. My fists are clenched and I am holding my breath. My mother is red. Her freckles stand out on her face. "You can leave this house right now," she says while barricading the door.

"All right!" I move past the closet, toward the door. She shuts it and snaps the lock before I can leave.

"You will not embarrass me that way," she says. "You're crazy. I don't know what is wrong with you. There are places where they put girls like you who don't get along with their parents!

"I will call your friends and tell them that you're crazy," she says and begins to move toward the phone.

"I hate you!" I yell back at her. "I hate you." My body wants to choke her, kick her, bite her.

I run down the carpeted stairs to my room instead.◆
The memory is packaged in old rage, laced with hopeless-

ness. I am startled by the vividness of it. It's as if I was a teenager in my mother's house again. I feel like I'm losing my
mind.

"This is another form of vision. It focuses on past experiences, called forth by your need to come to new understand-
ings. You are learning about craziness because a part of you is
trapped by the fear of it," Sure Voice explains.

I'm not sure I want any more of this type of vision. The
feelings bubble inside, chasing each other around in a circle. I
haven't thought about that incident in a long time. My childhood is mainly a gray vapor of bad feeling. It hasn't made me
feel any better to remember being called "crazy," no matter
what Sure Voice says.

I look at Sally again as if she could answer my questions.
She talks into the air, gesturing with her hands, sitting alone at
a table. Her shopping bag is filled with papers that "prove" the
conspiracies around her. Sally has other voices too, but she
doesn't think that they are a part of her. Sometimes just feeling
confused feels like the same thing as being crazy. I know that
Sarah, Fuckit and Sure Voice are part of me, but I don't understand why I'm always fighting with myself.

◇

Despite Fuckit's delight in the current situation, Sure Voice
decides that a career in waitressing is not my destiny. She waits
until I'm reading the ads in the local alternative newspaper. My
eyes fix on an ad for massage school. I try to move them on to
the Personals, but they keep returning, as if bonded with the
logo.

"Massage school? You've got to be kidding! I mean, you're
talking to the woman who hid behind the rows of wire baskets
in high school PE until the room was empty before I'd take my
shower. I blush if anyone even talks about being naked. I could
never take off my clothes in front of anyone." I cross my legs
and slouch into my chair.

Fuckit shakes her head. "No way are you going to throw

me in the midst of those mellow carrot-juiced sissies. They're health freaks. Boring! Plus, I don't care about bodies. I'm just fine without one. You're going too far this time, Sure Voice!"

"They'll hate me because my body's ugly," I inform Sure Voice, aware as I speak that I've said this to myself many times in the past. My stomach hardens with fear.

Sure Voice is accustomed to causing waves however. My eyes continue to rest on the massage school ad.

"But me?" I try to be rational with her. "Look, maybe I'm not hearing you right. I've never even had a massage. I just don't get along very well with bodies. I probably have one of the worst bodies in the world. Even if I manage to survive the classroom experience, I can't imagine people blind enough to want my ugly body to give them a massage."

"But what can it hurt?" Sure Voice asks. "After all, Fuckit enjoys unconventional occupations."

Fuckit stops arguing when Sure Voice presents the issue as one of rebellion.

◊

The first class confirms my initial doubts. My classmates awe me with their feats of Yogic pretzel contortion and bottles of homemade, freshly-squeezed, organic massage oil.

"Shit!" Fuckit exclaims inside of me, "They're all fucking perfect." I walk several blocks to secretly indulge in an evil and imperfect cigarette.

"You shouldn't smoke," Sarah grabs the opportunity to nudge Fuckit.

"Aw lay off me!" Fuckit growls. "I don't care!"

"You are a fake," Sarah retorts.

"Gentle. Be gentle." An unfamiliar voice speaks.

"And who are you?" I ask somewhat fearfully. I'm not sure how many more voices I want to have. It would be less complicated if I only had one voice. There's no immediate response, so I tell myself I'm imagining it and walk back so that I won't be late.

We're doing legs today in class. I rub warm oil between my fingers and place my hands on Jody's feet while staring at the cue sheet with words like efflaufage and petrassauge written on it. I'm surprised that I'm not frightened to touch someone like this. Instead I feel comfortable and almost trusting. The shells that Fuckit and Sarah have built to keep people out soften. My concentration overrides their conflict.

"I was born here," the voice says.

"So who are you?"

"Carrie. I was born in the pulsing of your hands. I began in touch when you felt another's body without hatred. I was birthed in the space of the table. I can travel under the skin, finding muscle. Textures and colors are alive for me. I like activities that are restful and herb tea, especially peppermint. I hold your dreams about the future." Her voice is soft, like that of my favorite Girl Scout leader when I was a kid.

"Herb tea," Fuckit says. "It figures you like herb tea better than Scotch. You're just another one of those airy-fairy mellow types. Blech."

When I close my eyes, I can see Carrie putting one hand on her hip, standing up real straight. She is my age, dressed in loose clothing. Her eyes are clear and calm. "You don't have to put me in a box, Fuckit. I am not the bastion of law and order. I like things that feel good, that's all. Besides, I think you're important."

Privately Fuckit thinks that she's important too, but she can't tell anybody. As far as Fuckit is concerned, Carrie is on probation.

◊

Chris says that massage is a healing art. She leads us in breathing through our arms and out our hands. Some of the tightness from my shoulders leaves in the breath. My hands pulse softly after the exercise. My hands have been with me for twenty-five years but I never noticed them before.

I don't know anything about healing. My classmates are

much more knowledgeable than I am. Chris says that I have a good touch. I don't know what touching has to do with healing. Chris says that healing may even make the symptoms worse before relieving them.

I look at my body. I begin to see my stories. I see my hating in the bowing of my head and the concavity of my chest. But I also learn that a million nerves respond in one second. My blood travels in circuits. I am ninety-eight percent salt water like the ocean.

Carrie practices on everyone I can get my hands on. I'm surprised to discover this gentleness inside myself. Carrie approaches each massage with patience and awe. I am learning how to feel calm from her. Sarah doesn't yell at me while I'm massaging. Fuckit is satisfied by the rhythm of the work. I notice that bodies are not at all the same.

◊

My body makes me feel unsafe.

I guess I must have been born hating my body because I don't remember a time when I didn't. Even before I was thirteen I hated it, before the blood and the breasts which grew in unevenly.

I don't have a body that's whistled at with appreciation. Nor is it the totally anonymous body. I can't get rid of the feeling that I'm perpetually conspicuous because of this body. Last night after work, Fuckit went bar hopping. I wanted to sit and contemplate, leaving pizza and service behind me. Silent men lined the barstools, immune from each other. But my body brings men over, like a magnet. Not interesting men either. Just ones that lean on my shoulders and touch me without permission. I moved my body away from them, but they kept following me until I was pressed between the corner and the lap of another man.

My breath came in shallow swallows. "Trap, trapped," my mind said. A familiar feeling of suffocation. A moment suspended in the evening. The panic peaked, I folded into the middle of my body. I didn't know how to get away. I froze. The feeling receded, but I remained cornered on the barstool while the man leaned against me.

"Let me buy you a drink," he said. But I knew that wasn't what he meant.

"Get your slimy hands off me, you toadstool," Fuckit said under her breath. I can't allow Fuckit's words to be heard. The words which might push them away feel dangerous.

"Be nice," Sarah said, "You mustn't say such things. Quit being ridiculous."

I cleared my throat. "Excuse me," came out in a tiny voice. I walked toward the bathroom, afraid of tripping, looking for sanctuary in the bar.

"Is that why you hate your body?" Sure Voice asks.

I've been writing in my journal in my room. I approach my body slowly in response to her. What if the darkness shows? What if it streams out of my eyes and is caught in unguarded glances? The blackness pulls me toward itself, a secret beckoning. I can no more avoid it than I could ignore the newspaper ad.

It is impossible to separate this dark feeling of decay from the rest of my woman's body. They are entwined, glued. For a long time I've been trying to throw the body into the trash heap so that I could get rid of the darkness. But I can't hate the body separate from the rest of me. The darkness that lurks like undiagnosed cancer is interwoven with me. There's a misery without a name. A flaw that makes me wrong and bad. I can't separate hating my body from hating myself. The truth of my romance with suicide is that bodily destruction will terminate my being. The separation is a lie. I and my body are fused, the body is I just as this voice is I.

I feel dizzy. I lie on the floor and my body starts to shake. My finger tips tingle and my toes spasm. My breathing comes very fast. I cannot hold a thought. I cannot dominate my flesh with my head. Even my head is body.

♦*Memory*. I am in the parking lot at high school waiting

for my friend, Paul. The sun makes my oversized body feel greasy. Paul's the only friend I have at school who's a boy. He never makes fun of me.

A group of boy/men dominate the parking lot with cigarettes, leather and leering.

"Look at her," one of them says. "Ain't she a cutie." "She sure is a fat one." "Hey, c'mon over baby." Someone whistles. Then they laugh.

I grow smaller and smaller. I send my consciousness into the size of a small dot. I hide in a tiny place that is deep inside of my soul. In that hiding place I take up no room at all, I don't even breathe.

I tell myself it's my body that they're making fun of. It's always my body that lets me down. It refuses to look like the bodies in *Seventeen* magazine.

I imagine that my body turns to stone. Hard. Cold. Unfeeling. I hide from them, following a familiar tunnel through the darkness to a place that is unreachable and separate. ♦

I am still shy of parking lots. I imagine the restaurant customers are whispering to each other about me. I know that some people would say that I'm being paranoid about it. But it's frightening to be noticed in innocuous places. I used to think I was anonymous, until mocking whistles and invasive eyes traveled my body from feet up while I walked on sidewalks, stood in line for movies, and sat alone in restaurants. I thought losing weight would help, but it hasn't made me feel thin or unnoticable. Fat is not a function of weight, but a state of mind. It is impossible to become invisible.

I thought that if I turned my body into stone I could save my spirit. But my martyrdom did not alter the situation. My spirit grew accustomed to living squelched in a dark place. I tore myself apart from myself and held my fragments in contempt because I wasn't whole.

I am still lying on the floor. A half hour has passed. A lump in my throat. Crying is heavy water in my chest. Crying is futile, meaningless. Crying never brings help. I don't know how to cry anymore.

Fuckit visualizes a picture of my mother with disgust. "I didn't want to be a woman! I didn't ask to be born!" Fuckit accuses the image. She remembers my mother replying that my birth was my fault. According to her, babies sit in heaven and point to the family they want to be born into. I feel myself holding heavy tears. "I will not cry," Fuckit says. "I won't let my mother win."

◆*Memory*. My body is very tiny and naked, wet. I enter brightness through a dark hot screaming place. My face is brand new. I am master of a thousand expressions.

As I smile my arms raise up and my throat tickles. I spend hours making sounds in that bed with the wooden bars. My mother makes funny noises back at me from her throat. She doesn't pick me up much because she's afraid of me. I don't know why.

The outside world is layers of color and sound dancing around the smells. At Safeway, I ride around on the cold metal bars in the shopping cart. A woman in line chews gum and smiles at me. Her glasses bob up and down and her nose wrinkles. A row of cans is reflected in colors on her glasses. I reach up to touch this wonder. My mother tells me to "be still" and gives me a swat on the leg.

I begin to scream because the swat is pulsing on my leg, but mostly because my mother is impatient; I know she wishes that she didn't have to be with me. She hits me across the mouth a couple of times, which makes me cry harder; she yanks me out of the cart by the arms and I am afraid my arm will come off. She is so big. ◆

Maybe I am going crazy. How can I remember such things? I am still on the floor; the room has darkened. I am clammy and in pain. If only I could cry. But I don't know how to cry. Crying is for babies.

I walk into the common area of the home I share with three other women. Belinda sits on the couch reading a magazine and crunching potato chips. I want to say "Hey Belinda, I'm having the strangest experiences. I just remembered being a little kid. Has that ever happened to you? It's more than remembering, it's being there again. A pond of salt water's trapped in my body and I can't let it out." But I'm afraid that if I say that she won't like me. I'm sure that no one wants a baby for a housemate. Belinda asks if I want to go to a movie. I say, "No, I just want to spend some time by myself." She goes to the movie anyway. I sit at home feeling lonely and out of control, drowning in my body. All I've really figured out is that not liking my body means not liking myself.

I try convincing myself. "I am an all right person. I am even learning a socially useful trade. I am good."

"I am not good!" Fuckit says inside of me. "And I refuse to be good just because I'm learning massage. That won't make me any better than getting A's did. Being good means being sweet and that's fucking boring anyway. Let's just forget the whole thing."

I don't feel good. Just saying that I'm good doesn't help anything. I'm still ugly. And now the darkness seems to be growing bigger instead of smaller. Like punishment.

"It's not nice to feel good," Sarah argues, "It's arrogant and vain and selfish. Besides, in order to actually be good, you have to love your family, stop smoking, stop carousing and quit making foolish, unthinking mistakes. This wanting to cry business has got to stop. You're bad. You were born bad and you make bad things happen."

I put my hands around my ears. Fresh insight makes the voices yell louder. My stomach is nauseous. I rush to the bathroom and put my fingers down my throat. If I can throw up, then the blackness will leave and my body will be clean. That would make me clean too. If I was clean I wouldn't be bad.

My body feels quieter, but it's still dark. Lying on my bed brings throat swelling. My nose crinkles. Soundless heat rolls in slow motion down my face. My pillow is damp under my cheeks. My chest heaves up and down. I bury my face deep into the feathers so that I won't make any noise. The thick pain in my chest threatens to swallow me within it, so I pull myself together and smoke a cigarette. Even though I cried for the first time in a long time, I am still weighted. Heavier than before I started crying. Now what? I wish someone would hold me.

Despair. There is no apparent direction: I think of suicide to still the hopelessness. Thinking of self-destruction makes the darkness larger, blacker. I always consider suicide when I don't know what else to do.

I pretend I am a bird and that I am safe and soft within my feather body. The tears roll off my fur like rain. Help me, I think, a distress signal dissipating in circles from a rock dropped into water. I don't know what to do.

"You do need help," Sure Voice begins to smooth out the stomach contractions and I feel calm, the voices quieted. "It is time to see a healer."

3 THE WELL

THE healer's office is in a house covered with cedar shakes. Through the window, trees change color. Carrie approves of the view. The wall is filled with quotations about growing and pictures of women. A children's story with a girl peeking through a spider's web is stapled to the wall. I'm too nervous to read anything. Maybe coming here wasn't such a good idea.

Two director's chairs and a small table fill one corner. On the floor a mattress is covered with golden brown fabric. I tuck my legs into yogic position and carefully place my cup of tea on the floor.

"Don't spill it or she'll know how clumsy you are," Sarah hisses. I sit on my hands so the healer won't see their shaking.

"I'm Kate," she announces, smiling and apparently perfectly at ease. She grabs a pillow and folds her long jean-clad legs underneath her.

I move backwards to increase the distance between us. "I'm Louise." My voice is barely audible over the sound of my heart thudding.

"We don't need any help," Fuckit insists, causing my calves to ache in longing for the exit.

A tennis racket leans against the wall, incongruous with the rest of the office. Kate's thin like a tennis player but she's not wearing tennis clothes. Just a slightly faded blouse and a brown sweater. The tennis racket looks a little frayed. A couple of maple leaves turning from green to red are strewn across the small table. Captured in their change.

Kate has been silent since she introduced herself. She doesn't hunch over herself like I do. Her grey eyes are soft, not filled with judgement.

"Um. I've never done this before. I'm not exactly sure why I'm here," I begin, feeling foolish. "I guess I just want to see myself more clearly." I want to say that I'm tired of feeling bad, but Sarah holds the words inside.

Kate nods, remaining silent.

"You're not going to make me do anything I don't want to are you?" Fuckit slips the words right out of my mouth before Sarah even knows what's happening.

Kate wrinkles her nose quizically.

"I mean," I hasten to cover up, "I don't know how this works."

"I believe that everyone's growth is different. I'll be here as you follow your own process. If it seems like you're stuck somewhere, I'll point it out to you. It may not always feel good."

"But I don't know where I'm going," I say, feeling discouraged. I had anticipated solving this in one session.

"That's all right," she says. "I'm sure you're going somewhere. That's how it works."

"Don't talk so much," Sarah warns, "You've got to make a good impression."

Kate asks me how old I am, how many siblings I have, where I grew up and what I'm doing now.

Fuckit inhales a cigarette. "Well, I'm currently engaged in a battle with God," she says, thinking to test the healer for any latent Sarah tendencies.

"That's interesting," Kate smiles.

◇

Kate and I sit in the same places, but she seems very far away. I am in the darkness and Kate's at the end of a long tunnel. I want her to reach in to me and pull me out, but she just sits quietly, like she's waiting for something. My skin feels like insulation, distant and dead.

I've felt this way before. My jaw is paralyzed. Captive

words crawl around and under my tonsils. I don't know if I can get the words to come out. I've never tried before.

"It is time to speak," Sure Voice encourages. "Try reaching forward. Vision requires risk."

I clear my throat. As I try to speak, a barrier of thick hot air pushes the words back down by throat. "I feel very far from you," my voice whispers against the resistence.

"You can come closer." Kate smiles and shifts on her pillow.

Then I'm back again, only three feet away from her, which is where I have been sitting the entire time.

"So big deal," Sarah says. "You're always dramatizing. You just want attention," she snorts.

But I'm shaking. I was sure Kate was going to tell me to stay inside that tunnel forever. I thought she'd want me to be as far away from her as possible.

"It's so dark inside of me," I tell her. I look at the carpet when we talk.

"What's in that darkness?" Kate asks.

I don't want to know, because it's awful and I'm awful because of it. I had, after all, abandoned my body because of this rotten, heavy place. Prodding around in it does not sound like a good idea. Kate is persistent, however.

It's so dark that I can hardly see anything. In my mind's eye, I slowly distinguish rough black obsidian walls which climb straight up for miles. The walls are part of a dry Well. I stand at the bottom of it. Next to me, a small fire dimly illuminates murky ground and an old man wearing only a loincloth. It embarrasses me that he's not wearing more clothes. He doesn't talk to me. He disappears from the image. The fire seems small next to the dark walls of obsidian. The light from the top of the Well is so far away that it looks like a star.

My neck aches from gazing upward. Even more distressing is Sure Voice's calm assurance that some day we will be out of here. I ask how we're going to do that. She says, "By climbing."

I was afraid of that. What I really want is for the healer to be God and zap me up and out of here. But she seems perfectly content asking me what kind of rock the walls are made of and whether I'm warm by the fire. She doesn't ask me about the man though.

"We'll just explore where you are right now." Kate stands to indicate that our time is over.

"But I don't like it in here. I thought you were going to help me." She probably hates me anyway.

"You can't be where you aren't," she says and gives me a hug.

This is not exactly what I want to hear. Not only is it dark in here, it's lonely. My street acquaintances are tolerant, but they're uncomfortable with non-material realities. My massage peers are kind, but they're impatient with my insistence that I'm trapped in the bottom of a Well. "Think of something nice, like a sunny field," they suggest.

The voices aren't exactly a lot of comfort either, even though I saw their images inside of the Well. Sarah says that the bottom of a deserted Well is my just punishment and that she's there to make sure I suffer. Fuckit says she doesn't give a shit and that she's going to pretend the Well doesn't exist. Carrie thinks the discovery is probably significant. Sure Voice just says, "Good. You see the Well."

I'm not so sure that I trust her anymore. I would like a little proof that she's working on our escape route. What if I can't ever get out of here?

◊

"It is important to walk," Sure Voice advises, "because then you cannot forget to take your body along with you."

I have dressed in anonymous clothes, a dark blue sweater and faded jeans. I'm afraid that other walkers will laugh at me or expect some conversation that I'll be incapable of providing. It sounds like a contradiction not to want to see anyone and then to feel lonely, but with all of these voices I am getting used to feeling many different ways at once. I have a disturbing sense that something will fall from the sky and assault me.

I used to hate my legs, but now, their motion reassures me that I'm not really stuck in a dark confined place. Frankly, since discovering the Well, I'm not sure of anything. I have the feeling that I want to be going somewhere, but how do I know that I'm going to the right place? Kate talks about process and transformation as if they were as certain as the existence of the kitchen table. But if this is really a journey, then where's the map? How do I know that Kate knows what she's talking about?

"Yeah," Fuckit agrees as I step squarely on unobserved dogshit, "I think we should just dump the healer, evict Sure Voice and put our thumb out on a road that has a map to go along with it. I refuse to be stuck in this Well. I want out now."

"Look at these walls." Carrie brushes some dust from the rough black rock. "They're so dark. It's as if they're holding secrets."

"Aw shit, you remind me of Pollyanna, Carrie. Always looking on the bright side. Yech. It's fucking dark and creepy in this Well. Every time I look around in here, all I see are these cold ugly walls. I don't think there's anything interesting about them," Fuckit growls. "You're just a newcomer here. I've been in this darkness for a long time."

The trees bare their branches like skeletons losing flesh. My mouth carries the tight plastic smile my mother insisted on. The smile was a lie required of "nice" girls and now I can't seem to take it off. I walk a zigzag path around mud puddles, waiting for quicksand to gobble up my tennis shoes. I'm afraid of how afraid I am.

I pause in front of a very large cedar tree. I throw my arms as far around her trunk as they can reach. When I close my eyes I am in a green mist and I feel calm, a welcome change from quicksand.

"There will not be an instant leap from the floor of the

Well to the outside." The words of Sure Voice are very clear. My shoulders relax for the first time in weeks. "Sometimes you will enjoy a delicious whiff of free outside air. But there will be days when you climb deeper into the bowels of the Well. You will wonder if you are going the right way."

The bottom of my feet tingle. I imagine sinking into the earth on the long sturdy roots of an old tree. My legs grow down past the Well, through layers of rock and caves of crystal. I draw my breath up, through the rock. Grounding is meeting the earth and accepting the support of being held upright.

"Louise, quit daydreaming!" Sarah begins another of her frequent attempts to discredit my experience. My shoulders start shrinking, binding my chest in guilt. I have no right to think I belong on earth with the rest of the animals. When I was an adolescent I believed that a flying saucer had abandoned me here. I don't belong.

But this experience stays past Sarah's inner words. Sure Voice didn't promise instant passage to the top but she's still talking to me. At least I know where I am. At least the ground is solid. It's more than I knew before. The air in the Well smells of fresh dirt instead of confinement.

The more I explore the inner ground of the Well in Kate's office, the more I notice. My closed eyes have adjusted to the darkness and I have acquired a peculiar kind of night vision. What once felt like a dark rotting mass in my stomach has specific features. The rocks lining the Well are dusty, jagged chunks of obsidian. The inner fire dims and quickens. Sarah, Fuckit and Carrie take form in the Well which houses them. Even more curious is that the more clearly I see the Well, the more I understand about how I move in the world.

◇

I spend a lot of time trying to fit in. I have to guess what's expected of me. Then I match it or refuse to conform depending upon whether Fuckit or Sarah is in charge at the moment. Now, in my dual career role, I imagine that my massage clients want me to be smiling and always loving. My pizza cohorts expect me to be rough and careless. I thought that any confusion had been solved when Carrie took over massage, leaving Fuckit free to roam the streets. But the voices refuse to stay conveniently boxed. Fuckit chafes at the bit as Carrie takes over the unconventionality of massage school. Fuckit sneaks along. "What are you doing?" Carrie inquires after Fuckit distributes business cards to pizza customers.

Carrie has a hard time ignoring Fuckit's other life. Fuckit's friends live dangerously. Craig, the cook, looks like my brother, Jim. Nightly, Craig reaches for a bottle of gin behind the stack of sixteen inch pizza pans. At 5:05 the fifth is full and sealed. By midnight, the eagle on the label is staring out from the rest of the garbage. Candy, who is sixteen, comes to the nightly post clean-up celebration with her cheek sliced by a knife. Her pimp was angry that she hadn't made more money. "But he loves me," she said as we reacted with outrage. Craig stationed the heavy oak stirring spoon near the entrance as a weapon in case her pimp followed her.

Because of Carrie's concern, Fuckit can't disregard the cost of this lifestyle. It's not fun to watch friends get hurt. The place where I once felt at home seems more like a nightmare, where teenagers grow old and forget their dreams. Like Stanford, it wears away at me, even though Fuckit's in charge instead of Sarah. It's hard for Fuckit to admit, but carousing is becoming painful.

◇

Faithful to Sure Voice's commitment to vision, I continue to explore the Well in Kate's office by visualizing it inside of me. Then "it" happens. "It" makes me wonder if I haven't been stumbling around blind this whole time. In a corner of the Well, the floor is parted from the wall, leaving a Pit the size of a small room. A narrow ledge extends from the floor, suspended over the gaping black hole. I stand on the ledge and look down into the most horrendous Pit I've ever seen, a Pit that compares with the swirling fogged scenes from the film *The Pit and the Pendulum*. I can't see the bottom of it. I can't imagine climbing down there despite anything Sure Voice might say. All around the Pit, a hideous murmuring makes me want to turn away.

"If you go down there you'll die!" Sarah threatens. "The devil lives in there."

"It's a secret route out," the rocks encourage.

And right then, looking down, I see her. An infant, six months old, covered with dirt. She wails. Awful screeches and crying fill my inner ears. The Well pounds my stomach. A grimy, neglected infant. YoungerOne. She is perched on the ledge, precariously close to the Pit.

"Uh-huh. This isn't part of me. I won't have anything inside of me that looks like that. I don't like kids anyway, they make me feel inadequate and shy. They ask all sorts of questions that I can't answer." I back away from her as if she could bite me. The obsidian walls amplify her crying.

"Naah!" Fuckit exclaims. "I put in my time babysitting! I didn't get sucked into this healer business to take care of babies. I don't like her. Get her out of here. You betrayed me, Sure Voice! I thought that things were going to get better. Then you lay this kid on me." Fuckit walks away in disgust.

"You've found a very young part of yourself," Kate says softly. "What is the baby saying?" she asks, leaning forward. She touches my hand.

I become the child. I can't talk. I roll around on the floor, gulping for breath. I make strange sounds, but all of the sounds are on the inhale. The exhale is silent.

Kate takes deep breaths, noisily expelling air as if she could breathe for both of us. "Let it out, don't take it in."

But I can't let it out because I know that I will get hurt. I am sure I will get hit in the stomach. Kate puts her arms around me. I flinch and back away. I roll over so that my stomach is under my back. I am rigid, waiting for a blow. I wrap my arms around my knees and tuck my head inside.

◆*Memory*. I am in a dark room lying in the bed with bars. I am playing with my fingers, running them over one another. Loud yelling shatters the stillness. Danger. I begin a whole body cry. My arms flail and my feet kick. I hear angry sound snowballed into words. "Shut up, shut up!" I can't stop my noise. A thud across my belly rolls me into a ball. As I suck in with my mouth, the sound is swallowed. I am very still. The mobile of plastic animals whirls above my face. The whole world is only the whisper of the air. I watch pink and blue animals go round and round. It seems that the mobile will melt into my eyes.◆

I know that Kate is holding me because I can hear her even breathing. Her arms touch my shirt but I am far away from the outside of my skin. My body is a heavy numbness wrapping me in a heartless cocoon. The Well is a thick weight in my belly.

Kate and I walk around the room before I leave. "Feel your legs," she reminds me. I don't tell her I can't find them. As I get in my car, I continue to feel like an infant. I have a list of errands to do. It's too much. I go to bed instead. I try sucking my thumb. My mind is a blackboard without words. Inside the Well, I hear the vicious snorting of monsters who are waiting to eat me. I look around for Sure Voice but I can't see her.

In the morning I look at myself in the bathroom mirror. My straight brown hair looks dull and dry. My eyes are red, distant behind glasses. I don't know my face, it's too old. A grownup has taken over. How can the infant I saw be related to this waitress in blue jeans and a baggy overshirt?

"I've been waiting ten minutes just to order," the suited man frowns. His girlfriend looks at the formica table top, embarrassed at his display. I feel as if he slapped my face. I can't defend myself. When I go behind the counter to place his order, Craig offers me a glass of gin. "To the waitress," he slurs his words together. The pizza will probably arrive in a rectangular shape. The man will deliver another blow. The waitress bears ultimate responsiblity. It's my fault, but it's not. I get the two confused. I take the drink because I don't know how else to protect myself.

I am reeling after work, but the infant remains. YoungerOne is small and naked. She shivers in the Well. She wants a mother. Mothers are unavailable to twenty-five-year-olds, no matter how young they feel.

"You're dirty!" Sarah tells her. "When are you going to grow up?"

I lose touch with the me that's an adult. The only solution seems to be lying in my basement bed. It's dark and cool there. I slosh in the waterbed. I pretend that I'm in the womb again. "I'm okay, I'm fine," I repeatedly tell myself. The knot in my stomach pulls my shoulders and knees together. I will never be able to untie it.

"Mommy, Mommy," YoungerOne wails, "Mommy, hold me."

◇

Kate tries to reach the YoungerOne inside of me. When I close my eyes, I see YoungerOne kicking, inching toward the edge. "No, you'll hurt me, you'll betray me, I know it."

YoungerOne is embarrassing. I'm scared of how helpless she makes me feel. She needs too much. Needs holding, needs soft words, needs people to reassure her, needs acceptance, gentleness, needs help. Kate says that YoungerOne is here because I didn't get the care I needed when I was a kid. She says that I don't like myself because I wasn't loved when I was little. I can't imagine ever feeling love. As a child, I pretended that my favorite teachers cared about me. I imagined them rocking me in their arms. Now I imagine Kate holding me. But even though YoungerOne wants to be held, she won't let Kate near. Despite numerous assurances to the contrary, I am convinced that Kate hates me.

"This is never going to get better! Sure Voice lied! This

hurts too much! Kill her, kill that kid!" Fuckit and Sarah act in chorus. "Kill her!"

Sarah picks up YoungerOne. She swings her over the ledge.

I want her to drop. I want to forget it all.

◆*Memory*. My mouth is open. I am staring back at myself through the mirror. Blood runs down my wrists. A moment before, I had decided. I would die. Thirteen years is enough.

I take my mother's razor blade out of the case. I stand in front of the mirror in my bedroom. In back of me, staring through the mirror, is a picture of Jesus that I sketched in pencil. He isn't looking at me, he is looking to the sky, at God. God is what he cares about, really. My fingers are steady, with ragged nail ends. I scratch back and forth with the razor on my wrist. I don't feel anything at first. There are no thoughts, no hunger. My skin changes shape. I would like to slide out of it. I change hands and begin on the other wrist. Back and forth. My sight seems to float from the ceiling. Red oozes out from little slits on my skin.

I look at my face in the mirror. Who is that person looking back at me? That little girl, with almost two chins. Her eyes are wide. Her face changes as I see myself looking back at me. No, I don't want to die. What will happen if I die? It is too scary to die. Her mouth forms a scream but no sound comes out.

The tape is in the same cabinet as the razor blades. White adhesive tape. My wrists are strong enough to pull it out from itself. I am surprised at that. Layer after layer, I unroll it to my skin, to cover up the redness, to hide the wounds. The girl looking out of the mirror folds her face in on itself, as if she has just closed the door between herself and her pain.

Fifteen minutes until the schoolbus. I sit next to the back seat and close my eyes. The tape catches on my long-sleeved shirt. ◆

It is twelve years later. I am in the healer's office. My legs tense, ready to leave.

"What happens then?" Kate asks.

"I got to school. I was there early, I caught the early bus. I went to Mrs. Sticks' room. She was my favorite teacher. I pulled the cuffs of my blouse up. I don't know what I said, except I told her that I tried to kill myself. She always seemed tall to me. I always liked the mischief in her eyes, but now they looked serious. She felt far away. Mrs. Sticks told me that everything would be better when I was eighteen. I felt her attention leave me. I felt ashamed, as if the red hot slits from my wrists were leaking over my body.

"After school, my mother's car was in the parking lot and I wanted to die all over again. I met her in the hallway. 'Go sit in the car,' she said, stern-faced. I watched her through the window. She sat in the principal's office. I'd never talked to the principal. He'd met my mother before though, because she was an elementary school teacher. I sat in the car and rolled down the windows because it felt like the car was running out of air. I didn' t think about what they were saying. I closed my eyes and pretended that I was a ghost. I sent my eyes out of my body and into the sky as if I were a robin.

"I opened them when the door creaked. I wanted to become an invisible speck of lint on the blue station wagon carpet.

"'If you ever try that again,' my mother informed me, 'I will kill you.'

"I closed my eyes and went about twenty miles into the air. I was sure that my brain died, because I saw a lot of colors. Red and blue, yellow, green. My brain was like an operator's switchboard at the telephone company and all of the wires went back into the wrong holes. Nothing made sense. I was sure that I had blown up. I thought that if I opened my eyes, there would be only specks of me, bloody bits of flesh scattered on the floor.

"'We won't mention this again,' my mother said in a tight voice as we pulled into the driveway of our house.

"What I felt most was that the teacher I loved betrayed me.

She gave me over to my mother. I am too horrible to save."

The words pour out in a monotone in Kate's office.

"Your mother really wasn't helping you. You wanted help," Kate says. Her voice is kind.

I stand with my back to her. My forehead leans against the door to her office. I want to bang my head again and again against the wood.

"You deserved to have someone listen to you and really try and help." Kate puts her arm around my shoulder. "She didn't hear you, your mother didn't hear how much pain you were in," she says.

I start crying ancient tears. Long tendrils reach for my eyes from my abdomen. Kate is the first one to take the thirteen-year-old inside of me seriously. She rubs my back. I want to believe that she does care what happened to me.

I visualize the Well. A thirteen-year-old child stands over a baby. I have more than one inner child. Hearing Kate's support releases feelings that had turned hard inside of me. The grief of YoungerOnes bounces against obsidian walls.

It's hard for me to believe that Kate believes me about my mother's meanness. Growing up, people saw my mother's roles as teacher and visitor to the sick, dying and newly born. They thought that made her a wonderful mother. When I complained about her reading my mail and diaries, people looked at me suspiciously. Some people even told me that my mother was a saint.

"You'd better not do that again," my brother said when I got home. "It'll just kill Mother or she'll go crazy or something. You know how she is." Many people treated my mother as if she were frail. She wanted others to think that a strong wind would blow her down. I was the only one who knew her viciousness. If there was a problem, my mother would say, "Let's just pretend this didn't happen," after we'd screamed with each other about it first. She never screamed in front of anyone else.

As I leave Kate's office, the craving for suicide is renewed.

Remembering these old feelings is too hard. I stand by the window at home and think about throwing myself out. "Kill her, kill her" is a low regular hum inside of me. I stand rooted in the ground, certain that the only force saving me from leaping is the inertia of my own body. I squirt massage lotion out of my two-story window onto the top of a garbage can below. Fuckit says, "There go our guts."

My friend Kim comes over for a visit. We commiserate about the sexism in her work. She wants me to go to the beach with her and "bake our troubles away." I try to tell her how I'm feeling. I pour more massage lotion out the window.

"Stop it, Louise!" she yells. Her voice is quivering.

"I can't stop it."

"I can't handle this, I'm leaving." Kim grabs her hat and canvas purse. "Just don't do it and stop fooling around." I hear the door close.

"Aw just leave me alone. Just leave me alone!" Fuckit reopens the door and slams it behind her for emphasis.

I keep coming back to dying. It's a familiar place. I don't ask why I wanted to die.

4 THE TOUCH

SOMETIMES I don't want to go to the health center where I'm working as a massage therapist. YoungerOnes fight to remain huddled and motionless. Fuckit complains because her time is not her own. Sarah questions my competence. But employment is not optional. I am forced to be functional. Working reminds me that I exist outside of the Well. Massage is the only time YoungerOnes don't control me with their crying.

Before I give a massage, I place my hands on my legs, palms up, receiving. The edges of my fingers curl like a bowl. "I am an open channel for the loving, healing energy moving through me," I say, exhaling and breathing slow long breaths. I imagine an ocean reaching through my body, vast and deep, holding life and tide. My body, for this time, is not filled with darkness.

I show Jackie to the room with the flowered sheet and the foot reflexology chart hanging from the wall.

I feel my feet on the ground and draw on the energy of the earth. I imagine a golden light at the top of my head and draw it inside of me, filling myself with energy.

From the base of my spine I imagine a cord leading into the ground. My own thoughts and feelings tumble down the cord. They don't go away, they are simply in storage for another time. The crying of a couple of hours ago waits.

I enjoy working with Jackie. A row of tight muscle knots cluster around both edges of her scapula. I soothe the skin first, adding embrocation oil to heat the muscle, softening the first layer of tissue. My thumbs move the locked fibers of deep muscle.

"Aah," Jackie makes sounds as I work. I used to stop when she did that. "No, don't quit," she said. "It hurts but it also feels good. I want to get through that pain."

"But we don't want to hurt anyone," YoungerOnes said, afraid.

"It is her hurt," Sure Voice said gently. "The pain is already there, woven into the muscles. You call her attention to it. You can not make it go away, unless Jackie allows it to leave. You assist her in healing."

Tonight, crying begins from a muscle spasm between her shoulder blades, in back of her heart. "I miss you, Ted," she says. At first, I was afraid of her crying. I worried that someone would come and tell us to be quiet. As I know my own grief, I become less afraid of Jackie's.

My hands are warm and curious. Tight muscles run like threads down her upper arms. A knot in the shape of a wooden baby block pulls her calf, shortening her leg. I smile to myself when I work on her feet, where her second toes tower above the others. I used to think all feet were like mine, with short stubby toes that form an orderly arch.

Lines from the corners of her eyes spread like a spider's web. Each line an expression, a laugh, a thought, a grief. I hold each hand and foot for a moment at the end. How many has this hand touched, trusted, reached out for, reached away from. People, occupations, emotion being held, then cleared away for new feeling.

I'm not sure what enables the healing. It has nothing to do with being good enough since I can do it. I'm calm when I am working, letting my hands think, focusing on the present. I imagine a stream of blue or light green light moving through my body and through her body. When I work, I can see sparks fly from her skin. I flick the energy from my hands into a corner of the room like used electricity.

The massage is more than prodding muscles this way or that. It's a connection within the space of the massage table. Thoughts that normally wander in the mind become temporarily silent. In those hours, the lesson is to experience feeling. I feel closer to Sure Voice when I massage. I don't have to worry about what I'm doing.

◊

Incense and oils fill my nose with roses, gardenias and cedar. The oil follows me home on the steering wheel. The oil comes with me into my apartment, lingering on doorknobs which slip as I turn them. Oil shines the fur of Crystal, my cat.

But I cannot hold onto the healing. It slips through my fingers so that I am locked inside myself, without solutions.

The rest of my life confronts me. YoungerOnes cry, "Mommy, Mommy," continually.

"Physician heal thyself," Sarah, trite and critical as usual, taunts me with sarcasm from the Well inside of me.

Why is it easier to see others more clearly than myself? Why can't I touch my own sore places and make them better?

"It's not fair that my clients get helped and I don't," Fuckit complains.

"There's no healing for you anyway. You're a phony, you're not really helping anyone," Sarah insists. "You don't really care about anyone but yourself. If they knew how bad you are. . . "

I wonder where the calm feeling of ease goes when I've finished giving a massage.

"There are many feelings, as diverse as the seasons of the ocean. Feelings are meant to change and provide variety," Sure Voice explains.

But it seems like the pain steals the pleasant feelings, tying them into a bundle that I only get to open for short glimpses. I feel like a child reaching for a tall shelf without a stool. Dreams and plans for the future seem increasingly impossible. Inside, I am a room where drawers have been turned out, spilling into sloppy piles. The suicide fantasies are a death movie in my mind. My arms ache, wanting touch. They fling up in the air waiting to be picked up. I wish someone would take care of me and show me what to do. How do I get what I've never had?

YoungerOne's thirst for a warm, soft mother touch feels unquenchable. I keep wishing that my roommate would hold me. But she talks about "neediness" and what a burden it is. I hold my breath and hope she won't notice the small grasping hands inside of me. YoungerOnes calm when Kate touches them, but when the touch is gone, their unending need for assurance comes back again as if there had never been any touch at all. They are always afraid that Kate doesn't really like them.

"Goddamn it YoungerOnes, there is no Mother!" I imagine Fuckit shaking them by the shoulders. "Quit crying, just shut up. It's too late. There's no one to pick you up, you've grown past that. You don't need it, you don't need it. You gotta quit crying."

I pace back and forth, frantic. What do I do? I can't handle this another minute. The phone looks up at me. No. I already called Kate this week. I shouldn't call her again.

"Help. Help," YoungerOnes plead.

"Kill them, kill them," urges Sarah.

"Shut up!" Fuckit yells.

I dial the phone, holding the receiver tightly. Kate answers.

"Um hi," I say in a very tentative voice. "This is Louise."

"Hello," she says. "I have to go to a meeting in about fifteen minutes so I don't have much time to talk."

"That's okay. I'm sorry I'm calling you again. I just keep feeling like dying. I want to jump out my windows, stick my head in the oven. I'm sorry I keep bothering you. I just don't know what to do. Is this ever going to get better?" The words tumble out in a pool of tears, circular, repeating themselves. Everything is moving around me faster and faster. I want Kate to hold onto me.

"I don't know how long it will take, Louise," she says.

"I'm sorry. I just feel so horrible. It keeps getting worse. I don't know what to do."

"Well," Kate pauses. "Why don't you call someone up and tell them that you love them?"

I hold my breath.

"We love her," YoungerOnes volunteer in small inside voices.

"I can't tell her that!" Fuckit says, "No way."

"She doesn't want someone like you to love her anyway," Sarah sneers.

"Come on," Carrie says, "tell her."

"I love you," I say into the receiver, a tiny voice, crossing wires. My heart races fast like it will catapult from my chest. I am afraid of the silence.

"I love you," Kate tells me.

"Really?"

"Yes."

When I hang up I don't feel frantic. "Someone loves us," YoungerOnes say. "Someone really cares about us." I don't remember feeling love before. The love comes inside like warm massage oil, spreading inside cold hard places.

◇

I've been depressed for months. I sit at home and cry. I'm tired of the baby and YoungerOne 13. I told Kate I just wanted to get rid of them. Not kill them exactly, just eliminate them from my personality. Kate doesn't think that's possible. She says that some day I'll probably be glad to know my inner children. I can't imagine what that would be like.

Now, a nagging ache in my stomach, like a small hand tugging at a sleeve. I pretend it's not there. The tugging grows more forceful. My chest feels strapped to my arms. My breasts hide in a cave which bulges at my middle back. I bend over in my chair, taking tiny sips of air.

I'm afraid of the intensity of my body's reactions. What if I'm dying? The pain pulls me away from my plans for the evening. I can't visit with Kim, Joan and Gretch. I can't talk to anyone. I feel uncomfortably transparent.

"Let's blow this joint! I can't stand it!" Fuckit reaches for a coat, the car keys, money. I walk out the door, obeying Fuckit.

The feeling seeps into a glass of white wine at the bar. I hear, "Help. Help," in a whining, insistent voice.

"You should be home cleaning the apartment," Sarah says. She sits like an obese troll on my shoulders, yelling into my ear.

The feeling in my stomach grows heavier, turns to lead, then iron.

"Tea. Let's just go home and have tea," Carrie whispers to Fuckit.

"I don't want to go home! I don't want to clean the apartment. Sarah will make me. I hate these feelings. They're a nuisance." Fuckit orders another glass of wine.

"They hurt," Carrie says. She sits next to Fuckit and takes a sip of wine. "You and Sarah forget that the pain is just YoungerOnes. They talk using feeling."

Fuckit stabs the cigarette into an ashtray. "I hate feeling this way!"

"It's never going to end," Sarah proclaims from her perch.

Carrie takes a notebook from the pack. "Well I'm going to listen to them," she says. Carrie writes long streaming sentences about darkness, terror and wishes into a spiral notebook. Writing eases the inner pressure but nothing makes it go away completely.

The feelings are finally released into water spots on my pillow that night. "I'm scared. I can't do anything. Something's wrong with me." The words hit the pillowcase, unquestioned, revolving around and around.

"I don't know what to do," Carrie says. The sobs thicken, caught in a spiral from pain to desperation. My face is tangled in a weave of mucus. The fear of pain surrenders to the pain.

"I wonder what it would be like if you were mother to these children?" Kate rests her hand on her chin.

"No way, no way, no way!!" Fuckit immediately rejects this idea. "They cry too much, they're ugly, they take too much time, they're mushy and they makes me feel like a fool. I never want to be a mother!

"They're only little girls." Kate addresses the part of me that's Fuckit. "What would be so awful about helping them out instead of ganging up against them with Sarah?"

Fuckit grows very quiet. Her words swell my throat. She waits a couple of minutes before speaking, swallowing the last bit of fear before she allows the words. "You see," Fuckit says in a very quiet voice, "if YoungerOnes get help they'll get hurt. They might even die. I protect them by hiding them. If people know they're here, bad things will start to happen. It's better if they don't get any attention." Fuckit sounds uncharacteristically serious.

"Well, maybe there's an adult voice inside that could let YoungerOnes know they're loved. You're pretty hard on these children. YoungerOnes need to know they're not all alone any more. They wouldn't be here now if it wasn't time for them to be known."

I hear an edge of impatience beneath Kate's reasonable words. YoungerOne 13 turns away, afraid of rejection, discounting a year of Kate's warm help. YoungerOne 13 looks over her shoulder to see if Kate notices her distance. I want Kate to put her arm around me. When she does that, everything feels okay. I want her to say she'll love me forever.

"I'm not going to hold you right now," Kate says, reading my longing. "It doesn't feel right to hold you when I don't want to. I'm afraid it's keeping you from taking care of yourself. It's become a rescue that stops your pain. I believe you can nurture yourself now."

Her words sting. She wants to get rid of me. I automatically harden with reflexes honed by past betrayals. A sharp pain in a soft place. The numb feeling of despair. I'm tired of having to take care of myself, it's always been that way.

Carrie comes out of the shadow of the Well and begins to move toward YoungerOnes. "I've learned about touching YoungerOnes by watching Kate. It's different now."

"This is the next step," Kate says. "Fuckit has protected YoungerOnes for a long time. There's a new way to take care of yourself."

It's hard for YoungerOnes to hear Kate. They want to hold onto the hurt of her earlier words. I wish she'd do something so that I could explode at her.

Carrie moves past Fuckit, carrying YoungerOnes away from the ledge. Carrie hugs YoungerOnes. I see the clear-eyed twenty-six-year-old part of myself holding two children on her lap. I rock back and forth, hugging a pillow against my belly. I didn't know I could hug myself and feel comforted. The desperate desire for contact and safety is eased. YoungerOne 13 gradually relaxes, a little relieved to move beyond such absolute dependence on Kate, but not sure what it means to trust her now either.

◇

Being a grownup has never been my idea of a good time. Grownups are people who have responsibilities they don't want. Grownups have to be serious, sensible and perfect. And most of all, grownups never have any fun.

Gradually, I break through my resistance to being an adult. I learn to include nurturing in my daily life. I take notes about the voices in my journal, even though there's a lot I don't understand. When I walk, I imagine YoungerOne 13 walking beside me with soft hands held between my bigger ones. The infant rides in a pack, close to my heart. I imitate Kate's gentle, non-judgemental touching. Carrie thinks of new ways of nurturing. She includes a non-traditional twist to intrigue Fuckit. We improvise songs on the guitar. Candles are lit and Tarot cards read. Carrie practices affirmations to create a new way of seeing the self, "I love my self unconditionally," she repeats ten times a day. Carrie sees the voices as being on a journey together like a quest, even though we haven't moved from the Well.

It's not always easy to reach inside my self and touch

YoungerOnes though. Today they've been unresponsive and annoying. Sad, frightened feelings make it hard to get out of bed. I consider helping Sarah throw them over the ledge into the Pit.

Fuckit turns up the radio, blaring rock, screaming guitars. Without plan, I find myself dancing across the living room, bare feet barely touching the rug. Arms alive, diving arches, spreading my body wide from my chest. A heron looping while rock turns to jazz. I circle in complex patterns of skip and jump. Round sounds roll through my throat, bubbles of ohs bursting to air. My body melts to ground, sweeps around in fluid slow-motion. I forget about the neighbors, like a child before learning to sit still and quiet.

Fuckit takes over from YoungerOnes, dancing adolescent edges, defining movement, contributing dash and flare. She rescues a purple scarf from the floor, draping it around my neck. I watch myself in the mirror. For a moment, the inner children aren't a pain-in-the-ass, but a symbol of freedom lost.

Fuckit and YoungerOnes even dance together, mixing play with sophistication. "See, you don't have to feel bad," Fuckit tells them.

They begin to lose energy. I can only feel so good before I have to feel bad. YoungerOne 13 looks at the dusty obsidian walls, then looks quickly away. "It's still dark in here," she says. The baby stops crawling.

Fuckit's irritated at their change of mood. She yells at them.

"You don't need to be scared, it's all right," Carrie reassures YoungerOnes. "It's okay to have fun with our body."

"It's never going to end," YoungerOne 13's whisper echoes against black walls.

I wonder if I'm ever going to feel safe or know what trust is. Maybe all I can do is bandaid YoungerOnes' discomfort. I still wake with a nervous knot in my belly. I'm always afraid when I start a massage. The fear goes away while I'm working, only to return when I finish. I'm never completely sure that my closest friends really like me. Maybe they're just being nice to me because they don't want to be rude. I know now that these feelings come from YoungerOnes but I don't know why they feel that way. I guess they just aren't very brave.

I tell Kate that it's too hard to feel the grief and the terror. Fuckit says it's Kate's fault. I never spent days huddled into a helpless, sobbing mass before this.

"Louise," she replies firmly, "you chose to come here. You chose to go through this."

It's better than graduate school. Today I felt good for a little while. I almost liked looking at myself in the mirror while I danced. I notice the hand tugging in my stomach more quickly than I used to. The sadness doesn't accumulate until it explodes. Now, when Carrie reaches YoungerOnes through the tears, through Fuckit's indifference and Sarah's belittling, I feel calmer. I feel my own strong arms around my shoulders. Sometimes I still pretend they're Kate's arms, holding my ears close to her heart.

◇

I keep telling Kate that I don't want to be in a relationship. I always knew I never wanted to get married or have children. I didn't understand why anyone would want that. Every once in a while I'd tell her about a man I picked up at the restaurant. But I never wanted to see any of them again after being sexual with them. I'd make them leave me alone by ignoring them.

I told Kate about the relationship I had in college with John. I was always scared that he'd go away. I'd do anything to please him. He responded with silence and absence. He said I was too intense. I guess I wanted him to take care of me, just like I want that from Kate. But I didn't really care about him. I confessed that sometimes I feel heartless. I finally told Kate that I was tired of having sex with men that I didn't care about. I was using them and I ended up feeling unknown.

I have friends who are lesbians. They seem happier in their relationships than I've ever been in mine with men. I've always been closer to my women friends. We share more feelings. We talk about what's going on inside of us.

Yesterday I went to a potluck where almost everyone was a lesbian. We laughed and ate and hugged. I felt comfortable in my body. I wanted to belong to that world.

The sun pools on the earth-brown carpet in Kate's office. I study the light and shadows while saying, "I think I'm a lesbian." Fuckit looks up to see how Kate's taking the announcement. When I see her smile, I grin. "When I was at that potluck, I felt at home as a woman for the first time. I like the variety in women's bodies," I tell Kate enthusiastically.

She smiles. I've told her how much I hate my own body about a thousand times.

I look down, suddenly feeling like a teenager, wondering how to go about being a lesbian. Those women seemed to know so much more than me. "I just know that I liked being a woman when I was with them," Carrie tells Kate. "I felt strong and proud."

"I think that's wonderful," Kate says. "You look happy when you talk about it. I'm glad for you."

"All right!" Fuckit says, wearing a purple scarf and dancing down the steps after my appointment. "I'm a dyke!"

◇

Kate says I've grown a lot in the two years I've seen her. She thinks I've learned all I can from her. "I just want you to think about it, that's all," Kate says. "You don't have to stop seeing me right away." She smiles warmly and reaches for my hand. "Think about coming in every couple weeks for a while if you want."

YoungerOnes want to pull away. "We must have done something wrong," they think while holding their breath. "She doesn't really like us."

"We don't need her anyway," Fuckit maintains, pushing YoungerOnes away. She doesn't want Kate to know how important she's been.

I came to the beach after the session with Kate. YoungerOnes cried on our way here. Leaving Kate makes my heart alternately soft and hard.

Carrie grows still for a moment. "She helped teach me how to care. She made me want to love YoungerOnes. She taught me that our growth is a journey."

"We love Kate," YoungerOnes say sadly, "Who will love us now?"

"We have friends." Carrie holds them, touching a hurt place inside my belly with warmth. I imagine my friends and Kate standing in a circle around the infant and the thirteen-year-old. I feel my chest expand, holding the caring close.

YoungerOnes collect shells from the beach. Fuckit practices the guitar. Carrie fashions figures out of clay. She secures a bare-breasted mother of clay onto a piece of driftwood. Feathers spring from her head, pointing in four directions.

For my final session with Kate, I perform a play with the clay figures of the voices I made at the ocean. I want to give her a gift of what she's given me.

"Once," I begin, "there was a woman who felt like a machine." I move a rock across the floor in heavy thudding sounds. "This woman felt that if she told anyone how she felt, they'd hate her."

"Sarah," the pointing clay figure gyrates, leaping an arm length toward Fuckit and YoungerOnes, "insists that crying is bad. 'You'll get in trouble if you cry. Quit it right now!'"

The clay statue of YoungerOnes dives into the carpet.

I hold up the distinguished stick. "Fuckit has naturally decided not to be clay like all the other voices," I tell Kate. "Fuckit said, 'Fuck this crap. I don't want to hear this boring fucking whining all the time.'" The driftwood turns away from the YoungerOnes. "'I just want to be cool!'"

"Carrie couldn't get to the YoungerOnes because Fuckit and Sarah kept her away." I am the narrator and the puppeteer. I arrange the stick and the pointing finger as a barricade in front of YoungerOnes.

Kate watches attentively, smiling a little with the corner of her mouth.

"But you," I move Carrie toward Kate, "thought that YoungerOnes were important enough to listen to. You touched them. YoungerOnes wanted to be touched but they were scared. Being touched meant being hurt. They held out arms for touching, but drew back when it came close, afraid to take in love. After a long time, they decided that you didn't want to hurt them.

"Carrie always knew that you aren't really my mother. I only saw you an hour a week," I tell Kate, moving Sarah and Fuckit away from YoungerOnes. "Little children need more attention that that. But there was a time when I lived to receive that hour, holding onto it like a lifejacket. I carried heavy luggage through the miles of days until I saw you. Carrie watched you, learning how to hug YoungerOnes, calm Sarah and have fun with Fuckit.

"Sarah eventually decided that you were good for me. She stopped screaming at me for making appointments with you. She kept yelling at me for needing you, though. Sometimes she even tried to use you against Fuckit." The clay figure of Sarah perches ontop the driftwood and says "blah, blah, blah," while stomping against the wood.

"You may wonder of course," Carrie steps forward again, stopping at the curve of Kate's knee, "what got Fuckit to come here."

The Fuckit stick plops itself in front of Carrie. "Wait a minute. Carrie does not speak for me. She's always trying to take over!"

"I was just introducing you, Fuckit," Carrie says.

"I'm going to sing you a song," Fuckit announces, loudly, for Carrie's benefit so that Carrie won't steal her moment. Fuckit loves attention.

The guitar strings are covered with a film of stage fright. I look at the floor, singing:

There's times it feels like dying,
like we'll never see the light again
So many questions bout where it is we've been
For the dawn opens slowly
through shattered plans that fall
to new horizons.

My face burns when I look at Kate. Fuckit congratulates herself, but is afraid to let in Kate's acceptance.

It's hard to leave Kate; an empty feeling rises and then dissipates.

I walk down the stairs after the session. As I look inside my self, Carrie, YoungerOnes, and Fuckit all hold hands. Sarah watches silently from a corner of the Well. We have come a long way together.

I can hear Sure Voice singing in a robin, perched in a fir tree by my car.

I thought I was done. Sure Voice didn't tell me we were just resting.

5 THE ROCK

I'D never had anyone to play with before I met Stephanie. When we went on vacation, Stephanie spontaneously stripped off her clothes and jumped into a glacial lake. Fuckit admits a grudging respect for Stephanie's style. We splashed our palms against the lake, pushing great tumbling walls of ice water toward each other like children. Giggling till we collapsed, holding each other with shivering arms. "Stephanie and Louise" in lipstick hearts decorated mirrors in service station bathrooms throughout Canada. We play with our bodies, tickling and wrestling without violence. Tumbling over each other like two kittens until we tire and curl together.

The first thing I noticed about Stephanie was the way her eyes danced when she laughed. I didn't really imagine it was possible to meet a warm, caring, lesbian, writer, artist, healer who was also articulate, self-perceptive and humorous. I was sure that anyone with those qualities wouldn't be interested in me. But Stephanie started leaving mushy romantic messages on my answering machine. Carrie tucks bits of romantic poetry into bundles of flowers at Stephanie's door.

Fuckit remains skeptical. "Uh-huh," she says. "None of this crap for me. I'll have to do what I don't want so that she'll like me. I won't have any time for myself. I can't be who I am if another person is around." But Fuckit enjoys play. She's glad that YoungerOnes are able to be spontaneous and childlike with Stephanie. "It's about time they did something other than whimper," she says.

Carrie thinks she's in love with Stephanie. I'm not sure. I get uncomfortable thinking about intimacy. I feel stimulated and accepted when I'm with Stephanie. But parts of me are hiding. My heart closes so that I don't feel anything. My genitals seem lost in the bottom of the Well. Sometimes Stephanie gets too close and I tell her that I don't want to see her for a week. Sometimes I'm not sure I want to see her at all. Then I remember all the friends and lovers I've lost in the past because I ran away from them instead of trying to work things out.

Sure Voice tells me that Stephanie and I are traveling together.

"I've never needed a relationship and I'm not about to start now," Fuckit says. "You can't trust people. People rob souls and carry them away if they get too close. No one ever really sees me." She turns away.

Stephanie's face gets sad and I can see her wondering what she's done wrong. "It's not you," I say, trying to reassure, while walking backwards at the same time.

I can't let Stephanie know that there's something wrong with me. I want her to like me. Sarah tells me that Stephanie will hate me if she knows about the Well. "You can't get along with anyone," she says.

The part of me that's Carrie draws closer, trusting Stephanie. Sometimes Carrie can open my heart, giving to Stephanie from an honest caring.

Mostly, I try to ignore the voices and just play.

But relationships involve sex. Sex confuses me. I feel stupid about not understanding it like everybody else does. When my friends talk about being sexual, I blush and my butt gets tight. I can't look them in the eyes. I try to act comfortable so that they don't know I'm so unsophisticated. The sexual revolution exploded during my lifetime, finally allowing women sexual freedom and choice. It's supposed to be healthy to enjoy my sexuality. But sex still feels dirty. I dropped men after being sexual with them. I felt used. I used them. I had sex with several men when I was in a relationship with John. John accused me of cheating on him. I lied and said that I hadn't slept with anyone else. I never felt bad about the lying. I could almost pretend that I hadn't really been sexual with those others.

It's different with Stephanie. We're more intimate, telling each other secrets we've never shared before, bringing ourselves into the open. We're both writers. We encourage each other. I never thought I would meet anyone that I could share with. Stephanie says that making love is just sharing. I don't seem to know how to share it. I get aroused with Stephanie but it fades away. I don't feel warm and close or playful with her when we're sexual. YoungerOnes hide. Sometimes I don't feel anything in my body when she touches me. I pretend that I do.

Carrie says, "I want to be able to feel sexual. It should feel good to receive pleasure and touch."

"It's too close. I don't like it. Sex is a trap." Fuckit and YoungerOnes agree.

When I have an orgasm I feel invisible as if I've been stolen. YoungerOnes start crying. I don't want anyone to touch me. I go to sleep quickly, turning from Stephanie on the edge of the mattress.

But in the morning, we hug and laugh. Stephanie placates Fuckit with a cup of freshly ground coffee, served in bed.

Brenda's hands rest lightly on my stomach. "Just breathe," she tells me.

A breath huddles in my chest, shallow. I feel exposed lying on the massage table, even though Brenda's one of my friends. We've given each other lots of massages. We take turns exchanging touch and giving each other feedback on our work.

"Let your breath come into my hand," her voice is patient.

"It won't," I say between clenched teeth. My body is connected with wires to my stomach. I am lost in the blackness behind my eyes. I tell Brenda I'm feeling dizzy.

"Just feel your feet." Brenda walks to the end of the table, closing her fingers around my feet like a glove.

My feet float, somehow cut off from the rest of my body. The Well rises steeply all around me. Breathing is short and rapid. I can't get out. I'm trapped.

I sit up on the table. My teeth chatter. I can't explain because I don't understand my reaction. It's too frightening to be touched. I feel a flash of anger. I don't know why.

Brenda holds my hand. She waits for me to tell her what I need.

"How about if you just massage my back?"

Strong fingers move the muscles. I hug the front of my body against the table.

When I get home, I pace the apartment floor, restless. I pick up a smooth grey rock I brought back from the beach. Black lines wrap around it, a web without pattern. I see myself stuck within its unchanging lines. Trapped in granite, caught between thin, ancient threads. I tell myself that's impossible, shouting reassurance over the mutiny of the voices. "YoungerOnes have Carrie. Our life isn't as destructive since we left the pizza parlor to work at massage." But I don't quite believe myself. I still hide in my room for days at a time, too timid to venture out even to see my friends. I write a song, or a poem and then hide them, guarding my words against discovery. I get angry about nothing. Anger dissipates to fear. I am always afraid.

Today Stephanie's going to do a trial hypnosis session with me to help me quit smoking. Fuckit isn't so sure about giving up cigarettes because they make her feel rebellious. Carrie tries to convince her that her noncomformity will remain intact.

When I was a kid, I thought that cigarettes were repulsive. I touched ashtrays with the tip of my fingers in the dishwater and washed my hands separately afterwards. My mother said that smoking was a filthy habit.

♦*Memory*. Jerry and I are sitting on a hillside. I know Jerry from high school. He hates his family, like me. It's a warm, star-filled evening. We kiss. He has a wart on his tongue. My body is overflowing with desire. The feelings are overpowering, I'm afraid and ashamed of them. I'm mad at my body for betraying me. God was supposed to make those feelings go away. Hours and hours of kissing. Jerry puts his hand in the crotch of my jeans.

Sarah says, "You're bad. You'll get in trouble. You're disgusting."

"I don't care. It doesn't matter anyhow," Fuckit says moving toward Jerry's touch. "It's no big deal. Leave me alone. I can do what I want."

Girls are supposed to be virgins until they're married. That's what the church says. I never want to get married. But my body feels urgent.

Jerry pulls away. He lights a cigarette and offers me one. I'm dizzy in a pleasant way that makes me forget the rest of my body. The hungry anguished feelings rise through my smoke and drift away on the white cloud. The thoughts slow down and I tuck the errant ones inside of a chest in my mind. I won't search between my guilt and my passion. I'll just smoke and pretend that I know how I feel. ♦

The habit remains, escalated twelve years later.

"Now this is just a trial run to see what kind of a subject you are," Stephanie says. We're camping. I'm lying on top of the sleeping bag in the tent.

"Begin to take deep breaths into your stomach," her voice is very calm and low. I feel myself floating. "Now breathe out the back of your head, letting yourself get very very relaxed, and drifting. Then imagine that you're walking down steps, counting very slowly."

I walk on steps chiseled into the earth. My body feels light and breathing is very easy.

"Now imagine that you're going into a cave. Lie down in the cave and allow yourself to know why you smoke."

I lie down in the entrance of the cave and curl up in a ball. I hear a far-off whimper that sounds like YoungerOnes.

"No. We can't go back there," Fuckit says urgently.

"Remember a time when you were sixteen," Stephanie's voice insists.

I float down further until I am no longer in the cave and there is no more sunlight. It is the Well. Dark, damp. A man stands in the Pit. He is naked, his penis is erect. He is bald-headed with a frightening, intense look in his eyes. I don't want to know who he is. But I do know. He is my stepfather.

"What do you see?" Stephanie's voice continues.

"No. No. No." I say quietly. I can feel Stephanie's breath as she leans close to hear me. My body rolls together more tightly, my throat closes, choking, a pain stabs my vagina.

"What is it?" Stephanie asks again.

"I can't tell you." The sixteen-year-old voice is like YoungerOnes.

"Tell me where you are," Stephanie says. I look around again. I'm not in the Well anymore. I see the Joan Baez lifesize poster on the wall above my twin bed. I see the bookcase with my record player sitting on it. It is dark outside, but there is moonlight so that I can see plants outlined through my basement window. I am sixteen years old in my bedroom.

I am in the bed, but I am not alone. There are hard mouth kisses. I've been asleep and at first, I think I'm dreaming. But the weight is too real: it presses my body into the bed. He puts a pillow over my face, catching my mouth open. Inside I think, can't breathe, can't breathe, I will die, it doesn't matter, I want to die, I want it to end. I hear a sound inside of me—a scream.

My body is underneath a rock, but it's not a rock because there is hair, it is rough and scratches. And there are hands pushing my legs apart and I can't get my legs to stay together. My legs are weak. Hardness. Tearing. The weight pounds against me I try to move my head and the pillow comes away. His eyes are blue and distant. He doesn't seem to see me. I close my eyes. I want to be anywhere else than where I am. I hold my breath to make it go away.

"No, no, no. This is not happening. Why isn't my ugliness protecting me? No. I won't believe it." I'm screaming in the tent. The scream seems to come from far away. Or I'm away, not inside the body.

"Tell the sixteen-year-old that the adult Louise will help her." It's Stephanie's voice talking. Her voice is like Sure Voice, it echoes on the inside of my body.

No. I don't want to hear any more about this. It couldn't have happened, I would have remembered it all the time. I couldn't have forgotten. I am older now, there's nothing to do about it. Go away, just leave me alone.

I want the sixteen-year-old to go away. She looks at me with dull eyes. She looks defeated. Her eyes say, "Listen to me. Make him go away, not me." Pleading.

Stephanie calls me out of the trance. YoungerOne 16 isn't so close. But whenever I close my eyes I see his eyes not looking at me and I see his penis, hard, standing in my room. The weight of his body is still on my chest and my heart is beating rapidly. "I will die now," YoungerOne 16 says. I can't live through this. My legs ache, I can't get up. My stomach begs to throw up. My vagina throbs, burning. It feels as if it has just happened, just now, rape.

My body and my mind go on even though my essence has disappeared, like when I was a kid. A familiar hollowness. A fragile eggshell with the inside sucked out through a hole. Sometimes I thought my soul had been taken but I couldn't remember how it happened.

"Push him off of you," Stephanie says. "Here take this pillow and push him away with your arms that are now strong and grown up."

I begin to push but a fear comes up from my solar plexus and my arms collapse around my chest again. I cry soundless tears. I don't want anyone to hear me. I will be punished. That's what the fear is. YoungerOnes grip the sides of my stomach. "We can't," they whisper. "I just can't. I'll die," YoungerOne 16 says.

I crawl out of the tent on my hands and knees. I find a spot and stick my thumb down my throat. I grab my journal and my cigarettes. I sit looking at the trees. I don't understand how the world can be so green and beautiful and so ugly. I reach for my pen but I can't write anything down. His hand is on my wrist and it stops me.

"Just pretend it didn't happen and it will go away," Sarah says, imitating my mother. I would like to follow her advice, but I can't erase the picture that follows me behind my eyes.

Thoughts run around in my mind. "This is madness, this is madness, you are crazy." I must be crazy. How can I see this? Why does it feel so real? I hate my body, I want to throw it away.

Who is this man, Don, my stepfather? It's peculiar. I've hated my mother for as long as I can remember, but I haven't had any feelings about this man, who shared my house from when I was fifteen till I left home. I never think about him, even in passing. My only reaction to him has been indifference. I don't think that I've ever felt less about anyone.

♦*Memory*. The chapel is filled with flowers and relatives. My mother has her arm around his sleeve. Aunts and uncles whisper to each other, "Ah, at last Carol has a man. Such a decent man too. She's had such a hard time by herself. And that daughter of hers shows no appreciation."

There are side glances at me because I've been living in a foster home. This is my first familial appearance in six months. I have never met the man my mother courted in my absence. I'm just relieved that there's someone to take her attention away from me. Maybe she'll forget about me and quit yelling that I am a communist and a crazy person. Maybe she'll stop talking about sending me to reform school.

I look at him again. He is balding, his face has a gremlin expression, smooth without lines. He is younger than her, but not by more than five years. His voice is barely audible at the altar. Squeaky, as if rusted from disuse.

"It will be better at home now, with this new man and all," the foster woman assures me. She reminds me that I could be sent to reform school if I misbehave. I thought leaving home would make things better but it hasn't helped at all.

I am home again and feeling shaky. He is in the living room. I decide to call him by his first name, Don. I spend time in my room. He buys me a guitar. He builds a house and we move into it. He hardly ever talks. He goes hunting with bows and arrows and guns. He comes home with deer that have bled. He raises cows, we eat them for dinner. I wonder what he and my mother talk about.

"It's so good to have someone to take care of me and protect me," my mother says.

Protect her from what?♦

My mind is clicking like a clock that won't run down. Who is this stepfather? I don't know him. I lived with him but I have no idea who he is. Everyone thought he was a good man. He hardly drank at all, he never stormed around the house, he went to church sporadically, and he was generous to my grandmother. I must be making this up.

"I'm not going to think about this anymore!" Fuckit declares. "This is a vacation. I want a beer."

"No one will believe me, I know that no one will believe me. They never have. I will not believe it. I will make it go away." Inside of me, YoungerOnes plead with the memories. I close my eyes, but I see him. He is coming closer to me.

"Why, why is he doing this to me? He is punishing me for being mad at my mother. I must have made him do it. I had sexual feelings, sometimes I rubbed myself and I knew that I was wrong, I knew that it was a sin to feel those feelings. Those feelings caught him. But I tried to hide them. I was afraid of those sexual feelings already. I tried to make them go away. I never felt sexual toward him. He was old. He hardly ever talked. Why is this happening to me? I'm bad. I'm evil. I made it happen, it was my fault, I should have stopped him. I must be making this up." YoungerOne 16 is talking too fast. I hate her. I hate my body. My body made it happen.

I walk to a cedar tree and hold the fraying bark. "Hold me up, I can't stand this," I whisper to the tree. "Make this go away. I don't know what to do. I don't want to think about this." The anxiety pauses while my feet feel the ground and my fingers press into the solid trunk.

"This will not go away," Sure Voice whispers from the tree. "This is the Pit in the Well. You will walk much farther before you see daylight again. But I am here to help you heal."

"Where were you then? How could you let that happen to me? Why didn't you send me someone that could help me? Goddamn you, Sure Voice!" I am shaking with fury and helplessness.

"The lives of people change when people change from the inside. I know you feel awful, but this is your changing. The only way out of the Well is to know the secrets held within the obsidian, seeing what you have hidden from yourself. Never forget that you survived these experiences. That is the proof of my presence within you."

I don't want to hear calm words. I feel ridiculed. "So rape is good for me," I ask, incensed. "Thanks a ton, you're all I need in my life. Fuck you!"

"I do not understand why you are mad at everyone but your stepfather," Sure Voice says, unleashing my arms and legs.

My fists fly into the air, my feet stomp against dirt. "I could kill him. Damn, damn, damn, how dare you! How dare you do that to me!" I tear rocks from the ground and throw them. I decimate his penis in every way imaginable. I am a mindless tornado of anger.

But then I see his eyes staring at me from the breakfast table and I begin to cry. No, I can't make it stop. He'll hurt me. He'll come right now and hurt me. I curl up in a ball on the ground and rock. I can't stop it. My body can be ripped apart like a jellyfish.

Stephanie comes over and puts her arms around me. "It's not your fault," she says, "He never should have done that."

I feel small, precariously balancing on an edge. "Are you going to go away because of this? I don't see how you could ever love me. I'm dirty and horrible. I'm crazy, I must be. . . " The words fall into shaking crying, incapable of describing the hole inside of me.

I look into Stephanie's brown eyes which are tender and close. "I'm sure glad you have brown eyes, I'm not sure I could handle it if they were blue," I tell her. I want to find something to laugh about.

"It happened to me too," she says. "It happens to a lot of children. The children almost always blame themselves. The secret gets held inside until it feels safe enough to come out.

"You're not alone this time," Stephanie whispers. "I love you."

6   THE THREAT

I DON'T know how to be safe.

Strolling in the arboretum, I squint against the sun. A man is walking toward me. No one else is here, four o'clock Friday afternoon. Leaves have begun to crumple and blend with the dirt. My heart beats quickly. A man. Walking toward me. Both arms lock at my sides. His face is hidden by sun glare. He pulls something white from his pocket. My knees are too weak for running. We pass. He says hello. He puts a handkerchief to his nose. I listen behind me, ears tight with searching for his footsteps, checking the distance between us.

"Parks are always dangerous." I don't remember how young I was when my mother began the warnings. "Never walk alone at night." Danger. "Strange men lurk behind bushes." The night is enemy. I'll make the night hurt me if I challenge it. If I behaved, I could dodge the nameless villains.

Last night, running through shadows, pursued in my sleep: I feel a touch against my arm. I wake up screaming. But it's only Stephanie, lying next to me.

"Another dream?" she asks with a sleepy voice. "Do you want to talk about it?"

I mumble a sentence. I cannot stay in bed. I put on my slippers and pad into her living room, checking corners for intruders.

"Lock the doors, don't forget!" "Check the back seat!" "Stay in after dark!" "Don't wear clothes that show your breasts, your thighs." "Keep your legs together." "Don't make eye contact, it invites them." "Girls make men do bad things." Someone is waiting to get me.

I hear a car door overhead, in the garage of the apartment building. Adolescent voices, slurred, tough. I check the lock on the door. My hand shakes. "They're going to get me, someone is going to get me," YoungerOnes say. They know it could happen to me.

My friends complain because I'm never home when they call. But home has always felt more dangerous than the park. The doorknob could turn, letting anyone in. I run away with Fuckit. I sit in restaurants and bars writing in my notebook. If I'm rude enough, I can keep those men away from me. When I go out, I look behind me, beside me, crossing streets to dodge casual looking men who could be serial killers. The street is supposed to be dangerous.

Home should be safe. A nest. I wasn't warned about Don. Marriage was supposed to make him harmless. During the day, Don is a distant figure in a flannel shirt outside the window, feeding cows and tending hay after coming home from a job with machines. The mounted mute heads of the deer and elk he hunted stare blindly above the couch in the basement. He ate lunch and dinner without talking. Home is sports announcers penetrating the silence from TV screens. Football, baseball, golf, basketball. Men playing games with each other. Normal. Family. Home.

I can't control the visits of memory. I don't want to believe them. It's easier to believe that checking the back seat of my car will make me safe. Sleeping brings repeating dreams of Don's hunting rifle propped against the twin bed in my room. Hunting season, early morning, before light. In the middle of the night he'll come shoot me. He knows where I live. He'll know I told Stephanie about what he did.

I must be making this up. It didn't really happen. I was sixteen years old. Old. Not a child. Strangers are the problem, not stepfathers. He doesn't even own an overcoat.

Strangers carry guns. Don's guns lean in a line back of the closet in the laundry room. Hidden till dawn. He lifts the gun from the opposite bed as he leaves my room, stroking the bar-

rel after ripping me. He's gentle with the gun. His eyes are re-
mote. I don't know what he's thinking. He says nothing, as if
nothing has happened, as if he's not there at all. He disappears
for three to ten days after he's stolen me. "He's out in the
woods, with the boys," my mother explains to her friends on
the phone.

"He's going to kill us," YoungerOnes whisper, squeezing
my breath into shallow nips of air.

Why did he do this to me?

When my mother has people over for dinner he smiles
without opening his mouth. He gravitates toward men,
awkward with women. His short sentences are about sports and
hunting.

Waiting for dinner, he reads the local paper. He never asks
if there's something he can do to help. My mother reports on
neighbors, students, relatives. He grits his teeth. His cheeks
twitch behind the newsprint. A television set faces the kitchen
table. My mother's voice competes with the six o'clock news.
He doesn't look like a rapist. Rapists look mean. I have pictures
in my scrapbook of me sitting with an arm around Don's
shoulder. We are smiling for the camera.

This couldn't happen. I am from a normal family.
Strangers were newcomers, city dwellers, poor people, those
with uncommon religions. My family was familiar in a small
town of familiar faces. Sex wasn't even discussed between hus-
band and wife. Never mentioned in front of children. Sex
wasn't nice. I read the word incest in a novel when I was at the
university. I'm going crazy.

Crazy is a feeling without legs rooting it to the ground. Pictures swirl together in oddly shaped puzzle pieces, but the
pieces don't fit together. The puzzle has pieces that don't have a
place.

I hear my mother threatening me with sizzling words.
"I'm going to send you to reform school. You're crazy," over
and over again. "Let's pretend nothing happened," she'd say
when she was through yelling. That was supposed to make

everything all right. I remember her laughing as she snapped a picture of the tears running down my face. I was sixteen. "I'll take this picture to show you how ugly you look," she said, "and then I'll show it to all of your girlfriends at school." A blue dot burned my eyes where the camera hit. Her laughter was the sound of hard hysterical feeling.

Nothing is safe.

◇

Stephanie touches my body gently, as a lover. I pull away from her, avoiding arousal. I want to disappear without having to provide an explanation.

"I'm sorry. I uh, uh, I'm not going to hurt you. Is there something wrong with me?" Stephanie asks. "I know this is your stuff, but I can't help feeling like there's something wrong with me." Stephanie looks hurt.

I force myself to respond. I would rather be still and pretend I'm invisible. I hate talking about sex. "No. No. It's not you. It's just that every time you reach for me, I see Don's hands coming toward me." I pat Stephanie's shoulder. "Right then, when you brushed my ankle with your foot, I felt his belt tying my feet together so that I couldn't move. Afterwards, he'd leave to go hunting. When he came back he had a deer tied to a pole, hanging by her feet. I know this is stupid. I know that I'm stupid. But I was sure that I was really the deer. Because I felt dead inside. And my head ached. Once I took twenty-two aspirin to make everything go away. But nothing went away at all, it just made my ears ring something awful and then I just stopped talking for awhile because my words echoed around inside my head." I am crying again, it seems like I will never get anywhere, never escape from my child-life.

Stephanie is holding me but my skin feels thick, like the hide of a dead animal. I know she's trying to comfort me but I have to keep her away or she'll want to be sexual.

◇

"This is purely a drag," Fuckit informs me. "I'm not having any fun. Let's just sell everything and leave town. I want out!" She glares at the obsidian of the Well.

"We tried getting out of here before, but it didn't work," Carrie says. "Stephanie says we can't go back to forgetting. When we try to make it go away, YoungerOnes just start screaming."

"Goddammit Carrie, you sound like Sure Voice. Jesus Christ, give me a break won't you," Fuckit responds with irritation. "YoungerOnes are lying. I never would have forgotten it."

It's hard to hear the inner voice of Carrie over YoungerOnes' crying and screaming. It's easier to walk out the door with Fuckit and try to make it all go away.

"I don't care if I am bad." Fuckit looks at YoungerOnes, a pathetic huddle on the cold circular floor. The baby found in Kate's office. The thirteen-year-old with bloody wrists. The YoungerOne raped by Don at sixteen. "Just don't think about it," Fuckit tells them.

"Sow as ye shall reap." The words of my grandfather, repeated by Sarah. "It's punishment. It's your fault. You should have stopped it."

"We're bad, bad, bad. Bad girl. Bad feelings. Bad Louise." YoungerOnes rock, repeating themselves.

"I think this stuff made us feel bad," Carrie begins.

Fuckit plugs her ears so she can't hear Carrie. She stands in front of the YoungerOnes so that Carrie can't get to them.

"You were born bad," Sarah screeches.

My stomach arches, blocking my breath. Something is on top of me. I can't roll into a ball for protection. Maybe this pain is cancer. Maybe the stomachache is really an ulcer. My heart can't keep pounding like this, it will break. I'm torn between the fear of dying and wanting to die. "Go away," YoungerOne 16 pleads with the memories.

"What do you see?" Sure Voice asks.

YoungerOne 16 talks in weary sentences. "High school. At

break, I slammed my locker like I wanted to destroy something. When I felt my body, I was crushed under its fat. My mind had a weight on it. I lost notebooks and pencils, everything seemed scattered, I couldn't pull it together. I kept wishing that I was someone else. I hated my body. I lied a lot. I couldn't figure out why I felt so bad.

"My teachers said that I had 'potential.' I wanted to do a lot of things but I couldn't reach out for what I wanted the most. Like brass rings hung just out of grasp. When I did well at something, I thought I'd only been lucky. I was never good enough. Pieces were missing inside me. They're still missing."

I remember being sixteen. I said things over and over again to memorize them for school, so I wouldn't forget. Memorizing kept me from thinking. "I can't do this, I can't," I clutched my stomach before each debate. A powerful moment where my tongue found arguments and flung them over the podium. I practiced being heard. I won trophies, but my mother didn't hear. She had already decided I was crazy. I tucked poems, songs and short stories in the back of schoolbooks so my mother wouldn't find them when she searched my drawers. The stories started stopping without endings.

"Don is upset because you won't let him adopt you," Jim said. He changed his name to match Don's. I didn't. I couldn't lose my name. I wouldn't know how to find my self.

Don gave me a guitar. Guitars don't kill anyone. A tiny hole, circled with red, took the life from the deer. Their eyes were replaced with glass. Mounted heads without bodies.

I debated on the Vietnam war. Eighteen was the magic number of freedoom. I crossed dates off a calendar with red Xs.

"I'm still scared of saying the wrong thing," YoungerOne 16 says slowly. "Everyone will hate me. The darkness is showing. Run, I tell myself. I can't. My legs don't move. My body won't help me."

Patterns repeated endlessly, without changing. Exhaustion. My mind keeps busy with worry. I am always afraid in the morning.

◆*Memory*. I watch Don walk out the door of my room. He takes the hunting rifle he had propped against the twin bed. It's about five o'clock in the morning. His truck idles, gravel under the wheels, sound becoming distant. I have no feelings, my body is a shell. No soreness. No marks. I am a hundred years old this morning. My vagina hides the evidence.

I will get up. I will not stay in this bed. This is a bad bed. The shower is hot, as hot as possible. Soap once, soap again. My skin is turning red. I don't use a washcloth. He might have used the same washcloth. I want him off of me. I would like to take a layer of skin off my body.

Outside it is foggy and cold. The first of November. I can hear my own breathing, shallow tugs of air. My mind doesn't work. I do not give one thought to what has happened. If I thought about it I couldn't pretend to be alive. I have to live till I reach eighteen when everything will be okay and I can escape.

I wander in a wooded lot, wearing my school clothes. I take a cigarette from my pocket. I look at trees. I wish I was a tree. Minutes, hours pass. I won't ever go home again. But running away didn't help before. They said that if I ran away from such a "good home" again, they'd put me in reform school.

The voices of the teachers come through a long corridor into my ears. I think that people are staring at me. I feel eyes on my shoulder. I turn around to catch them, but they're looking away. I put a long expression on my face. 'Help me, I'm feeling awful,' the expression says.

My friends in the hallway. Talking, chirping to each other. "Aw come on Louise, quit looking so bleak. I'm so tired of hearing about how awful your mother is. Plus she called my home and my mom says that maybe we shouldn't be together so much. So get off it. I'm tired of hearing you complain." Leslie looks at me, rolling her eyes.

"I've got to go now." I back away, because that crying feeling is getting strong. I lock the stall in the girl's bathroom. I decide to hide in the middle of my body. I won't ever come out. YoungerOne 16 disappears. I swallow the ball of tears. It lands in my stomach and turns hard, salt without water. I put on a smile, locking my back teeth together. ♦

Why do I have to remember this? Why can't I just leave it back there? I'd rather be doing something else.

"You cannot leave it," Sure Voice says, looking to memory. "Everything that happened to you taught you something. You learned to hate yourself. You learned to live in fear. You became afraid of the fear. You blame yourself for events you did not cause."

"But I did well at school," I tell Sure Voice. "I don't want to believe this. If someone else told me it happened, then I'd know it was true."

"Your muscles have locked the secrets inside of your body. Healing begins with the pain. The pain is evidence." Sure Voice pauses.

I remember Brenda massaging the band of muscle around my ankles. Loosening the stiffness caused by Don's belt. My right shoulder aches where Don's hand caught to roll me over. I tense that shoulder whenever I feel anxious.

"Your experiences have hardened into your posture, affecting the way you move through the world. You repeat the same reactions you had as a child whenever you are scared now, even though the situations are different. Unless you remember what happened, YoungerOnes will never know the difference between the past and the present. You still believe that nothing is safe and that you are powerless. You are learning to see with the eyes of an adult."

Well, I'm seeing. But I don't know what to do with what I'm finding out. I pick up the grey rock crossed with lines. I look hard at it but I don't see how to untangle myself. I want to find the answer outside of myself.

The Well is cold and damp. Don stands in the Pit. YoungerOnes feel his breath on their faces, even though they are on the ledge, away from him. "Help," they say, repeating it without hope.

"It is time for telling," Sure Voice says. "Tell" echoes through the Well.

"Wait a minute," Fuckit objects. "We can't tell anybody about this. Don't tell anyone. He said that. Or. Or. He'll kill us. That bastard." I feel like running away.

"I thought you weren't scared, Fuckit," Carrie challenges.

Fuckit sticks her hands in her pockets. "Well, listen to smart-ass goody-twoshoes who thinks that she has all of the answers. Guns scare me, that's what. I may be a rebel, but I'm a pacifist rebel and that's one wierd man. Besides we don't need anybody. Nobody needs to help us, I'm doing just fine." Fuckit paces with agitation.

"You're just making a big deal out of nothing," Sarah says. "So what if he did rape you? If you weren't feeling horny as a teenager, it wouldn't have happened."

"Help. Help." YoungerOnes sound increasingly frightened.

I feel very alone. I don't think I'll ever get out of the Well. I smoke a lot of cigarettes. Sarah tells me I'm bad because I smoke.

◇

It took two days and four crossed answering machine messages to reach the healer, Jean, for an appointment.

"Well, finally," she says after we reach each other.

My hand sweats profusely against the phone.

"What did you want?" Her voice sounds abrupt. I imagine that she's looking at her watch.

My mind loses all sentences. The words I find come out in spurts and pauses. "Um. . . I wanted. . . to see you for help. Kim said. . . you might be a good person to see," my voice trails to a whisper.

"No one will be able to help us," YoungerOnes say inside of me.

"Be cool," Fuckit says, inhaling a cigarette.

"Um... I'm a lesbian. I guess I need to know if you've worked with lesbians before." I don't need anyone trying to fix what little feels right about me.

"Yes. I've worked with lesbians. Is it a relationship issue?"

"No. I like being a lesbian, that's not a problem." How do I find out where this woman is coming from on the phone? I don't trust anyone.

"Um are you a lesbian?" I ask her.

"I'm a lesbian at heart," she says.

I'm not sure exactly what that means, but at least it doesn't sound antagonistic. The next problem is that I don't have much money. We agree on a temporary payment arrangement. I want to talk about anything but the reason I need to see her.

The word "incest" comes out quickly with a question mark attached to it. My voice rises out of my body, too loud inside my ears, then dropping to a murmur. I make an appointment to see her. I need a drink of water. My mouth tastes like chalk.

"We're not taking them," Fuckit points to YoungerOnes as I sit in Jean's waiting room, twisting my fingers around each other.

"They get too attached, always wanting a mother like they did with Kate. I'm not going through that again! I'm just going to act cool." Fuckit picks up a magazine, but I'm too nervous to read.

Jean doesn't have tennis rackets or mattresses in her office. Papers and books form several scattered mountains on her desk. Her office is more formal than Kate's, with a filing cabinet and a velvet chair. No floor sitting here.

Jean sits back and swivels a bit in her chair. She seems awfully tall. She raises her eyebrows at me with a question.

I hug the corner of the couch as if I was sharing it in a crowded room.

"Don't let her know you're nervous," Fuckit reminds me. I

sit on my hands and clear my throat.

Jean just keeps sitting there. She's a lot older than Kate. She's as old as my mother. Does that mean she won't like me? Right now she looks pretty serious, businesslike. Her eyes are very blue and interesting. I wish she'd quit looking at me though. She intimidates me. I wish I was as good as her. I must look pretty stupid sitting here, shrinking into her couch.

On her wall, there's a sign that says, "All you have to do is breathe."

"A lot of good that's going to do," Sarah says cynically.

"I am not going to let her intimidate me," Fuckit announces. I force myself to sit straight in the couch.

I'm still trying to find words to say out loud. Is she frowning at me? I know that I have to say something. I can't just pretend that I'm not here after being desperate to get here in the first place. She has a pen and paper for taking notes.

"Well," I begin. She's looking at me so I decide to tilt my head to one side and look out the window. If I hide my eyes, maybe she won't know I'm a bad person.

"Um, I saw Kate for a couple years. I haven't seen anyone for a year and Kate's gone. . . . I'm here because I've been remembering some memories that I didn't remember before and um, um, I am feeling pretty bad a lot of the time. I've been realizing that for a long time my past was just a big black blur with a couple of moments sticking out of it. When these memories come up, my body hurts and chokes and feels sick. It's not like looking at pictures. It's like being there again: feeling it, seeing it, hearing it, smelling it. I get lost. So sometimes I um, can't remember that I'm a twenty-eight-year-old person."

She raises one eyebrow and writes a note. She'll never believe me. I would like to crawl under my armpit. I am probably the most inarticulate person that she has ever worked with.

"What have you remembered?" she asks.

I wish that she'd say something reassuring. "Um, my step-father, he um, raped me. Ha ha. You see, he'd come into my room before he went hunting and I'd wake up and it was real weird, ha ha. But I forgot about it until just recently, so maybe it didn't happen and I'm just crazy, ha, ha." I can't stop laughing, right when I'm going to say something serious, my mouth takes over and I'm grinning.

"Can you say that without laughing?" she asks.

It's funny that she can say that and I don't feel hurt like I do when someone says I'm doing something wrong. I guess I want her to understand.

I slow down and relate the events of the last few weeks. I have to push the words out through a wall of air blocking my mouth. The muscles in my butt are very tight, holding me together. I check to make sure that the doorknob is not moving, so that I am sure Don won't come in and kill me for telling.

As I tell her about the memories, the sixteen-year-old seems very far away. I don't feel anything when I tell her about Don. Suddenly the carpet is waving and moving. My body gets very still and it seems like I don't have to breathe. I am standing behind my body. I have gone away to a place where it is perfectly still, where there are no feelings, a vacuum, clean and solitary.

"Where are you?" she asks. Her words hang in my ears. I left through a tunnel to a place where no one can get me. I see thoughts form. "I went away," the thought says, it's almost in writing. I can see it standing at the back of my throat. But I can't say it because I am not in my body and my body can't talk without me in it.

I gradually seep back inside myself. "I um, well it feels like I go out of my body. And sometimes when I am remembering what happened to me, I see it from the ceiling, at least at first. I see Don's back as he's lying on top of me. You know, I want it to have happened to some girl that isn't me. If it gets too close, I just want to die."

"Next time that happens, call yourself back to your body," Jean suggests. "You can have some control." She gives me a book about incest from the many books in her office.

We stand at the end of the session. I want to leave as if nothing has happened here. I ask for a hug but I don't want to feel it. I don't want to feel anything about her. Carrie thinks that Jean is wise. She likes her solidness. I wonder what Jean thinks about me.

"I don't care what she thinks," Fuckit says. "I'm not going to try and get her to like me."

YoungerOnes start crying. "We want someone to care about us."

Sarah tells them that no one ever really will.

Carrie takes out her journal and writes it all down.

◇

"Hi, Louise." Judy comes over to my table at Cevies. She pats my arm affectionately. "It's good to see you, my dear." Judy picks up the book Jean gave me, bringing her dark eyebrows together in a frown. "Incest. It's horrible to even think about something like this... I can't imagine someone doing that to a child... "

It's hard to tell her I've remembered my stepfather raping me. I can't talk about the feelings. I can't find words for the fear. I stop myself from talking too much. "Oh, it's just a bunch of weird past stuff that feels bad. It doesn't matter. How are you doing?" She reaches to touch my hand with reassurance, but I feel like crawling under the table and hiding.

I can't tell her the details, but words like rape and incest don't describe it. She'll think I'm bad if I tell her what happened. Or she won't believe me. A lot of people have it worse than me, anyway it's not important. Talking about incest isn't like sharing the usual daily information. It's acceptable to talk about Stephanie or about my work. Sharing is like newspapers, if an event happened twelve years ago it's old news that's irrelevant.

I told another friend about the incest, in a swift short rush of distant words. She said, "But it's not that common is it? Let's talk about something else." Sharing a secret has two parts. One is the telling. The other is being heard. Talking about incest feels like saying dirty words out loud. I never know who will back away and tell me to make the words secret again. I don't want to talk to that friend any more.

Stephanie's the only one besides Jean who sees the feelings. When the grief and fear overtake me, I become a child again. All I can think about is how much I hurt. I cried about having a flat tire. I knew it must have happened as punishment. Stephanie dragged me to the tire store. She talked to the man at the service station. It's too hard to take care of myself.

I keep asking Stephanie if she still loves me. I can't believe her when she says that she does. She told me she's tired of my asking. I pulled away from her, afraid of criticsm. If I do something wrong, then I really am a bad person.

I open the book. I read myself in another woman's words when she talks about being so afraid of the world and of everything around her; of feeling like she has no self-confidence. I close the book again. I don't want it to remind me of how I am.

Carrie says, "But someone else felt this way too. We're not the only one this happened to."

I'm too tired to care. I think about dying a lot. I consider checking myself into a hospital as a mental patient and letting someone else take care of me. Maybe there I could let go of the horrible feelings in a big blast of electricity, flying apart without having to pretend that I'm normal. But I'm afraid of what they'd do to me there. What if they never let me out again?

It's hard to go to work. I push against the heaviness of the Well as I climb the stairs to my office. Sometimes I feel better when I'm doing massage. Sometimes YoungerOnes are quiet and Carrie takes over without conflict. I'd rather lose myself in someone else's body. But by the end of my day, the tension has built up again. My throat is full of mucus that I can't seem to swallow.

My mind is a wind-up toy that moves in clattering circles. If this didn't happen, why would I make it up? Why did he do it? What was I being punished for? Why did he act so normal and passive during the day? Why? How could anyone do something like that?

"Why" swings from question to question but I don't know how to answer myself. Why did I forget? Why do I have to pay for his desire, his crime? Why doesn't he suffer for it? I've never seen him try to kill himself. He's not afraid, he does whatever he wants. But I don't know him. Maybe he is afraid. He hardly talked, never cried, never yelled, never swore. His body was tight hard muscle, he kept his fingers locked inside his hands. His footsteps were solid, claiming chunks of ground. He held everything inside his body. He never told about himself, rationing his words.

Why didn't my mother see it? Why didn't she stop it? Why did she always blame me? Why did I always blame her? But it has always been easier to blame women, a string of lies tied to an apple. No one blames Adam for taking a bite of his own volition. No one blames God for the harshness of the punishment. Eve always pays for the sins.

Jean tells me to write letters, without mailing them to Don, to practice confronting him. The first letter says "Don, Die. Louise." It's all I can think of to say. I am telling him to go away over and over again.

But I'm the one who's driven away. I am the one who sits shaking and crying and waiting for the doorknob to open my room at night. My anger is like throwing darts at a giant. Then I'm afraid God or Don will punish me for being angry. It's only safe to be mad at myself.

I was arguing with my mother in the kitchen once, roundly denouncing the hypocrisy of the church, which I was very familiar with at the time. Don was sitting at the table with a newspaper. "Sit down and don't ever talk against the church that way in this house," he said with a slightly louder voice. I sat down immediately, shaking inside. I could yell at my mother, but not at him.

"As long as you're under this roof," my mother would say, "you will do as you're told." Everyone only gets one family. There was no place else to go.

◇

Fuckit chain-smokes by the fire in the Well. "I just don't give a shit," she says when YoungerOnes start to cry. Memories and shadows speak from the obsidian. Carrie nurtures YoungerOnes but it's not enough.

"Sing," Sure Voice whispers into the echo of the Well.

♦*Memory*. This morning a wonderful thing happened. I made up a song. It has five verses and a melody. It's called "The Misfit Song." In the song I sing that nobody loves me but that I don't care because I don't belong to them. I sang it to my best friend, Jeri. She said she liked the song a lot and wants to learn it. Even though it's a sad song I feel better when I sing it.

My song echoes against the pink tile in the eighth-grade girl's bathroom after school, filling the room with my sound. The singing reaches into my feelings and makes them real. ♦

I sing the first verse of that first song aloud while YoungerOnes hum inside me. Fuckit's love of music pulls her out of lethargy. I take my guitar from its case. My fingers play with the instrument that Don gave me and play the songs that his abuse of me did not take away. My breath sings songs of my feelings and songs I collected around girl scout campfires. The music sends my breath deep into my body and shakes loose feelings from the past.

◇

The massage table is solid underneath my stomach. My back feels like a sheath of thick matted leather between my shoulder blades. The knots are so ingrained I suspect nothing short of a hammer and chisel would dislodge them. "What's in here?" Brenda asks while pressing her thumbs into my back.

She is respectful as she touches me, always asking my permission. I've told her about the incest.

What I see is slack and wrinkled, with a texture like cottage cheese. Old. Surrounded by white hair. I saw this memory several years ago. I was in Kate's office. YoungerOne wanted to hide in a closet. I faced into a corner, trying to disappear into the seam. A momentary flash of my grandfather's penis, it made me sick to my stomach. I stuck my thumb down my throat in her bathroom. I told Kate what I'd seen, but we were talking about the closet. We skipped over my brief mention of my grandfather.

"What do you see?" Brenda asks again, encouraging me to break the silence. The question echoes inside my back as if Sure Voice was repeating it. I'm choking and my nose is plugged up. My legs are short. My arms are pressed close to my sides.

♦*Memory.* It is taller than my eyes by just a bit. "Candy," he says, "it's like candy. Help Grandpa and eat his candy." His pants are hanging around his knees. His suspenders flap loose above his shirt tail. We are in the "berry house," in the back by the canned pears neat and white in clear jars. I helped my grandma can them. They're next to the string beans in shiny metal cans. I got up when the sun was hardly in the sky to pick beans and the leaves stuck to my hands and I was full of itches. This does not look like candy. It smells of wee wee.

"No, no," but my voice is very small and catches around my tonsils. This is my grandpa and my mother said we should never tell him "no" because he is taking care of us. "Children are to be seen and not heard," she says and she is always making me be quiet, even when the clouds make pictures in the sky and I know there's a movie up there. But she says be quiet when I try to tell her about the elephants in the sky.

My grandfather's hands are very big and scratchy. He doesn't put lotion on them like Grandma. When he puts his hands on my shoulders they cover my arms and his hands pull me toward his candy. But it doesn't smell good, it smells like the bathroom. "Open your mouth," he says and his voice is tight like a piece of twine. He moves my arms around his legs, they are bigger than tree trunks and my fists hold on because everything is swimming and I'm going to fall down soon.

"Put it in your mouth," he says, "suck it." It tastes like raw sausages. My tongue curls inside of my mouth. I try to pull away, but his big hands are cupped around the back of my head. His hair bristles my cheeks, my face is lifted up and I cannot even see him, for that blob in my mouth is in the way. I close my eyes. "That's it Loueezy," he says.

When I close my eyes, I climb out of myself. I become a hollow tube and that bad taste goes away and my body is limp. I don't have to breathe. I can't breathe. I will die. There's something in my mouth and there's hair in my nose, there's no air any more. I will float.

I leave to play in the sunshine. I throw my ball hard into the rosebush. I go get it. But I don't pick it up. I run my hands back and forth against the thorns and watch them bleed. I hope I die because God wants me to. My grandmother puts salve on my hands and says I'm foolish to play so near the roses. ◆

My throat is choked off. I can't move my body. I spit up long strings of gooey white mucus into a paper bag. Part of it rolls down my chin. Brenda encourages me to get it out of my body.

My stomach feels better, but my heart's raw, as if I fell and skinned it. My grandfather died five years ago. At the time I felt guilty because I wasn't sad. I thought I just didn't care about him. Now I feel bruised by him. The place in my chest that loved him was too badly hurt to continue. When I visited him, he'd rub my hands and arms with his aging fingers. My adult skin wanted to crawl off my body. I hated it when he touched me.

"You're a bad girl for making Grandpa do this," Grandpa had said. His voice sounded different, frantic, gruff. I knew that what was happening was bad. "Sow as ye shall reap." The test was in what happened to me. I had severe sore throats when we lived with him. God punishes.

"Don't tell, Loueezy. Be a good girl now." He patted me on the head like a dog that he was training.

I couldn't tell because I didn't know the words for what he was doing. Maybe I could have drawn a picture if someone had encouraged me. But I knew those parts of the body were dirty because that's where pee comes from and the bathroom is a dirty place. I had never heard the word "penis" spoken out loud.

"Always obey Grandpa." "Don't get dirty." "Seen and not heard." "Be still Loueezy." I never let the kids at school call me Loueezy. I must have done something very bad to make that happen.

My body turned awkward and clumsy. I fell from the monkey bars, the merry-go-round, and the swings. I fell off about everything I climbed onto. My body felt weighted from the shoulders. My calves were made of hard steel which kept me from walking away.

I've always remembered when my grandmother and my mother pulled my pants down and held me on the bed while my mother probed inside my vagina. I was nine years old. They said they saw blood on my underwear and I must have fallen from my bike. I screamed that I didn't fall from my bicycle. They weren't listening to me. Now I wonder if they knew what Grandpa was doing. I don't know what they found. I don't know how the blood got there. No one stopped him.

7 THE RESPONSE

♦MEMORY. I told my friend Sally that my mother said her mother had a big mouth. We were talking about how our mothers always sounded like teachers, talking in loud-speaker voices that drowned us out.

The next day, my fifth grade teacher calls me into the hall. Dressed in black, she stands next to Sally's mother. Sally's mother teaches fourth grade, mine teaches sixth. "Mrs. Richards is upset because Sally came home telling her that you said your mother said Mrs. Richards has a big mouth. Your mother says she'd never say anything like that! So apologize to Mrs. Richards for telling that awful lie about her." My teacher waits with one hand on her hip.

My voice is tight in my throat. I've never been called into the hall before. I try to be good but I'm bad. My mother did say that about Mrs. Richards—a couple of times. And Sally told on me, just like my brother Jim would do.

They don't ask me if I heard my mother say that. They don't want to believe me. I look across to Mrs. Richard's belt, a circle of black around a print dress. I look down and sweat from my face. A whisper. "I'm sorry, Mrs. Richards."

"And your mother didn't say any such thing about Mrs. Richards now did she?" my teacher asks in a loud voice.

"Uh-uh." The lines on the forest green linoleum start wiggling like white snakes.

The whole class looks at me as I take my seat. Don't

86

tell. Don't tell. "No one believes you," Sarah says.

Telling in the hands of a grownup was a weapon. My mother told on me. "I'll call that teacher who thinks you're sosmart and tell her how disrespectful you are at home," she threatened when I balked instead of agreeing with her. She often mentioned "having trouble with me" when she spoke to my teachers. After I ran away at fourteen, my mother contacted the parents of my friends to tell them I was "crazy," to warn them that I might influence their daughters. She seemed able to control how others thought about me through telling. Teachers would never lie, so she wasn't questioned. My friends backed away, the school counselor told me to shape up, teachers called me for conferences. It didn't matter whether I was quiet and depressed or trying to kill myself. The most important goal involved placating my mother.

It always seemed like I had something I wanted to tell someone. But I couldn't remember what it was. It was a secret.

Anyone could tell on a child. Children could tell on each other. But children couldn't tell on adults. Seventh grade, the year when we learned world history. My social studies teacher said that communists encourage children to "turn in" their parents. She said that's why we must fight communism. "In the United States," she continued while pointing to the flag hanging next to the blackboard, "we don't have a police state. We don't turn in our families." It is more important to be loyal than honest. Families had to be protected at all cost.

Telling was never about getting help.

◊

In the last four months, my body's been in daily pain from the memories. Relief is always temporary. After I remember an incident involving my grandfather or Don, the pain lets up a bit. But then a different pain starts, in my eyes or shoulder or thighs. My body's out of my control, as if it's still not mine. Sure Voice told me that my body only experiences in present time. That's why the memories feel so real years after they happened. "In healing, your body reopens wounds from the past," she said. "It is as if you kept an infection covered, hoping it would mend without your attention. Now it needs light to heal."

Sure Voice sounds logical. But it doesn't help the anxiety. Words don't convince the voices. They hardly hear her or Jean. Carrie tries. I tell myself to be calm. I try to eat right, to get up instead of hiding in bed, to go to work doing massage. But my will has a hole in it. I spend my days with memories. I'm closer to my past than to the present. My pubic bone aches when I wake up, as if it's been banged against something hard. My pubic hair burns as if someone has been pulling at it. I imagine my vulva to be a large raw, ugly sore. I've had these pelvic sensations intermittently for years. It was less intense then than it is now, wrapped in conscious memory. Before, I accepted it without thought, along with sore throats and anxiety attacks.

Sure Voice says that it's important to talk about the incest so that I can get it out of my body. She says that's the only way YoungerOnes will start talking again. They need to know that I can tell.

I'm ashamed of what was done to me. The incidents are ugly, furtive and wrapped in violence. The memories make me feel ugly. I shovel cigarettes and extra food into my mouth. I eat from the refrigerator, grabbing food from the shelves and eating it with my hands. Gagging, I feel my tongue pressed against a penis. I can't get anything that feels good inside of me. Childhood rooms haunt me. The bathroom, the berry house, my mother's room, Grandpa's car. My breath sticks to my throat. I can't swallow.

I sit like a statue, unable to move. My voice frightens me when it tells secrets. I hold my head tilted back, waiting for God to punish me. Waiting for Grandpa's penis. The incest has become part of me, absorbed into my skin, my vagina, my mind. If someone sees it, they'll hate me.

It's hard to tell Jean. When I talk about my grandfather I

feel young and unimportant. I hear my grandfather's judgements. "You play too much," he'd say in the voice he used to officiate grace at the dinner table. "Come help Grandpa." I'm sure I did something that made him hurt me. But I couldn't be good enough to stop it. I brought my report card to Grandpa to get dimes for A's. I washed the dishes, took care of Jim, sat quiet and still. Trying to earn safe passage.

Jean says, "You look like a little girl when you talk." She wrinkles her face up and makes her voice sound like she's talking to a kid. "You can grow up," she says, reminding me that although I was the child this happened to, I'm not a child anymore. But YoungerOnes' feelings are more compelling than those of my adult life.

When Fuckit tells Jean about the sexual abuse I sound tough and removed. "So what?" Fuckit says. "Nothing hurts me." Then YoungerOnes start to cry and I turn into them again.

YoungerOne 16 always talks in a flat, low voice. She tries not to feel. "We might as well die," she repeats. She's given up trying to change what happens to her. She's afraid to finish projects. Don was the last straw. After him, she surrendered to Christianity and worked at being perfect in school.

Jean tries to get closer to YoungerOne 16. She's gentle with that part of me. But YoungerOne 16 feels invisible. "It's no use to fight back," she says. "I don't exist. You don't really care about me." Nothing changes her mind. It's too hard to try and hope if I'll end up failing.

The smaller YoungerOnes want Jean to love them. It seems like they'll never feel cared about. At the end of one session, YoungerOne 7 tells Jean, "I really like seeing you." She says it shyly, looking at the floor, waiting for love to come back.

Jean holds the door open and says, "I like that you like me."

"We want her to say she likes us too," they say, disappointed. "If someone cared about us, we wouldn't get hurt."

Carrie reaches over to touch them. She laughs gently.

"Well, Jean is not going to say she likes us just because we like her. That feels good but I don't know why."

◇

Jean looks concerned when I walk into her office the next week. "What's up?" she asks, peering at me through her glasses.

I am a frazzle of tear trails and rumpled, slept-in clothing. The blackness and monsters are gone from the Well. The solid shapes of Grandpa and Don have replaced them. I am tiny next to grown men. My arms and legs are tired. When I try to avoid them, it feels like the obsidian walls are closing in on me.

I think of my life in the last week. When Stephanie reaches out to give me a hug, I don't see her. Instead I am on my grandfather's lap again. He rubs me up and down against his crotch. The room is full of Christmas visitors. No one seems to notice what my grandfather's doing. Too much of my fear makes sense too suddenly. I don't want to believe the evidence of my memory. I take three or four scalding showers a day to make myself clean. I would like to pour scalding water inside of myself because the dirt feels so deep. Nothing that happens in my twenty-eight-year-old life feels real.

YoungerOnes are never comfortable. "Hide, hide, hide," they say.

"Die, die, die," Sarah tells them.

I curve over the end of Jean's couch. I hold the corner pillow in front of my stomach for protection.

"I don't want to live anymore," I announce. Jean made me promise, in the beginning, that I'd talk to her before I tried to kill myself. So I'm telling her now. It feels like my skeleton has melted. I can't stand upright or move forward. "I don't want to remember anymore. Nothing is ever going to change, these nightmares are going to last forever. I can't love Stephanie right. I don't believe I'll get out of the Well. I'm too scared. It's too hard. I hate myself for what happened to me."

Jean watches me while I watch the roof through the

window in her office. YoungerOnes wish that she'd hold me and tell me that everything's all right, but she never does that.

"Men with bald heads remind me of my stepfather. I get sick to my stomach just passing them. I shrink when they look at me. I'm suspicious of grandfathers playing with children in the park. I hear noises at night. In the morning, my jaw aches from grinding my teeth." I'm desperate for her to hear me. Remembering has irrevocably changed my perceptions of my family, my childhood and myself. I can't live with knowing this.

Years of wanting to tell clash with years of terrified silence. "I hurt all the time... "

"What?" she says sharply. "I can't hear you."

Maybe I don't want her to hear me. She doesn't care anyway. She probably thinks I'm lying or crazy. She just listens because I pay her. Fuckit turns from Jean. I feel unreachable.

"Please believe me. Please make it stop." YoungerOnes stretch a tentative hand toward Jean.

"Do you believe you?" she asks.

"Nobody hurts me!" Fuckit says stubbornly.

I want to believe that if Jean believes me, she'll make it go away. But it's already happened. It's too late to get an adult to stop it.

I tell Jean that I want to die. I don't feel anything when I tell her that. The rug seems to wave like grass moving in wind. I'm tired of my endless debate between life and death. I want a decision. Dying seems more plausible.

I look up at Jean. Her eyes are soft. I don't really think she thinks I'm bad. I can't even pretend that she hates me—I have gotten more honest with myself. I have to keep checking though, because I never know when someone will turn on me.

She takes her glasses off, leans back in her chair and closes her eyes. She does that when she's thinking of what to say.

"I wonder what it would be like if you decided to live," she says slowly.

"The more I live, the more I hurt. I thought I could escape

my past. But I can't stop feeling it, seeing it or thinking about it. I must have made it happen."

"You know, I tried to kill myself once." Jean looks directly at me. "I was about sixteen, older than you were when you first tried it. I decided that if I was supposed to die, then I'd die. And if I didn't die, then I might as well commit myself to being alive."

Jean's words stop my long familiar recital of why I should kill myself. She hardly ever talks about herself. She seems so powerful now, it's hard to imagine she ever wanted to die.

"But how do you do that?" I want her to hand me a formula.

"You decide to live. Then when you're feeling suicidal, you remind yourself that you're not going to act on that."

"But there's no purpose to being here." I don't think making a decision is going to make me feel any better.

"Oh, some people think that you have to search for purpose. I think you just make one up and follow it."

I look out the window. I wish I could fly away. I don't know what I want. What will I do if I can't think about dying? What if there isn't another escape? A decision might work for Jean, but she's stronger than I am. Sometimes Jean makes hard things sound easier than they are.

"You might be more creative if killing yourself was not a solution," Sure Voice whispers to Carrie.

"Louise," Jean searches for my eyes. "You are in charge of the decision. You can decide not to kill yourself. But it's more than deciding not to die. It's also deciding to live."

The session ends without resolution. Jean hugs me. "Think about it," she says as she often does. I feel grumpy. YoungerOnes want her to do something to make it better. Instead, she stirs things up and sends me home with questions. I don't feel any better than when I came.

I suppose this decision should be easy, but it's not. I have to pay attention to each voice. If I try to leave any of them out, I feel worse. Decisions are by consensus. The voices are all talking at once, pulling my body between them. That's why I'm staring at the walls of my room. I know that I ought to just say, "Okay, I commit to living. I will not kill myself, ever. I am already guaranteed the experience of death, so what's the hurry?"

"Die, die. You are bad, you should die," Sarah chants.

Fuckit paces restlessly and hardens her chin. "I don't care if I die. I just want to relax!" She reaches for my coat.

A small voice speaks from beneath the weight in my stomach. "I am bad," she says, "but I'm scared of dying."

Grandpa and Don move closer and closer to YoungerOnes in the Well. "You've told, you'll die," they threaten.

"I don't want to die," Carrie says. "I want to live. She tries to reach YoungerOne but there's a tight layer of muscle between them. YoungerOnes aren't letting anyone touch them.

◇

"Nothing changes. Bad things always happen to me. I can't keep going through it," YoungerOne 16 says desperately.

"But things did change, even for you," Sure Voice says softly, looking past her toward YoungerOne 17. "Even though you were afraid to believe it."

Inside I see YoungerOne 17 smoking in a niche in the Well, leaning against the obsidian. She's wearing the green school uniform of Bomaderry High School in Australia where I spent my senior year as an exchange student.

♦*Memory.* I am crying in the deserted hallway of Bryce High School after school. Last week I heard that I was going to be the Rotary Exchange Student. But the school counselor just told me that she'd met with my mother who told her I couldn't get along with anyone and shouldn't be an exchange student. Now I might not get to go; the counselor said it would depend on my behavior. I wander around looking for something to hold onto. A friend tells me that it will help to give my life to Jesus so I do, but it makes me feel guilty. The Rotary decides that I can go.

Australia's a lot different than Bryce. I don't miss my family. But sometimes I feel very alone in a vast dark hole with no floor. I like giving speeches to the Rotary though. I feel important when I drink beer in the pub with the chairman of the exchange program and the president of the Rotary. Being an exchange student is special—even though I get worried that I'll mess up and they'll see I'm not good enough to be here.

The best part about being here is staying with the Gumms. I've never met anyone like May before. She's sixty years old. Her fingers are spotted with clay from the pottery classes she teaches to the women in the neighborhood. Her cigarettes burn long ashes while she's at the potter's wheel but they never fall into the swirling clay. She tells me never to get married, that I should just explore life. I've never heard an adult say that it's okay not to want marriage. We have real conversations too; she asks me what I think and she listens to my answers. After dinner she lets me sing to her instead of drying the dishes. Her favorite song is "500 Miles," it makes her cry.

I feel like she likes the true me, or at least the parts of the true me that stick out from the darkness. She looked at my fingers once and said I had the hands of a writer. ♦

I smile with the memory of May. I remember feeling that she honestly liked me. Knowing her gave me hope for growing old. I see how she fed the vision inside of me and made it sound possible.

"The worst part was when I had to leave Australia at the end of the year," YoungerOne 17 stubs out the cigarette and doubles over. "I never cried that much before. May and I were sitting in her car, the 'Mini,' waiting for the truck of friends to pick me up and take me to the airport. May and I were saying goodbye and saying we loved each other and I was crying loud with sound, I thought I would dissolve and I didn't care because I didn't want to leave her. I didn't want to let go of that love. I wanted to keep talking with her."

When I first got back to Bryce from Australia, I wrote her long letters. I held the koala bear she'd given me and ached with missing her. Over time I closed my heart again, forgetting the love, shutting away my loss of May. Australia was too far away. The darkness kept growing inside of me. Love was too rare to hope for. Now it seems like a long time away from May.

"She touched the life in you when you most needed it," Sure Voice tells YoungerOne 17. "The incest wasn't the only things that molded you. May's caring fed who you are, her vision of you fed your dreams and helped you keep walking."

◊

I walk to Cevies, my favorite gathering place, anxious to escape the turmoil of the voices. It's November. I don't feel the cold. I don't feel my feet walking or the rock in my pocket.

"How are you?" Judy asks from a table near the window. "It's good to see you, my dear. Have a seat." She smiles warmly at me, welcoming. She's dressed in the colors of fall, burnt yellows and browns. She easily pushes a chair aside to make room for me. Unlike me, Judy appears to function with a natural grace. Theresa is here too, wearing a new burgundy parka over her shoulders. She broadens her smile as I sit and moves her purse so that there's no barrier between us. Gretch completes the circle, nodding at my arrival and moving a stray long blond hair to the side of her face. I sigh and lower my shoulders. Sometimes I forget about the warmth of sitting in a circle of women. I met Gretch and Theresa at Cevies and I don't know them as well as Judy, but every couple weeks we run into each other here and talk.

Theresa grins, Gretch sighs and Judy says, "Arg, I've been working all day." It's my turn. They know about the incest. When I told them, Gretch said that she was raped by her uncle as a teenager. She told her mother, who believed her. But to this day, ten years later, her uncle maintains that Gretch tried to seduce him. He says he told her that would be a sin. Sometimes I catch her looking at nothing through the window and I wonder if she's thinking about her uncle's lies.

"Well," I gulp a breath of air and reach for a cigarette. "I've been, uh, thinking about life and death a lot lately."

"Nothing like a light conversation opener," Judy remarks. I lock my jaw self-consciously. Judy pats my arm. "I'm just kidding, dear. Come on, don't stop."

"Um. Well. Do you ever think about committing suicide?"

"Well for God's sake, don't do it," Theresa says immediately. "We'd miss you!"

"I didn't say I was going to kill myself." I say defensively. No wonder nobody talks about this stuff. "It's just that I think about it sometimes and I wondered if everybody thought about it or if it was just me." My stomach tightens.

Everyone's quiet. Judy slowly twists a brown curl around her finger. Gretch fidgets with a coaster.

Theresa looks up, thoughtful. She's stopped her usual smile. "Oh, I think about it sometimes." I'm surprised to hear that from her; she has children she speaks of warmly. She sips Chablis. "But I'd never do it. I'm basically a coward." She looks over to Judy and starts smiling again.

"I never think about killing myself," Judy says. "Who knows what happens when you die? Playing a harp with a bunch of other dead people?" She rolls her eyes. "I think I believe in reincarnation. If that's true, I'd just get sent back again anyway."

"Stephanie believes that if you kill youself, you return to similar circumstances until you've learned from them. Blech." I shudder considering the prospect of going through all this again.

Gretch has been stirring her ice with a straw. "I think about suicide, but I probably wouldn't do it. But I think about it when I feel bad." She blushes and looks at the tabletop.

"Sometimes I think that suicide is an addiction," I tell them. "I've thought about killing myself since I was a kid. I think it will cure everything. . . that I could rest and not struggle any more. But every time I have the flu or after a day of smoking too many cigarettes I'm terrified that I really am dying because I feel so shitty." Everyone nods agreement.

"I think there's a difference between being scared to die and wanting to live," Theresa volunteers.

"That's what Jean says. I wonder if that's why some people look alive, with light sparkling in their eyes. It doesn't seem to matter how old they are. I have a couple massage clients who are like that. Jean has that intensity in her eyes too."

"I always imagine that those people get up in the morning, look outside their window and say good morning to the tree," Theresa grins. "It's some attitude that keeps life from greying."

"That's what I want," I say, "but I don't know how to feel enthusiastic about being alive. I want to learn. I want to notice everything. It's not that I only want to feel happy... I don't think I could ever only feel one emotion. I just want living to be interesting... and less grueling."

Theresa purses her mouth together, puzzled. "I don't think I'm committed to life. Mostly I think it's important to have a good relationship. I'd settle for that. When you expect too much from life, you get disappointed."

"I set goals for myself—things to do. I do some of them because they're good for me. After a week I get tired of them so I come here and have a glass of wine to recover," Judy sighs, "but it's not a bad life." I've always marveled at Judy's ability to cook herself exquisite healthy meals, get enough sleep and keep her apartment in genteel order. Being alive sounds like too much work to me.

"But it sounds like you want a 'feeling' about life, Louise," Judy continues. "I don't know how to be that enthusiastic. Maybe that's what positive thinking is about. I'm not very good at convincing myself that way though."

"Me either," I admit. "I just can't seem to talk myself into feeling how I don't feel. I don't want to pretend that things are fine when they're not. I want to combine reality with passion. I just can't figure out how to do it."

Theresa looks up from her study of the table. "I've had some wonderful moments though. When I woke on Saturday I could see fresh snow on the mountain sparkling against the clear sky outside my window. I felt happy."

I feel better after talking with my friends. The voices are still. I don't feel like I deserve my friends. And I'm afraid of them because they're people. But I'm lucky to know them.

◊

I've been trying to take a nap. When I close my eyes, I see a garage door. It's Uncle Kevin's garage. I haven't thought about Uncle Kevin for a long time. I can feel the muscles of my inner thighs straining to hold my legs together. I am in Uncle Kevin's station wagon. We're stopped in front of the garage. Then everything is black and damp like the Well. Pieces of memory. The door comes back again and again. A movie frame, repeated, stuck. Driving up, stopping. My stomach doubles up like a clam trying to protect itself from being pried open.

What is it about the garage door? Why can't the voices just shut up and lay off for a while. Damn! There is no more! There can't be any more.

My thirteen-year-old self looks into the mirror while blood runs down her wrists. I hate her right now. She's ugly.

"She should have died," Sarah says.

"We want to die. Make it stop. Nothing will ever change," YoungerOnes whine. Hate is slimy and dark like dirty oil. Hate got inside us."

"Oh shut up!" Fuckit says. "I've had enough of this. Go ahead and die and get it over with!"

I'm lost between bits of memory and undefined terror. It's hard to think. I have a cup of Valerian root tea made by Carrie instead of Fuckit's prefered Scotch. I lay down again. I go to sleep looking at the garage door.

"They're called flashbacks," Stephanie says the next day.

"Bits and pieces of memories. They're like the tabs of file folders that the labels attach to. Once you start remembering, it's like opening the file and seeing everything that's been closed for you. You can't stop the process that you've started."

My mind filed complete memories under small remembered scenes that have always seemed unaccountably vivid. Memories of Grandpa stored under the long-remembered rosebush thorns. Memories of Don kept in a bottle of aspirin and the gun closet. But Uncle Kevin died six years ago of lung cancer. My mother called to tell me. It was like hearing the death of a stranger, casual news that didn't evoke mourning. I never think about Kevin. Nothing happened. I must be making this up.

♦*Memory*. "And so you're Louise." He pats my eleven-year-old head. His British accent has faded with the years of immigration. He wears a plaid shirt and baggy grey pants that are so big they pucker with his belt.

I'm supposed to call him Uncle Kevin. He's my aunt's brother.

"How nice that you've moved to Bryce with your parents," my mother says to him. "Martha says that you're going to open a watch repair shop."

Uncle Kevin lives with his parents? He looks too old to have any parents. He's at least fifty-five, with a round shiny spot on top of his head. Strands of greased grey hair lie on top like snakes sunning themselves on a rock. I heard my mother talking to Aunt Martha about him. He was divorced several years ago. He has a grown daughter who never visits him. My aunt's voice sounded disgusted and hard when she talked about his daughter.

"Do you have a watch, Louise?" he asks, while moving closer to me.

"No." I look at my bare white wrists. I feel nervous around him.

"Would you like one? You'd have to take good care of it. And not get it wet."

I look at him and feel shy, which is usually how I feel when adult men talk to me. He is very tall. I don't know whether I like him. Nobody gives me presents except on my birthday or some holiday. He's just told Jim he'll give him a watch too.

That's not fair. Jim's only nine. He's not big enough to get a watch.

"Well, I'll be over with the watches tomorrow," he says looking at me.

"Thank you," I say like my mother says I'm supposed to. She'll have me write him a thank you note. She always makes Jim and me do that.

After he leaves, my mother says, "Oh, how nice for you kids."

I hear her on the phone with my grandmother, talking about Uncle Kevin and how good he is with the youngsters. ◆

Morning. I wake with a rash on the back of my left wrist, where I used to wear a watch, years ago. My anus is sore and itchy like hemorrhoids. My stomach hurts. The radio alarm is blaring about Christmas shopping. Forty days left.

I rumble out of bed and away from the garage door that chased me through my sleep. "Give me a break!" Fuckit says to God. I am not in a good mood.

The rash itches. I thought I'd outgrown it. About six months after Kevin gave me a watch, I developed a metal allergy. My wrist oozed a sticky infected discharge despite prescribed ointments. It itched constantly. Taking the watch off didn't make the rash go away. I began to break out in little itching bumps around my navel too. The rash came back several times after I'd left home, when I was being sexual with men. I haven't had the rashes for about three years though. Now I wonder if I'm allergic to Kevin.

◆*Memory.* The garage door is white, criss-crossed with blue trim like his house. Even in the laundry room I can hear the ticking of fifteen clocks. A cuckoo strikes a quarter past. Inside the watch shop a display case protects exotic clocks. Round glass globes surround gold workings and moving disks.

I move toward the shop door since that's usually where I wait. Mother and Jim are going to pick me up.

"No," Uncle Kevin says. "They won't be here for a while. I have something to show you."

He leads me through the living room to his elderly parents' bedroom. Figurines of porcelain from England curtsey on the dresser. Little girls painted in pastels. I don't like frilly stuff like that. The windows are behind lace crocheted curtains. My stomach is jumping up and down. I turn to leave the room, not sure of what he wanted me to see.

Uncle Kevin has folded down the fine white bedspread to white sheets underneath. "Lie down," he snaps like a drill corp commander.

I pause. Why does he want me to lie down? I don't want to. I am eleven years old. I don't take naps anymore. Maybe he doesn't know that. I want to tell him I don't want to lie down. I would rather look at the clocks. But my mouth is too dry. My tongue is rolled into a ball. Sometimes I can't talk.

"Lie down there, you bitch." He's not shouting but his voice is hard like steel. I am afraid to look at his face. I don't think that I can move, but I do. He pulls my pants to my ankles.

He lies on top of me after unzipping his pants. He pushes up and down, wrapping his arms around my ribs. I can't breathe. My pubic bone feels sore. "You cunt," he says. His anger comes out on his breath. I try not to breathe his words into my body but they come in anyway.

My body is confused. Thick, strange feelings come from between my legs. But Kevin feels horrible. He feels hating. He feels old. This is dying. It seems like he will crush my body underneath his weight. I cannot breathe. I cannot move. Every time he bears down on me he calls me a name. No one has ever called me these names before. But I know what they mean. They mean I'm bad. "Bitch. Cunt. Whore." My body stops feeling. I become vacant. He is sneering. "You're liking this aren't you?" he whispers. I can't talk. He doesn't wait for an answer. He is six-foot-two but he seems ten feet tall, towering over and stretching far beyond me. I have no room.

It ends. He gets up, pulls up his pants and leaves with a curt "Put on your clothes." I get up and zip my pants. I hurt. Will it be bruised in that place that has new bits of hair?

I look at my face in the mirror. She looks like a ghost to me. "You liked it," his voice sounds in the back of my mind. "I hate me," I say back to the voice.

I don't want to go to the clock shop, but I don't want to stay in his parents' bedroom looking at lace. My arms are frozen or I would smash the little porcelain girl onto the ground.

Too tired. Tired. Sick. I don't feel good. I'm just sick. No thinking. What happened. Don't know. Just sick.

He is behind his workbench with monacles that clip to his glasses. He peers at miniature pieces. His hands are steady. He looks like he always does as if nothing has happened.

I study the floor. I don't want to see him. A blushing shame rolls over me. I pretend to look at the clocks in the case. I let the ticking take over my brain. Ticking never stops.

"Your watch working okay," he says, but not as a question. "You take good care of that watch." ♦

I am on my knees throwing up into the toilet. I imagine falling through the round white hole, drowning in toilet water. My wrist itches and starts to ooze.

"What good is knowing this stuff? Get me out of here. My fault. I just want to die." YoungerOne 11. She looks miserable.

"Louise." I hear Sure Voice. "It is time for your decision," she speaks slowly. "Your life-story will not always be the way you might have wished. If you give up, you will stop learning. Your grandfather is dead. He is not God. He cannot kill you. Don is miles away—he does not even know that you have told his secret. You do not need to kill yourself for them." For a moment, I can see Sure Voice. An ancient woman with silver hair, standing close to YoungerOnes. "Your life will change. You must trust that. If you kill yourself, Kevin wins because he takes you with him to the grave. You are an adult." She looks at Carrie. "You can help YoungerOnes. You must choose life or you will not be able to stand to hear any more of what they have to tell you."

Right now I'd rather die.

"Your feelings will not kill you," Sure Voice says.

"He's not going to win! I hate him!" Fuckit says suddenly. "I've had enough of this shit!" She starts screaming, "He tried to stomp the life out of me! I won't let him have us!" I begin pounding pillows, alive with furious energy. "No more!"

Carrie joins Fuckit. "We have to change this," she says. "We can't keep feeling helpless, like they wanted us to."

"You asked for it, you should pay," Sarah contradicts them. "Sow as ye shall reap. You made it happen. Die."

"We never asked for anything from that bastard," Fuckit yells at Sarah.

"No. We will not die. We will heal." Carrie faces Sarah. "To heal is to believe in life."

Something has snapped inside of me. Maybe it's the greasy voice of Kevin swearing into my ears. A hard, long-hidden redness spreads through my body, furious. I would like to kill him.

YoungerOnes are shaking. "We want to die. We want out of here. Help."

"YoungerOne 11 is very frightened," Sure Voice says. "She has kept these secrets for a long time. She hated herself, unable to express anger at what was happening to her." Sure

Voice is a healing light in my solar plexus. "YoungerOnes still feel trapped under all those bodies," she tells Fuckit.

Carrie and Fuckit whisper to each other. "Now here's the plan," Fuckit announces.

I close my eyes and imagine another ending. Carrie and Fuckit storm Kevin's clock shop. Fuckit shouts, "Let her go!" while Carrie takes the watch off YoungerOne's wrist. Fuckit grinds the watch under her heel. "You bastard!" she yells, throwing pieces of the watch in his face. She and Carrie move the display case in front of Kevin so that he's locked in a corner of his shop.

They lead YoungerOne out of his house. They drive to my adult apartment in another city. Carrie holds YoungerOne and keeps saying, "You're safe, you're here now." Fuckit shouts, "We're not going to let him have you. We're going to get free of him! We're not going to carry him around anymore!"

I feel exhilarated and clear inside, hopeful. I don't know all the steps to healing. I only know that each step follows the one before it.

8   THE STARE

My body's will is separate from mine. I cannot bring myself into harmony. I feel sexual and begin to masturbate. But no matter what fantasy I choose, I see Kevin instead, leering over me. I can't make him go away for good. I hear YoungerOnes whimpering in the Well. I pull my hands away from my own body. I hate my body for being sexual. I hate my mind for showing the memories.

Before each memory my stomach tightens, cutting my breath in half. Today my knees hurt, the muscles lining my shins ache. My anus has been itching, embarrassing me, causing the heavy muscles of my buttocks to squeeze together. From my buttocks past my thighs a band of fatty, sagging flesh with a rough bumpy texture is numb. I have had burning diarrhea for the past three days, cramping my abdomen.

Brenda's office is warm and inviting. A flowered sheet covers the massage table. It's warmed by two red heat lamps hung from the ceiling. A thriving begonia in the corner enhances the feeling of calm within this room.

When Brenda begins massaging my lower back and gluteal muscles, I feel her hand but nothing else. My skin is dead.

"Why is this numbness here?" she asks, while tracing the outline of my hip joint with her fingers.

"To keep him out," I hear the inner words clearly, as if my thigh was speaking. My body squeezes together in response, making me long and narrow.

"I don't want to talk to my butt!" Fuckit says. "It's just something to sit on. It's not important. I just want a relaxing massage. I always have to work."

"You're making this up," Sarah says.

"What would happen if you weren't numb here?" Brenda asks, going deeper into tissue with her fists and thumbs.

I gasp as white-hot pain radiates from a spot under her thumb, spreading to my knees like branches of lightning. My upper back stiffens, while my forehead digs into the massage table.

My neck arches as if my head were trying to crawl away from my body. Bits of memory: A white towel. My head is pressed against the edge where the towel and the brown tweed living room carpet meet. My inner voice is ragged and hoarse, tinged with screaming. "No. No. No."

"Breathe." Brenda stops working on my buttocks and lightly places her hand between my shoulder blades. "What's happening?"

"I remember lying on a towel on the living room floor. I'm about thirteen. I can't move my body, an arm is across my thighs, a big body is leaning on the arm, anchoring me. It's cutting my legs off, pressing them into the towel."

"Ask your butt what the tension is."

All I hear is a horrified "No, I can't, I can't." A sharp pain travels up my rectum. I hold the sides of the table, curling my fingers around the upholstery.

"What do you need to be safe enough to know what's locked inside of you?" Brenda asks, moving her hands from my body and covering me with the towel.

YoungerOne 13 feels naked inside of the Well. With my inner eyes, I see her leaning into the walls, wishing the rocks would swallow her. Her knees are jammed close to her stomach, supporting her head. Her eyes are closed tight, causing a helmet of tension around my head.

"I'll blow up inside," YoungerOne says. "My insides will be shredded, torn by the sharp points. I'm so dirty. I just want to die."

"I'm afraid it will kill me to see it," I tell Brenda. "I feel like someone's slashing my intestines. My grandmother used to give me enemas when I was constipated. My abdomen would bloat and bulge. I thought I could just pop open, spilling out of my belly."

"Touch your abdomen for a minute," Brenda suggests.

I feel the soft skin of my belly moving in and out with my breath.

"We're not going to blow up," Carrie tells YoungerOne 13, putting an arm around her shoulders. "I won't let him get us."

I ask Brenda to lock the door to keep Kevin out, even though he's dead. When I was growing up, I longed for a door that I could lock, but my mother wouldn't let me have one.

Brenda resumes massaging my buttocks and thighs. I try to relax so that she can reach the deep tension in that area.

♦*Memory*. Kevin tells me to take off my pants while he holds my shoulder. He puts a towel from the linen closet on the rug. "Lie down," he says. I close my eyes, but not before seeing the plastic and wood toys lying next to my left thigh. He took them from his pocket. Red hotels from a Monopoly game, Scrabble letters, plastic animals. He leans against the back of my legs, pushing them into my anus. I want to scream but I can't breathe. I have to go to the bathroom. I want to pass out, to faint. I can't. I pretend that my body belongs to a rubber doll. Nothing hurts the doll, she can be stretched and twisted. "Asshole, bitch, cunt," Kevin breathes dirty words, panting.

The next day in school, I faint during art class. I begin fainting every day. The school nurse offers to call my mother but I know I'll get in trouble. Now I go to the bathroom and put my head on my lap when I feel dizzy, hiding it from them. ♦

"Let the sound out from here," Brenda says. My "Noooo" is a long screech.

"Say 'This is my body. My buttocks. Get him out of there!'" Brenda says the words easily.

I can't say them. I don't want this body. This body has too

many holes in it. Everything comes inside through the holes. I want to sew my body shut, close all the openings, the anus, the vagina, the mouth, the ears, the eyes, the nose.

"Don't keep it inside of you," Brenda whispers. "It doesn't belong in you."

"Leave me alone you bastard!" Fuckit screams out loud, heaving the force of the no's up through my throat.

I turn over, relieved to rest my back against the table. "I felt like dirt." My fists clench. "My family thought Kevin was a generous man who had trouble getting along with adults but was good with children. No one asked what I thought about him. No one cared." I cry until I'm limp and tired.

Brenda massages my feet. Her hands warm my toes. "Take some breaths. You've worked hard enough for today," she says. "Imagine that you are rocking in a boat on the ocean, lying on your back, watching seagulls in easy flight across the sky. A rainbow forms above you, red, blue, purple, yellow, green. The rainbow moves across your body, blanketing you with its colors. As you breathe, the colors circulate around and through you, washing away pain, filling you with light and vibration. Ask your buttocks and intestines to show you the colors you need for healing."

A flower of carmine red, opening slowly in my uterus, brushing my moist walls with delicate beauty. Red petals scatter through my vagina, reawakening dead tissue. I imagine orange, the color of laughing flames. I draw the orange through my buttocks. With my mind's eye, I watch the scarred tissues absorb the healing. The cells soften, bathed in a pool of cornelian light. Brenda gently rocks my belly with her hand. I imagine yellow blossoms of forsythia sheltering the raw nerves of my solar plexus. Stretched nerves healing, resting. I wrap my heart in lush green ferns. Green washes dried black tears from my chest, removing soot, planting seeds. I wash my throat with the blue water of the sea. I open the eye of my forehead with the azure blue of lapis and look full into the stars of a midnight sky. Amethyst light washes through my hair.

The rainbow dances around and through my body, like spark-
lers of colored light. Carrie holds YoungerOne 13, massaging
her back with round calming circles.

◇

Stephanie sighs when she sees my wet red eyes.

"I'm not doing very well either," she begins.

I don't want to hear her.

"I was hoping you could hold me for awhile," she says.
"I've been having awful nightmares about my family."

Stephanie needs something from me. Her feelings grab at
me like the arms of an octopus. I step backwards.

♦Memory. At the end, Grandpa says, "That's a girl,"
and pats me on the head. I want him to hold me. I want
him to say that I'm his good little girl and that he loves me.
I'm too alone. I can't talk. The taste won't go away. He
pushes his skin back in his underpants and goes outside.

I walk out of the bathroom, but I feel like I'll fall down.
My mother is wearing a green housedress which buttons
down the front. She picks me up and I want her to tell me
that she loves me. I want her to make Grandpa and the bad
feelings go away. I want her to give me a mint to chase
away the taste in in my mouth.

She says, "It's so hard for me to live with my parents.
You're all I've got. You've got to help take care of your
mommy." She holds me tight.

I have to help her, poor Mommy. I pat her back. I am a
milk carton. She drinks me, then she crumples me and puts
me down.

If I take care of her, who will take care of me? But if I
don't take care of her, there will be no one to take care of
me either. Then I would die. ♦

But this is not my mother! This is Stephanie. She's listened
patiently to more than four months of hysterical feelings and
sickening details of abuse. She was abused as a child too. While
I remember, her own memories are reawakened, throwing her

inner children into old betrayals. What happened to her was worse than what happened to me. I've got to help her.

"I don't want to. I can't." YoungerOnes withdraw to the ledge in the Well, away from Stephanie.

"Sure, I'll hold you. I'm sorry. Come here." I wrap my arms around her but I feel hollow as I do it. She starts to cry and talk about being bad.

"You're not bad. You had bad things done to you. You were just a child," I tell her in a firm voice. But I can feel myself being angry at Stephanie. She reminds me of me but I don't want to be reminded.

"Oh, it's oookay." She sniffs and pulls away. Her words stutter and crack.

But it's not. I should be there for her. I don't want to be. "You only think about yourself," Sarah recites.

Stephanie looks five years old, lip hanging, arms behind her back. "Your stuff is bigger than mine . . . " she says, putting herself away.

"No it's not!" Now I'm really pissed at her. Fuckit is walking away from Stephanie. "I just—I just feel too full to listen to you right now. I'm sorry. I think I need to go away and write or something . . . "

My body sags under guilt. I'm not being fair. I owe Stephanie my support. I have to pay for the support and love she's given me.

When Stephanie and I both feel bad, an enormous ball of yarn seems to tangle and twist us together. I can't find the loose end that would unwind us. Past and present merge. We both become symbols for the other. Our feelings slop together until it's hard to separate myself. When I try saving her, I become an abrasive instead, hating her helplessness and my own.

"We've got to get out of here!" Fuckit says urgently.

"Stephanie's going to hate me. I want her to love me. She needs me. She can't make it without me. I can't make it without her," YoungerOnes whisper frantically to themselves. I run toward Stephanie. Before I get too close I turn and run back. Inside, YoungerOnes sit on the ledge of the Well, looking into the Pit.

Carrie looks at Fuckit and then watches YoungerOnes. "I don't know how to love anybody," she says. "I don't even know how to learn. I don't have a vision of loving. How can I take care of YoungerOnes and love Stephanie at the same time?" She shakes her head and says "Someone ought to write a book about how to do this. But for now. . . . "

"I can't hold you right now, but I want to," I tell Stephanie. Stephanie looks hurt and disappointed. "But later I can. I just need some time to be with myself."

Stephanie looks at me. Her eyes are flat and far-away. "I guess we both just have too much going on, huh? You don't have to be with me today if you don't want to." She looks at the ground.

Why did she say that? I know that she doesn't mean it! "Oh, so you don't want me to be with you?" Fuckit says sarcastically to Stephanie, letting poison arrows fly from my tongue. Carrie tries to hush her, but once started Fuckit continues on her own momentum, as if saying "fuck you" to someone I care about will make me feel better.

Stephanie really just wants reassurance. Why can't I just give it to her?

"I'll be back," I say, resisting the urge to apologize and make everything all right. Fuckit's footsteps pound the cement stairs.

"I can't stand it when she calls herself bad. It drives me crazy!" Fuckit stomps so hard that my head shakes like a ceramic doll with a spring neck.

YoungerOnes are scared. They can only see my mother's unpredictable neediness and the tricks of Grandpa, Kevin and Don. I learned that people take while pretending to give. I learned that I could lose who I was and what I needed for my self.

"I am a total shit," I tell myself, remembering the scene with Stephanie. "How can I be so goddamned selfish? She listens to me. She holds me. I reject her sexually because of my stuff. I control the roller coaster. But as soon as she has a need I don't want anything to do with her."

A scruffy brown terrier calls attention to the anonymous suburban neighborhood that I'm stumbling through. Separating the two off-green identical post-war houses on the left is a tall cedar fence. It's not a remarkable fence in any way, but I can't stop looking at it.

"Okay Sure Voice, speak up." I know by now that when my eyes lock into place, Sure Voice is trying to speak. But inside I'm talking to the voices, not listening for Sure Voice at all.

"What do you see?" I dimly hear her ask.

On one side of the fence the yard is full of toys and chaos. The neighboring yard is neatly trimmed with plaster of Paris elves peeking from behind juniper bushes. The fence divides the yards, giving a boundry to the property of each one, separating the toys from the ceramic artifacts. "Big deal," Fuckit says inside of me.

"Breathe," Sure Voice says calmly. My breath is an impatient sigh blown with force through my nostrils. Fuckit taps her foot in the background preparing for what she is convinced will be a long lecture from Sure Voice.

"You are angry, Fuckit?" Sure Voice touches Fuckit's clamped jaw.

"I wish I had a fence like that so I could keep out Stephanie! I don't want to be needed. I hate it. I can never give enough to satisfy the other person. And the other person always wants more than they ask for. Stephanie doesn't just want me to hold her. She wants me to cook dinner and give her a bubble bath. She wants me to be grown-up. And I don't want to."

"We're not grown-up," YoungerOnes get smaller and smaller as my family, joined by Stephanie, grow taller in the Pit.

"You are afraid Stephanie can take what you do not want to give. YoungerOnes confuse a gift with an obligation. They were used by the offenders and by your mother without regard for their welfare. But giving can be a natural expression of the heart," Sure Voice touches Fuckit's chest gently.

Fuckit kicks a stone as I walk.

"Your mother wanted you to be an adult instead of a child. You tried, even though you needed her to protect you from the incest. You did not know you could not really take care of her."

"I'm just fucking tired of feeling responsible for everything!" Fuckit explodes, irritated. "Why didn't she teach me how to be strong, instead of insisting I was the problem?"

I watch Fuckit doing what I couldn't do as a child. She feigns indifference, then she leaves. It's safer to be alone. I never learned how to work through conflict with another person.

"Stephanie's feelings frighten me. I'm afraid I'll get sucked in and disappear. I don't know how to set limits with her. I don't trust how nice she is to me. I'm not sure what she wants in return. Like Kevin's watches, every present has a price. That fence you showed me is so stark and clearcut. The boundaries are measured," Carrie says, running fingers through her hair. "But one minute I'm warm and loving—with no fence at all. Then Stephanie reaches toward me at my invitation and I slam the fence into her face."

"No one is going to trap me ever again," Fuckit says. She wants barbed wire on the fences that separate me from others.

Stephanie and I always seem to be taking care of each other. I'm afraid that if I tell her how I feel, I'll hurt her. Lovers are supposed to be supportive. Lovers are supposed to be there for the other person. But how do I give to both of us at the same time?

"Carrie?" Sure Voice pauses before Carrie's drawn features.

"I want us to dance and play and have a good time." Carrie looks up for a minute. "I don't want Stephanie to have been hurt like that. And no matter how we are," she gestures to include YoungerOnes and Fuckit, "we seem to hurt her. Just by having been abused ourselves. I wish that there was something I could give her to make it up to her. Maybe she really deserves someone better than us."

"You wish to make her whole and you cannot," Sure Voice pauses. The bottom layer of leaves have decayed into a brown mash. Only on the top are the forms still distinct. "You do not have that power in your wand, no matter how many people you help to heal, Carrie."

When I return to Stephanie's apartment she's in her over-stuffed chair hugging the teddy bear I gave her for Valentine's Day.

"I'm sorry," I say.

Stephanie still looks little and sad. "I'm sorry. I—uh—shouldn't have any expectations I guess. I just shouldn't ask you for anything." Her chin hardens. "I don't need nothin' anyway," she declares while her chin shakes.

I see Stephanie's child self console herself with these words, not wholly meaning them. She, too, is trying to help herself the best she can.

I reach out and hug her. Another small girl. And inside I hug my own small self. Even as a grownup, it's hard to live in a world that hurts.

◇

"Get me out of here!" Fuckit demands, pounding fists against the Well. "What the hell's going on? I stormed Kevin's house. I brought her here." Fuckit points at the eleven-year-old trembling against the cold floor. "I told him to leave us alone. So get me out of here, Sure Voice."

"YoungerOnes are not ready to leave," Sure Voice replies. "You have to leave together or not at all. You are all parts of the same self."

"I'm not taking them with me," Fuckit says, indignant. "They can stay in here. I want out."

"You are not separate," Sure Voice continues. "Each of

you grew in response to Louise's life. Your healing is inter-connected."

I feel the Well as a pain in my stomach. When I'm close to a memory, I imagine I can feel the jagged walls of obsidian rough against my wounds.

The Well holds fear. The obsidian held these secrets until I was able to look inside. In a way, the Well has protected me. It kept me from too much knowing.

Now I feel trapped and frustrated banging my fists against rough walls. I hunch over the Well in my body, afraid to walk fearlessly. Afraid to meet Don's guns. Shrinking to a five-year-old with a small weak body. Feeling dizzy with confusion. Grandpa with candy that was a penis telling me to "come help him." Spanking me if I told a lie.

Fear has scorched stiff limbs. "Don't go any farther with this," the fear says. "You are crazy. Forget again. The Well will fall on you, trapping you beneath boulders." I see Don, Kevin and Grandpa coming too close. "I'll never be safe. Some-one will always get me," YoungerOnes say over and over again.

"I want to die," YoungerOne 13 says. "Nothing stays still. When I got my period I tried to hide it. I thought it would go away, but there was more and more blood. I thought I was bleeding from cuts inside me. Mother said I was a 'young lady.' I didn't want to be one but I couldn't stop it. I touched myself through my jeans like Uncle Kevin did in his car. I wanted the good feelings of my body but they made me feel bad. Uncle Kevin knew I was bad. His voice was dirty and it crawled inside of me. I thought that if I looked unhappy someone might help me. But I kept getting in trouble. I have to die. It's too much."

♦*Memory. Taylor's Medical Dictionary* is in the book-case next to the *Illustrated Bible Stories*. I'm home alone, Saturday. Mother and Jim went shopping. I take the dic-tionary off the shelf and sit down in the upholstered rock-ing chair. I open to the section on reproduction. I don't understand what sex is. My crotch is warm, pulsing. I want the feelings to stay and go away at the same time. The medical dictionary has a diagram of a penis. It also shows fallopian tubes and ovaries. The medical dictionary doesn't talk about why my body feels this way.

A car door slams outside in the driveway. I close the dictionary. When I look up, Kevin is standing in the living room, unannounced. I hide the medical dictionary behind the chair. I know I can't let anyone know that I'm reading it.

"What are you reading?" he moves toward me.

"Aw nothing," I look at my lap searching for something to say. Trying to remember what my mother would say to him when he comes to visit.

"Come here." His voice is to the left, past the hallway, in my mother's room. "I can't find your mom's watch. I was going to fix the band on it."

"Lie down," he walks toward my mother's bed. He loosens a thin black belt on his baggy grey pants, the ends stick out.

He pulls my dress up with rough hands. I am lying on my back. He bounces up and down on me, pounding. "Cunt. Bitch."

My pelvis is full of sexual feelings. They go away, leaving bruising. His eyes, grey, glaring, hate me. He keeps them open right on my face, punching me with his eyes.

When I close my eyes I am lost in the darkness inside. I grit my teeth. Tiny spurts of pleasure are turned dirty, sooted by horror. Too many feelings, my body will burst. I want to go to the bathroom. But I can't breathe. I'm drowning. The feelings are a thousand needles poking into me.

Kevin bangs, feeling heavier, swearing into my ears. "Whore," "Cunt," "You like this," "Bitch." My legs are numb. The complexion of feelings has gone. I don't feel. I don't hear. I can float on the ceiling. It is someone else down there in that fragile dirty body.

My mother stands in the doorway, reflected in the mirror on her dressing table. She leaves quickly. She walks away from him on top of my body. Footsteps walking to the door.

The front door slams. Kevin gets up. He narrows his eyes, his face is close to me. Dangerous hard eyes. Eyes that hurt, eyes that could kill. He pulls my dress over my legs. I hear him greet my mother. He left me lying on the bed. "Louise isn't feeling well," he tells her. I don't hear what my mother says.

I get up and walk into the dining room. "Go down into the basement," she tells me.

It's dark in the basement, damp. I'm glad it's dark and that no one will see me.

I go upstairs after my mother yells "Louise." Kevin has his hand on her shoulder. My mother looks stern. "Set the table," she says.

Fuckit shakes her head. But instead of walking away, she moves closer to YoungerOne 12. "That bitch! I wish she'd have helped us. She could have stopped it right then!"

◇

"But this is so awful," I tell Jean. "How could something like this happen? I never read about things like this, other than in Amnesty International reports of the torture of political prisoners. Or newspaper accounts of rapes by strangers. But this was happening within my own house. No one drank, no one was in jail. Everyone went to church. I feel crazy trying to fit this into the 'perfect' family I was told I had. My body keeps telling me this happened. When I see how I've lived my life, hating myself, feeling terrified all the time... remembering the incest has made everything fall into place. I can see why I'm the way I am. But still... there was so much abuse and no one seemed to notice it."

"A lot of awful abuse is never talked about," Jean says, frowning. "I've heard of grown women forced to eat from dog food bowls, tied to beds, beaten, locked in closets. No one wants to believe this stuff. Most of us can't stand to read about it. It makes us wonder about ourselves and our capacity to abuse each other. That's uncomfortable."

YoungerOne 12 rocks back and forth inside of me. "I should have stopped it," she whispers. "I should have told someone. I should have said 'no.' I shouldn't have let him do it. Those feelings in my body made him act that way. It was punishment for reading the medical dictionary."

"Who would you have told?" Jean asks, leaning forward as if she's listening carefully to the twelve-year-old.

"It didn't make sense. Kevin ate with us. I knew how mean he was. He hated me. I saw my mother see him on top of me. I knew she would never help me. I didn't know how to talk about it. The way Kevin just showed up, the things that happened when I had to ride in his car. He was so nice to my mother, he always brought her presents. He told her how hard it must be to raise two children by herself.

"No one at school talked about anything like this. None of my friends, none of my teachers. My mind took the words away, the words didn't fit how I felt. I wouldn't know how to tell. It's hard to tell you, fifteen years later."

"We should have stopped him," YoungerOnes repeat.

"It doesn't sound like it was safe for you to get help," Jean says.

Her words won't come into the Well. YoungerOnes can't hear her.

Talking aloud or writing it in my journal are both telling. When I talk with Jean, the hot air wall blocks my mouth and fingers squeeze my throat. I am fragile like glass. My body can be broken. The journey of telling is a long distance from the deep Well to spoken words.

"What do you want me to do?" Jean asks.

"I want to you to stop it, but I know you can't. I guess I

just need to keep telling you what I remember. I'm tired of running away from myself." I look in her eyes instead of avoiding them.

She nods her head, agreeing to hear me. I think she must be the most patient person in the world to keep listening to me.

"Now that I know why I've always felt so awful, I feel worse. Memories and feelings hold hands and charge to the surface. Sometimes I don't know if I'm physically sick or if it's the remembering."

"It seems to work that way," Jean says. "In healing, there's a place where you feel worse before feeling better."

"Brenda says it's like cleaning your room—it gets messier before it gets tidy." I sneak a glance at Jean, suddenly afraid she'll go away. What if I'm too horrible to work with?

"I want you to practice being a brat this week," Jean says, smiling mischievously.

"Brats are bad," YoungerOnes whisper to each other.

"I can handle that," Fuckit thinks. She sticks her tongue out at Jean as I leave.

9   THE FIRE

"GRRR!"

I wonder what that is. I try to ignore it.

My legs begin to move without my permission, pacing with a floor-jarring intensity that is probably shaking my neighbor's ceiling. I have been trying to do my taxes. Why do I have to listen to myself right now? Why can't the voices just wait? I still try to avoid them. Then they yell at me until I'm so miserable that I have to pay attention. My arms stop recording the carefully calculated numbers. They have been stapled in place by clenched fists that extend up my arms into the mountains that bury my shoulders. Fuckit, Carrie and Sarah are fighting. My upper body is in a traction of metal bands.

"Grrr!"

"Hello Fuckit." I surrender to interruption.

"I hate him. Goddamn asshole! How could he do that to me? I'd like to rip his penis off and stomp on it." Fuckit jumps up and down.

Carrie holds Fuckit's arms behind her back. "I'm afraid she might hurt somebody. We're making a lot of noise—she's shaking the whole apartment building. I don't know what'll happen if I let her arms go. She's terrifying YoungerOnes."

YoungerOnes hide in a corner of the Well, against the obsidian. "Don will shoot us. God will kill us with lightning."

"Wait a minute! Fuckit, what's going on?" I ask.

"That fucker. When I think about Don hurting her," Fuckit jerks a thumb toward YoungerOne 16, "I want to scream and kick and hurt him the way he hurt her...The way he hurt me! That jerk. I'd throw a celebration if he dropped dead right now. And I'm glad. I mean fucking glad that Kevin and Grandpa are dead. It serves 'em right. But in a way I wish they were here because I'd like to have the sheer pleasure of punching them out myself." The floor shakes again.

Heat collects in my throat, burning in my upper arms and thighs. If the feeling gets out nothing will be left of me.

♦*Memory*. Jim grabs my crayons and walks across my mother's room with them. I run after him, putting my short five-year-old fingers around the square box. "Give them back to me, you can't have them." I make a high whining wailing sound. Jim pulls, the box collapses, colors fall into a mound on the floor. I push him, looking for a way to grab his hair.

"You kids quit fighting. . . right now!" My mother is clapping her hands and looking for the yardstick she hits us with.

"Jim took my crayons." I'm sure she will make him give them back to me.

"Just calm down right now." My mother's voice isn't calm, it's collecting steam, boiling the air. "Go to your room if you're going to act like that!"

"No. No. I don't want to." The red feeling is big and hot. It will swallow me.

"Don't you say 'no' to me!" The yardstick gets closer, stinging. "Don't you talk back to me!"

The yardstick is tall, made of thick golden wood. I hate the yardstick. My nose runs, I taste salt on my lips.

"Stop that noise right now or I'll give you something to cry about. God is watching you!" The yardstick hits my back with a smack.

I try to find my breath to take it back and hold onto it. My eyes are stuck open. My mother picks up Jim. ♦

Anger was a hot plume falling down on top of me, like lava smothering dirt. My own anger has accumulated, clotting my throat, heavy in my upper arms, growing beneath the fat on my thighs.

The fury of my family was funneled through unacknowledged channels. My mother would get mad at me. She wouldn't say, "I am angry." Instead she said that God would punish me, that I was bad and evil. "Don't act that way, Louise, it's not nice," my grandmother said when I was little. "Little girls don't look nice when they're mad."

No one yelled at my grandfather. Once in a while, my mother told me, "He is so stubborn," while she knotted her hands together. When my grandfather got mad, he yelled about communists and Catholics or at my grandmother. His opinion was the only one that mattered. He made the decisions like fathers were supposed to do. His anger flowed out from him like a wrathful God, punishing others who "made him act that way."

Don and my mother never argued either. He presided over disagreements. His response to my heated arguments with my mother was, "Don't talk back to your mother."

My fury circles back inside of me, hitting me with myself. I take it out on my body, slashing and pushing, unable to be gentle. The anger crowds out softness, making me rough and hard.

It's safer to be sad and helpless. "Then eventually people will just go away and leave us alone. Being mad is just asking for trouble," YoungerOne 16 says.

"You shouldn't be angry," Sarah says, "It's bad."

"Fuckit's feelings aren't going to go away, we already know that," Carrie tells her impatiently. "But we could try an anger exercise."

I lock my apartment. I stand with my legs a shoulder and a half width apart. My hands are laced together. I swing them between my legs like a woodchopper, bending and straightening from my waist. I clear a path for the fury to come out of my body as my arms swing through my legs. My breath reaches into my abdomen. Sound burns my throat. My thighs ache with supporting me. Screams. The swinging is interrupted by spasms in my solar plexus. The fear of being discovered. I look out the window for police cars.

"Damn you Don! (swing) You suffer you, bastard! (swing) Get your body off me! (swing) Put that ugly smelly worm you carry (swing) in a meat grinder (swing) and turn it! (swing) Lash your tongue to an iron (swing) and burn slowly! You bastard! (swing) It's not my fault! (swing) I am not bad, you shithead... " Crash.

Scream. The floor meets my hand with momentum built from the gush of red words and the slamming of my fists. My hand pulses from crashing into the floor instead of sweeping back and forth above it. The anger vanishes like a ghost in daylight.

Swelling starts immediately, stretching from my little finger to my wrist. When I try to move my fingers, pain flushes up my arm. Taxes mock me from my desk. I return, bandaged and diagnosed from the emergency room. No massage work for a week, at least.

"That's what happens," Sarah intones. "Sow as ye shall reap." Get angry, go straight to hell.

Fuckit seethes, wordless.

Stephanie heats the water for soaking. I don't know how she can keep loving me. I didn't tell the physician at the hospital that I hurt my hand doing an anger exercise. I told him that I hit my hand on a table. All he said was, "It's not broken."

♦*Memory.* My mother and I are watching the river view from the window of a restaurant. As she remembers, her body turns away from me. She tips her chin toward the sky, removing her eyes.

She says to me, "When I'd go to the doctor, he'd say, 'Carol, how did you get those bruises?' I'd tell him that I fell down the stairs or that I'd stumbled over a desk. But it was Sam hitting me. Your grandmother didn't want me to marry him. I couldn't let anyone know about the hitting. I was ashamed that I married him. And then, two weeks after your brother was born—your grandma was visiting. We were sitting at the table and Sam knocked me to the floor. You started screaming 'Daddy hit Mommy, Daddy hit Mommy.' Grandma got her suitcases and told Sam off. As she walked out the door she told me that I could come home any time with you kids. So I left.

"No one else was divorced then. When Sam refused to pay alimony, the lawyer said, 'Carol, you were lucky to get out of there.' It's not right to divorce, marriage should last forever. I shouldn't have married him—my folks were right. I should have listened to them."♦

"I never get mad," my mother told her friends, "I just get hurt."

◇

Lately, whenever I play my guitar, I feel nauseous. My voice is thin like a diluted beverage. The pain in my body has been getting worse the way it does when Sure Voice is bringing up a memory. "I don't want to see any more. This is taking too long," I tell her. I've been remembering for five months. Sometimes the memories come rapidly, like when Stephanie touches me or when I work with Brenda. But sometimes the memories come in bits and pieces, filling in like a jigsaw puzzle. I've felt every obsidian rock in the reachable circumference of the Well.

"You must finish seeing the past or there will be no room for the future," Sure Voice says.

I eat for distraction. I throw food into my mouth so quickly that everything tastes anonymous. My abdomen feels extended and clogged. I feel uneasy in the bathroom. I leave the door open. At night I see the same scene again and again: A piece of shit floating in a toilet. Then I want to kill myself but I can't because I promised myself that I wouldn't.

♦*Memory.* I'm in the open closet in my room, playing the guitar and singing "If I Had a Hammer." The door to my room is closed. Sometimes I like to play my guitar in the closet, sitting on a blanket on the floor. The sketched picture of Jesus is reflected on the mirror on my dresser.

I'm the only one home this Saturday, mother and Jim just left to go shopping.

The bathroom is next to my room. I hear noises from there. I put my guitar across my bed, careful so that it doesn't hit the wall. When I open the door to my room, Uncle Kevin is coming out of the bathroom, buckling his pants.

He smiles when he sees me. "I'm just bringing your mom's watch back," he says.

I slide back toward the open door of my room.

"Let's see your watch," he grabs my twelve-year-old hand. The rash that has formed under the watch face is spreading across my wrist. He keeps a tight hold on my arm, reaching his fingers all the way around it. His hands are large and hard with trimmed, tidy fingernails. My nails are bitten into ragged edges. My guitar teacher has me do stretching exercises because he says my hands are small.

"Come in the bathroom," Uncle Kevin says, pulling my left arm, the weakest one. I don't want to go anywhere with him. My feet follow, stiff under locked knees.

"Now," he says, closing the bathroom door. We stand in front of the toilet. He moves the lock across the door. The bathroom's crowded because he's so tall. I don't want to look down.

"Get on your knees," he pushes my shoulders with both hands. His voice is low and slippery. The linoleum is cold on my legs. He shoves my head down. Shit floats in the toilet. I don't want to look at it, I never look at it. I want to flush the toilet and make it go away.

I close my eyes. "This will go away," I tell myself. "This isn't really happening." I pretend that I'm in my closet, playing my guitar, singing "We Shall Overcome."

The toilet paper roll makes a wobbling sound. Uncle Kevin keeps his hand on my shoulder and leans down into the toilet, scooping with the paper. He carries the shit, smeared brown like leaves rotted and slimy on the sidewalk. I want to be white like the toilet paper. He brings it to my nose. It smells foul, like the manure used on the garden. I try to move my head back but he holds it with his hand.

"Eat it," he says.

I can't open my mouth, my molars are holding onto each other. It touches my lips. A throwing up feeling moves up from my stomach. I hold it back with my teeth.

"Open your mouth and eat it, you bitch." He pushes it hard against my mouth, it sticks against my lips. My mouth opens. I hold my breath. It spreads across my tongue, a brown carpet of slime, sticky. It tastes like it smells. My throat gags closing, refusing.

"Swallow it. Swallow." His voice falls down on me. He closes his fingers around my hair, pulling.

My tongue arches up in the back. I have to make the taste go away. He rubs the tissue against my face breathing hard. I hate smelling. I never want to breathe again. My eyes are punched tight together. He moves his pelvis against my back.

The swallowing makes a hard feeling in my stomach. It will never go away. His dirt is inside me.

The toilet flushes.

He washes off my face with a washcloth. "Such a dirty little girl. You better not tell how dirty you are."

He unlocks the door and leaves me kneeling in the bathroom. I can't throw up because I'd have to taste it all over again. I take a handful of chocolate chip cookies from the freezer, chewing, chewing, biting hard, trying to erase the taste. I keep eating handfuls of cookies even though it makes my stomach hurt more. ◆

The pain in my knees that has followed my twenty-eight-year-old self for days, lessens after remembering. My jaw is clamped tight, sending pain down my neck. No. This couldn't have happened.

The Well is cold and damp. The fire is too small to provide

comfort. I wear layers of clothes but I don't feel them against my skin. Fuckit looks past YoungerOnes. Her shoulders hang, her eyes are glazed. "I don't want to know anymore. This didn't happen." Her anger has dissipated like sparks doused with water. "What's the use of yelling about it?" she says.

I've never heard of anything like this. What's wrong with my mind and my body that I see such things? Why do I have to feel so horrible?

My stomach hurts. I make a sandwich. I smoke cigarettes. My body feels limp, paralyzed. The only motion is food coming into my body. Food that has no taste. I stay up late, refusing to sleep, drinking coffee. I know I'm making myself feel worse but I don't care.

"You're crazy," Sarah says. "You're just sick, that's what this is. No one would do that!"

YoungerOne 12 lies face down in a muddy place in the Well. Dirty.

♦*Memory.* I am twelve years old at a Girl Scout meeting. In the bathroom the soap is dispensed in white paper-thin slices. They smell like ivory soap, clean, spotless white like Kleenex. The soap dissolves against my tongue. My tongue tries to move away, rejecting the soap taste. Washing out my mouth with soap. My hands reach for another and another.

A couple hours later my intestines are burning. It's hard to walk to the car because I'm doubled over. The Girl Scout leader wants to know what's wrong, afraid of food poisoning. "I ate soap," I tell her.

"Why?" she asks. The lines on her forehead form a question mark.

My face turns hot. "I don't know." I'm confused. I shouldn't have said anything. "I'm okay. It's okay," I tell her.♦

In the Well, YoungerOne 13 looks at the scars on her wrists. "I ate from the toilet. I feel like a toilet, holding dirty, bad things. I can't get it out of me. It lives inside of me next to

Grandpa's penis, covered with urine and things that smell bad. Nothing I eat makes it go away."

YoungerOne 13 digs her fingers into her legs as she speaks. "My body was like the fat lady at the circus that everyone laughs at. I didn't seem to know how to move it right. If I thought that people were watching me walk, I tripped over my feet. My mother said I was clumsy. She sent me to charm school, held in a large cold room on the second floor of J.C. Penney's. 'Walk tall, ladies,' the instructor said, while balancing a hardcover book on top of sprayed brunette hair. Her high heels tapped delicately across the linoleum floor. I shifted in my beige folding chair, feeling my body around me like sandbags. The book fell from my head on the solo walk from wall to wall. I knew it would but the laughter bothered me anyway. The instructor shook her head. Not one strand of her hair moved from its place. I should be able to make things stay still. 'Pick up your feet,' she said. My mother said that too. I couldn't find my feet, they were miles away.

"I gave up on being like other girls. The ones that could run and turn somersaults on the uneven parallel bars. When I was seven or eight I thought maybe if I got older I'd turn into a graceful young woman like the teenagers I saw around me. But after Uncle Kevin I knew I wouldn't ever be like them. Charm school didn't help.

"My friends were talking about boys then. Because I was fat and ugly my friends decided I should like the fat, ugly and very boring boy in my class in junior high. I tried to make myself like him but I didn't.

"My friends and I talked a little about sex at slumber parties. I knew my body felt that way sometimes. I turned red when they talked and all the words left my head. I thought boys were supposed to make me feel that way but they didn't. I had to pretend all the time... Except sometimes I didn't think I could pretend anymore." YoungerOne 13 touches her left wrist with her fingers. "Mostly I just wanted to tear my skin off."

◇

It would be impossible for Jean to ignore my bandaged arm, hung in a sling. I might as well wear a sign saying, "I am disabled."

She raises her eyebrows. "Need a vacation?" she suggests.

"Aw shit!" Fuckit says outloud. "I was just doing some stupid anger exercise, when the fucking floor bit me!"

Jean laughs briefly, struggling to call her face back to attentive neutral listening.

"Does your anger have to hurt you?" Jean asks. I can tell she thinks it shouldn't work that way.

Her words bring tears that fall with a thud and a shake. "I guess I'm afraid I'll get punished for being mad at Don or Kevin or Grandpa. Sometimes I think I punish myself for them. It's not like I plan to hurt myself. I just can't believe I can be mad at them without being hurt.

"I feel crazy with these memories. Do you think I'm crazy?" I ask. I want her to say, "Of course not. I believe in you. You're doing a good job. You're really growing."

"'Crazy' doesn't really mean anything," she says instead. "Sometimes it's just a label used to describe differences or things we don't understand. Quit calling yourself crazy. I want you to find other words that describe how you feel."

"What should I say to myself then?" I want Jean to define me. I want her approval.

"You'll think of something," she says.

"Sometimes I feel crazy because this stuff is so bizarre and hateful," I tell her. "After I remembered Kevin forcing me to eat feces I thought that I'd lost my mind, because I'd never heard of anything like that. When I went to a workshop on incest at the Association of Women in Psychology conference, one of the presenters said that ten percent of the abused children she worked with were forced to eat fecal matter. I didn't feel so crazy then... "

"But we deserved for those things to happen," Younger-

Ones whisper inside me. "We made them happen."

"I want you to hear something." Jean takes a small tape recorder from the top of her desk. Her voice comes from the miniature speakers. She's reading from a book. "And then he made me put it in my mouth. It was wrinkled and smelly and felt bad. . . . I knew there was something wrong with me. I should have stopped it."

I recognize the words from one of the books about incest that Jean gave me to read.

"What would you tell her, if she came to you for help?" Jean begins, motioning to the tape recorder as if it was another person sitting here with us in the room.

"I'd tell her it wasn't her fault. She was just a kid being told what to do by an adult. It's the grownup's responsibility, not hers." Carrie knows that's what I'm supposed to say to her. That's what I tell my clients.

"Are you sure she didn't do something to encourage him?" Jean asks. I look at the tape recorder as if I could see her.

"No, she couldn't cause that. . . "

But YoungerOnes aren't sure, they're wavering inside. "Well, what if. What if. . . "

"Well, maybe she did something?" I say tentatively. "But she didn't really make it happen. She probably couldn't have stopped it," I insist out of duty to the sister tape.

Jean looks at me silently.

"Well, maybe I was bad." YoungerOnes seize the silence to speak, but the words are muffled like drizzle.

Jean's eyebrows lift and say, "Go on. Tell me what you mean." She leans back in her chair with an open expression on her face. Sometimes I just wish she'd tell me the right answer so I wouldn't have to go through all this stuff.

YoungerOnes step into the silence. "I mean, maybe there was something about us that kept making it happen. First there was Grandpa, then Uncle Kevin, then Don. It even happened in a family we stayed with in Australia as an exchange student. The elderly man French kissed me. So, if one thing happens a lot, there must be a reason."

"What is bad about you?" Jean asks conversationally. My ears search for the sound of judgement, but I don't hear it from her.

"I let it happen." The first answer.

"Could you have stopped it?"

I close my eyes and imagine YoungerOnes next to the shadows of Grandpa, Don and Uncle Kevin in the Well. In my family, a child who said "no" was willful and had to be broken. "Don't talk back," the adults said. "Do what grownups tell you to do." I see my mother calling me names, "bad girl" over and over again. I see my mother seeing Kevin on top of me. School and church taught that parents were good, that children had to be disciplined. "No" was a bad word.

"No. I couldn't have stopped it. I was too little. Even if I'd had someone to tell, I didn't have words for what was happening."

"You couldn't stop it," Jean repeats, leaning forward and touching her fingertips together like she does when she's making a point.

I know we've moved from the woman's tape recorded story to mine. I think that was Jean's idea all along. I can't seem to make myself go back to the other woman. She has become me.

I see Don on top of me. I am sixteen years old. I see a gun, early morning, the enormity of an adult male body. I hear the praise of adults, "He's such a good man," they said. No one suggested he had any other aspects.

"No, I couldn't have stopped it," I say, looking at the tweed carpet.

"But we could have made it happen," YoungerOnes assert fearfully.

"How?" Jean asks, curious.

"Well." I search for a reason. "I felt sexual sometimes. I couldn't quit masturbating."

"When?" Jean asks.

"Well, when I was sixteen."

"What about when you were five."

YoungerOne 5 shakes her head. "Not Grandpa's candy. Grandpa's candy makes me throw up.

"I remember being told that 'girls make men do bad things.' Grandma said, 'Sit with your legs together. Men just can't control themselves.' She made it sound like a girl had power: that if I dressed right and sat correctly, I wouldn't get hurt.

"But I always felt guilty about feeling sexual. I know now that feeling sexual is supposed to be a natural feeling. If those feelings cause incest then everyone would be incested or raped. In my head, I know that the men around me imposed their sexual feelings on me."

"They had no fucking right!" Fuckit erupts like a flare.

"We were bad, we made it happen," YoungerOnes insist. Sarah agrees.

"What if you didn't make it happen?" Jean asks. "What if you had very little control over what happened to you at all as a child? How would that feel?"

"As long as your under this roof, young lady, you will do what you're told!" my mother yelled, the closing sentence of adolescent arguments. I remember how helpless I felt, depending on my mother for shelter, meals, clothing. I could not drive away. Adults made all the decisions; it didn't occur to them to ask how I felt. If I'm not bad, then I have to admit that I didn't have any control over the adults around me. If it is my fault and I'm bad, then trying to be good offers hope. "If we're not bad," YoungerOnes say, "then maybe we can't make anything happen, not even bad things."

Carrie kneels beside YoungerOnes. "We can make things happen now without being bad," she tells them. "We're finding ways to help our self. We come here. We learn from our feelings. We don't live with those people anymore. We don't have to be bad for them."

"But we're still bad," YoungerOnes tell Carrie.

"So what makes you bad?" Jean asks again.

Sure Voice touches the YoungestOne. Fuckit looks at her shoes. Sarah and Carrie are quiet. I forget to breathe. Sure Voice draws a long sigh and turns to YoungestOne. "What is it? What do you think is bad about you.?"

"It's bad. . . " YoungestOne begins, feeling the continuing touch of Sure Voice on her shoulder, "to be a girl."

The words sprout in the air, coming out small like a flash card, becoming giant like a bulletin board.

Stephanie was a girl, and Jean and Kate, even Joan Baez was a girl. It can't be bad to born as I was. I enjoy women, they're my chosen partners. I can't hate my own birthright. That can't be bad.

Sparks fly inside the Well. My favorite writers, my friends, my clients were all girls. Sometimes I thought my mother didn't like me because I was a girl, boys were better, they carried on the family name. But I didn't want to be a boy. Around me now, it's women who support and teach me.

"No. No. No. That's not bad," Carrie tells the Younger-Ones, excited. She shows them pictures of girls and women they admire.

"It's great to be a woman!" Fuckit says. "Women are doing important things in the world! Women are a lot more interesting than anyone else! We don't even have to wear those disgusting dresses any more." She struts around the Well.

"But you don't belong with other women," Sarah objects. "You're not good enough."

"It's indisputable, Sarah, we are women." Carrie points to Sarah's body. "Look for yourself."

The old reason for being bad leaves my body as I exhale. A hidden dishonesty that can be rejected once I've defined it. The shame of being female was poured inside of me, not born in. It was injected through incest, through my family's belief that boys were more important, and through the messages of this culture. My arms and legs tingle as if the old ideas were moving out through my hands and feet.

The small fire in the Well brightens as if dry wood has been added. The fire has always been inside me. The fire planted questions about was happening to me even when the Well seemed inescapable. The flames represent my desire to embrace myself.

"I'm not bad. Being a girl isn't bad." The YoungerOnes say it out loud, tentatively at first and then with a growing intensity, that echoes in the obsidian that surrounds them.

I had to become a woman before I could understand my birth rights.

10 THE MASK

"I DON'T want to go there for Christmas," YoungerOnes say.

"Me neither," Fuckit says. "I wouldn't miss them if I never saw them again."

"Dinner will be at about 5:00," my mother is saying on the phone. "The candlelight service is at 7:30. Then we'll come home for dessert and to open the presents."

"I'll be there at 5:00," I tell her while Carrie tries to placate Fuckit and YoungerOnes.

"It'll only be a couple of hours," Carrie tells YoungerOnes. "It's easier to go than explain why we'd miss Christmas. We're not going to lie for them anymore. But we're not ready to talk to them about the incest."

"I'm never going to talk with them," Fuckit declares. "We speak different languages. They've never listened to me and they never will. They want me to be shallow, silent and ladylike or else they think I'm a communist. Fuck them!"

"Are you going to stay overnight?" my mother asks. "We're going to Cindy's parents on Christmas Day. It'd be nice if you... "

"No." I cut in rapidly, "I have plans on Christmas." I never stay overnight in their house, it's always made me nervous.

"We're scared." YoungerOnes remember when I couldn't leave their house. They remember how the inner darkness clashed with the required festive mask. They decided that Christmas was a lie.

"We'll be with Stephanie the next day," Carrie reminds them. "I want to see them. Maybe I can understand why the incest happened if I look hard enough."

I don't have much contact with my family. This year I have consciously avoided it, never initiating a phone call or a visit. I don't want to be around them. The memories make it difficult to maintain the superficial conventions I adopted once I moved out of their house. I'm not sure I can handle four hours with them for Christmas.

My mother calls periodically. I never talk with Don on the phone. My mother asks how I am and then starts talking about the neighbors and which local restaurants she's eaten in lately—before I've even said that I'm fine. I always say that I'm fine. I fill in small appropriate blanks with condolences. She talks about births, deaths and people I don't know who are in the hospital. She tells me how many deer, elk, goats and fish Don has caught. The conversation is like the small-town news-paper's vital statistic column. Personal emotion and ideas are censored, leaving a bone skeleton of words.

I don't try to convert them politically anymore, though Fuckit leaps automatically when the discussion turns to a bar-rage of labels; communist, Democrat, colored, Oriental, wel-fare bums, loafers. I don't discuss relationships, either. Les-bians are considered a sin and a perversion. Lesbians are com-munists who molest children. But the family is blessed by God, sacred. We have never been a family that encourages differen-ces.

It's safest to keep locked inside myself when I'm around them. We have little in common, held together by the expecta-tion of blood-ties. The past has never been discussed. The glue that has bound us disintegrates with memory.

◊

The presents are wrapped, bowed and paper-sacked in the back seat of my car. I am wary of gifts. Giving presents is ex-pected. Receiving presents obligates. "After all I've given you," my mother would say, "how dare you act like that." Kevin bought me with a watch. Don gave me a car after I graduated from the university. Did he think he was buying my silence? Will I ever know what he thought?

I hated shopping for my family—especially for Don. I was going to get him wool socks, but he would wear them hunting. I settled on a wallet which was on sale at the bookstore.

It was hard to shop for my mother, despite pages of Christmas ads suggesting ideas for the "lady of the house." I refused to buy her appliances, presents for the "housewife." I wanted to give her *Of Woman Born* by Adrienne Rich or *The Female Eunuch* by Germaine Greer. Or a record by Cris Williamson, Holly Near or Meg Christian. YoungerOnes still believe that if I do the right thing, I can change her. But she doesn't read. Her favorite singers are Bing Crosby and Mitch Miller. It's hard to remember what I got her as the freeway replicates itself like a habit. A pottery bowl in the blues and greens that she likes. I can imagine it lost between the tupperware and the Melmac.

I like the kite I bought for Jim and his wife, Cindy. Wind strong nylon, pyramids of red, blue and purples. I thought of it flying like a giant giddy bird secured to invisible string. I realize now that they probably won't fly it. My brother never was a child. At best it will hang on the wall of their house.

YoungerOnes huddle against me, looking pale and small. Fuckit stands on the other side of them, chain-smoking. "Do we have to do this? God, I hate Christmas! I can hardly wait until this is over."

Panic is unpredictable, piling debris in front of exits. What if Don attacks me, what if he shoots me with the guns in the closet, what if my mother commits me to a mental institution? What if I freeze, unable to get away? What if I am captured by memory and the scenes roll by without stopping? What if my body fails me again? I might scream or cry or throw things. What if I shoot Don first? What if I can't ever leave there?

"Breathe!"

Fuckit takes this interjection from Sure Voice as an opportunity to light a cigarette.

Sure Voice puts an ancient arm around YoungerOnes.

"Listen," Sure Voice says in a low steady voice. "You do not live there anymore, you have already left. You have survived them and escaped. Just watch, see if you can understand what you could not know before. They do not own you."

◊

The packages form a shifting weight against my breast. Fuckit clutches the keys in my coat pocket.

"We can do this. We've done it a thousand times," Carrie repeats inside the Well.

I put on the familiar mask that YoungerOnes designed during the years of concealment. I call feeling away from my eyes, they stay flat in my face, allowing nothing to sink inside. A smile staples the corners of my mouth in place. My jaw waits, tense, ready to push my words back down my throat. When I wear this mask I can pretend that nothing happened. I can pretend that my body doesn't exist and my soul is out of reach.

I wore this face at school. I ate dinners seated beside Uncle Kevin clutching this expression while my mother passed the peas. When I got older Fuckit added a sneer to the mask, drawing my chin forward, silently protesting. I took the sneer off after I left home; it just caused trouble. I wore this face in the living room watching TV with Don, Jim and my mother. This is the mask of "daughter." I have to remind myself not to let the mask fall away. It doesn't fit like it used to.

I feel the grey sky darkening as I open the door that leads through the garage. A "No Smoking" sign from the American Lung Association is scotch taped to the door. Fuckit glares at it. When I started smoking I stood on the toilet seat and blew smoke into the fan. Or I sneaked outside at night, smoking under starlight. My mother used to send me *Reader's Digest* reprints which threatened lung cancer, emphesyma and heart attacks. The threats of my family often involve death.

I pause at the threshold of another closed door. I'll see my mother in the kitchen when I open it. On the left, in the laundry room, the rifles wait in a closet beneath the red hunting hats and flannel shirts. The stand-up freezer guards the corner with the key hanging from a lock on its door. My mother freezes cookies, stacking them between sectioned pieces of deer and elk. Cold chocolate chips mashed between my teeth. Mother opening the freezer door yelling, "Louise, have you been eating those cookies?" "No, it wasn't me." I knew I was lying. But lying never seemed wrong when I was growing up. I pass by the freezer without taking cookies.

"Oh there you are. Dinner's almost ready." My mother's head dives under the counter, her hands emerge balancing tupperware. "Jack and Linda will be over shortly, Jim and Cindy just called. It's cold out. Are you wearing that to church? Poor Joanna's arthritis is getting so bad she can hardly walk anymore. Jim's going to drop these cookies by for her."

The kitchen fills with my mother's voice. We hug without touching. Some beast is tied around her vocal chords, making her voice dive up and down nervously. She wears a pastel blue polyester pant suit, a white nylon blouse, and blue clip-on earrings. Her hair has just been curled, the grey is hidden under the red at the beauty shop. She wears gold wire-rimmed glasses.

"How are you? How was the traffic?" She holds both hands together in front of her stomach, looking toward the table while she talks to me.

"Fine. Heavier between Greenwood and here."

"I can't stand this," Fuckit mutters.

"Go down and see the tree. I decorated it by myself again this year."

The dining room. Wax candle angels. China and silver, mother's marriage gifts on their annual display, out from the cupboards that hold them the rest of the year. Soon, turkey, salads, jello and sweet potatoes will be self-served and then carried below to the tableclothed ping pong table in the rec room.

The living room to the side is undisturbed, symmetrically tidy. A clear sheet of glass covers the coffee table, forever untouched by rings from coffee cups or magazines. An old wood high chair from my grandmother holds a doll with glass eyes. Through the window I can see the row of plastic daffodils my mother has interspered between the vines on the hill. An oil painting of Mount Rainier with overly blue water is framed in gold painted wood. The couch with large orange brown flowers matches the large chair. 1971. An organic layer of aging grey settles into spaces that were off-white. The furniture wears from standing on display, not from use.

I stop in the guest bathroom. Struggle to dry my hands with tiny initialed hand towels. I pick up and put down the December issue of *Guidepost for Christian Living. Guidepost* never printed the appropriate prayers for me. I don't want to think. I look at my mask in the mirror, yanking the smile on. Don't remember. Just keep going. Carrie tells YoungerOnes that we can take off the mask later. It will not stick to my face.

"The tree looks great, Mother," I yell toward the stairs from the rec room. I put the heap of packages next to a long present for Jim from my aunt and uncle, Linda and Jack. Four stockings hang suspended from elk antlers on the wall. I want to rip my stocking from the antler. My name in glitter hangs from the dead elk. I know that inside is a toothbrush, a tube of Colgate toothpaste, an anonymous toy from the drugstore, a tube of Head and Shoulders shampoo and mandarin oranges. I want to squish them, squeeze them, and stomp them into a blue-orange bristly sticky puddle. A pile that can't be ignored. A spot of ruin that shouts at the tidiness and splashes against the the perfect picture of Christmas.

"Down Fuckit." A cold numb sensation deadens my stomach through my thighs, curling around my chest. The fireplace has been boarded off and connected to a brown tank that burns wood and generates more heat. In the rec room, appearance is sacrificed for efficiency. I remember lying on that brown couch when I had the flu. The seams have unraveled in wiry thread loops. The stuffed rocking chair carries the prints of repeated sitting. *Taylor's Medical Dictionary* peers out from the bookshelf next to *Illustrated Stories of the Bible*. Dust.

Down the hall, Jim's room is now Don's den. Fishing tackle is hooked to a baseball hat. A deer with brown glass eyes stares in silence. The mounted never tell. *Sports Illustrated* magazines clutter the corner of the dresser. A box of rifle shells waits on the floor. One strung bow hangs on the wall, with no signs of blood. A bumper sticker on the mirror from Jim. "Square dancers call it." No letters, no shaving lotion, no diaries, newspaper articles, photographs or books. Reminders from a sporting goods store. Weapons looking for targets.

My room was next door to Jim's. It was my waking refuge from the twelve hour television, demands of mother and silence of Don. The built-in desk I never used has Jim's square dance award, a model plane, a couple of his old square dance shirts from high school and his stereo, abandoned to upward mobility. My mother's pleated plaid skirts hang in plastic cocoons in the closet, saved until fashion repeats itself. The twin beds I slept in are gone. The double makes the room smaller. It holds ribbons and gift tags with pictures of Santa. This room houses the past of everyone but me.

I hear Don's footsteps descending the stairs. My left shoulder jerks forward like a door slamming in my chest. I close the door of my room and lean against it. My heart is moving too fast, like a clock counting quarter-seconds. The television sings White Christmas. "We'll die," YoungerOnes say faster and faster till the words join each other, "We'll die we'll die we'll die."

"We've seen him before," I remind myself, calling back the mask. "He doesn't fly around in an angry rage of breaking furniture. He's doesn't drink. He's normal during the day. This is Christmas. Everyone is 'perfect.' We're safe." Carrie moves close to YoungerOnes. I hug my shoulders with my arms. My arms have muscles from working. Long breaths, breathe in, breathe out, make a rhythm. Pretend I'm in a boat alone, rocking on the ocean, under stars.

Don sits in the rocking chair, straightening the newspaper.

The reading glasses make him look like an aging cobbler. The top of his head reflects the lighting—he was bald at twenty-eight. I imagine the unsaid words and unfelt feelings collecting like sediment. The brown suit fits uneasily on his body, making him look stiff like a mummy.

"Uh hi," I croak in his direction.

"Carol said you were home. Cold out." He sits, waits. This is the time I always ask him about hunting, fishing or hiking boots. I can't. I won't. Don fidgets with the paper.

"Well I should go up and help Mother." I edge toward the stairs. Don nods. We don't usually talk much anyway. He does not reminisce. His past is a rumor from his seldom seen relatives. I am behind Plexiglas, far away, on an ocean. My smile stays in place like make-up.

My mother hands me a bowl, a can of cranberries. I battle with the electric can opener. My arm moves forward, as if I would touch my mother. Fuckit stops the motion. "No. Don't trust her. She'll use it against us." In the last few years I've noticed how solely responsible my mother is for the holidays. I want her to know that I notice. It's hard to stop wanting to bond with her as a woman. YoungerOnes remember when I softened in the past and reached out to her only to be betrayed by her name-calling and threats. Fuckit built a barrier to help me stop caring about what she said. "The house looks nice, all decorated and everything," I tell her.

"Oh that's nice," she says automatically.

"She'll never hear anything good about herself," Fuckit fumes. "Nothing gets through to her." I take deep breaths. I am accustomed to being mad at my mother. My anger toward her lives in easy-to-reach accusations.

But I don't want to pretend that she's a poor, defenseless woman and condescend to her. I know how abusive she's been. Over and over again she'd yell, "Show some respect for this family. I don't know what's wrong with you. Why aren't you more like Janice or Karen? They don't treat their mothers this way. You must be crazy. Other girls don't talk that way about the church. You're always making trouble, I don't understand what's wrong with you. If you don't straighten up I'll call and tell your teachers how crazy you are." Craziness was a fortress that kept my mother from seeing me. It was an understanding that did not implicate the rest of the family. Respect meant never disagreeing. She did call the parents of my friends and tell them I was "seriously disturbed." She arranged clandestine meetings with my teachers to discuss my "emotional nature." The school counselor even called me to her office and told me I shouldn't treat my mother badly. My mother searched my drawers and my diaries. We never talk about our past.

Linda arrives bearing Christmas bowls of green salad and her usual efficiency. Greetings are exchanged and dropped into talk of dinner preparation. My mother repeats "It's almost ready" three times. She and my Aunt Linda stir, dish and walk between the stove and the counter. They busy my extraneous hands with dishes and silverware. I don't have a fixed place in the kitchen, even though this is where the women are kept. I am supposed to fit in this room. My mother says she confides in Linda, but I've never heard them talk about how they feel, only about what they do.

Jack follows, looking ill at ease in the church required suit. "How ya doin'," he asks without pausing for an answer as he wanders through the kitchen with a box of presents. He and Don wait downstairs for the women to order and arrange the dinner. Men are for football and outside work. Women are for creating holidays.

My brother Jim and his wife arrive, tailed by my cousin Craig and his wife. Boy men of twenty-six years in suits, followed by delicate feminine women. The women remain in the kitchen. Craig folds his long legs down the stairs. Jim pauses in front of me, we hug. "So hi, sis," he says. He and my sister-in-law live next door in a house they rent from my parents. My brother manages Jack and Linda's business.

Jim looks down at my mother, dwarfing her with his height. He clicks his tongue and wrinkles his forehead in the serious discussion of how many cars it will require to transport us to church. Mother nods, saying, "You'll figure it out." I remember her telling him, in the same solemn distressed voice that he was "the man of the house." He was six years old. All my uncles told Jim, "Take good care of your mother." He's always taken the injunction seriously. He takes two steps forward and then returns for approval and further instruction.

I'm glad Jim's here. I like him. In early childhood Jim and I formed an alliance against the grownups. But our partnership was not stronger than our assigned roles. He was supposed to protect mother. As older sister, I was supposed to take care of him. I didn't understand why he was the head of the house. I was the older sister. I figured I was smarter, wiser and perfectly capable of running things. But I was a girl. Girls don't head the family.

What would he say if he knew about the incest? Or does he already know? YoungerOnes tug at my stomach when I think about the incest. I make my mind turn off the questions. Jean and I agreed that the best way to survive Christmas was to pretend that I'm an outsider visiting my family. But the roles fell in place as soon as I opened the kitchen door. Without them, we wouldn't know how to act with each other. I used to be surprised when my friends looked forward to spending time with their families. It didn't make sense.

Don says grace. When I was small my grandfather preceeded each meal with words to God. He grew particularly long-winded when there was company, perhaps to impress listeners with his intimate and comfortable manner with the Almighty. Jim and I used to steal glimpses of each other and at the rapidly cooling food. But at this meal, because the speaker is Don, the blessing is short and standard. "Dear God, Thank you for this opportunity for all of us to be together. Bless this food to our use. Amen." Clatter of silverware.

It's business talk between Jim and my cousin, joined by Jack. Women talk of marriage, birth and death. The men move to sports. Linda asks me how I like the city. "Fine," I say.

I am a ghost at the table, an apparition. If I were not here, it would be noted. My place would be empty. But it wouldn't make a difference to anything that's happening here. Perhaps that's why incest was possible. I was not essential.

I make myself stay quiet. I take the crystal stone from my pocket and hold it. I imagine myself sitting inside of it filling with light. I don't start throwing dishes off the table. I don't leap at Don with the dinner knife. A raw red rush of feeling shoots through my arms and legs like a drug. I hate Don for his "normal" life. It's not fair. I'm the one with nightmares and nausea. I'm the one who runs away from red hunting clothes. For Don, hunting season is still sport. Why am I paying for him? Why isn't he feeling bad? Why doesn't he hate himself? Why doesn't he try to change?

He sits at the table quietly, grinding his teeth. His palms are concealed under fists. Tension merges with him like a favorite sweatshirt.

For a moment I forget the fear of being shot. My feet become solid and strong, capable of trampling him. I imagine rising from the table and telling everyone that Don raped me. That it felt awful, like being a can opener or a broom, instead of a person. Another used item. I would say that we must talk about it, because it has to stop. The silence breeds it, encourages it, allows it to continue. "Quit being so invested in being good," I'd yell, "it only makes you blind!"

And what would happen then? Silence. Guns? Screaming. Bodily tossed out? Denial. Would the plate of white turkey meat simply go the rounds again while Jim speaks in favor of nuclear power? Would my mother say that I'm home on a pass from a mental institution, that I'm crazy like she's always said?

Suddenly I want them to act like something has happened. I want Don to pinch my breasts in public. I want him to tell a dirty joke. I want him to threaten me with a rifle, here, in front of everyone. The dinner table conversation says nothing. Words form in the air and disappear without impact. The dinner is a picture from a Christmas card. The embarrassing items are hidden away. "Don't ever talk about the family, it's private," my mother said. The family never talks about itself either.

When I was seven, Jim and I watched General Hospital with my grandmother every day until the episode where sixteen-year-old Angela got pregnant out of wedlock. My brother and I were promptly put outside, with instructions to play and not disturb Grandma. We weren't supposed to know about things like that. Outside, Grandpa led me to the berry house and had me suck his cock.

Silence covers the abuse. This room is devoid of intimacy, shellacked in gossip. Problems are hidden in prayer. The minister dispenses assurance. Christians are saved, chosen. No examination is necessary. To peer too closely is to to challenge God's order.

Christmas. The rifles stay on the porch. My mother doesn't say I'm crazy and had better straighten up my act right now young lady. We're not driving past the reform school on the way home from Auntie Sue's house. She's not telling me that she'll send me there if I don't shape up. They're all only eating dinner. Consuming sweet potatoes and olives.

I feel the lifelong fear come to a point in my stomach. My feelings pendulate from anger to humiliation. My body was stolen. It's so hard to get it back. Nothing happens now because happenings only occur when they can be hidden away in early morning hours, in a separate compartment from the breakfast table. Just as I was seen as crazy, in isolation, not a part of the whole.

Jim takes care of mother. I take care of Jim. Don takes care of mother, but she really takes care of him, feeding, clothing, arranging a social life. I take care of Don, not telling, protecting. No one takes care of themselves. Hands reach to give while trying to take. All bodies are dirty. We can't talk about them. The holiday hides it. We're eating together at this table, Christmas.

The pews will always be hard bare wood. The large white

cross hangs from the front. Jesus looks out from stained glass on two sides. In twenty-five years the church has added a room to the back and ushered through three sets of ministers and their families. It's crowded as we sit, nine in the same pew, squeezing over and touching each other to make room for new-comers. The elderly are outnumbered by young visiting families.

The minister says the same thing every Christmas. I don't listen. The birth of Jesus did not help me. The pastor will look down from the pulpit and see rows of contentment, mouths moving only on cue, the best clothes that the congregation closets hold, faces that come this once a year for tradition. From his viewpoint, my family looks like all the rest.

My mask begins to falter because my mouth is tired of being told to smile when I don't feel like it. Jim elbows me because I've been sighing at regular intervals. His job, once we got past the point of wrestling quietly in church, was to keep me civil once we arrived. It started the Sunday that I was thirteen and refused to go to church. I was bodily pushed to the car by Jim and my mother. "I will not allow you to shame this family! I'll tell the minister about your disgraceful behavior," she said. The minister wanted me to write a prayer for the congregation. "Atheists do not write prayers," Fuckit decided. I did not want assimilation. The reader is finishing the last gospel. No one told Christ to be seen and not heard.

Christmas cookies and pumpkin pie. I play with my food, watching the clock. My body feels heavier with each hour, gaining weight by the minute. My face sags into discontent. A frilly blouse from Penney's from my mother. "Ladylike," two sizes too large. One hundred dollars from Don, traditional. I'll take it. One hundred dollars will almost pay for three sessions with Jean. One hundred dollars is not enough. I thank him with a voice that sounds like tin. I unwrap make-up that I don't know how to use. A plate of white turkey meat is wrapped to go. I am a corpse hugging my mother. A sister hugging my brother. Goodbyes. I nod my head at Don.

I slide with relief into my Volkswagen. My hands shake as I aim the match for the cigarette. The blessing is being able to leave. Cigarette smoke thickens the air. Power is in car keys.

The mask drops off. "We did it," Carrie congratulates YoungerOnes. "Tomorrow we'll have a fun Christmas." My first Christmas with Stephanie. Our presents to each other are mountains under the tree we chose together. Paul, my long-time friend from high school and his lover, Dennis, will be there too. "It'll be like having a family," Carrie tells YoungerOnes. "We won't have to wear a mask."

11   THE SONG

"What do you think you're doing?" Sarah walks up behind Fuckit. Fuckit's been playing the guitar and singing. She likes to pretend that she's performing in front of other women. I don't really perform though, it frightens YoungerOnes. They let Fuckit sing in campgrounds where they can hide while Fuckit pretends that the campers are applauding.

"I'm practicing being an inspired and gifted folksinger, that's what. Blow off, Sarah." Fuckit strikes an A minor chord, hitting the strings with fingernails, then catching them with the soft part of the finger.

"You're not good enough," Sarah chides while sitting on my upper chest, locking my voice inside.

Fuckit pushes her off. "This is my stage Sarah, get the fuck off. I can't hear the music when you're yelling at me. Shit. Take a vacation."

YoungerOne 7 used to strum a tennis racket on the front lawn of my grandparent's house. Grandpa told me to stop that "foolishness" even though he beat the piano so hard the house rattled with the Battle Hymn of the Republic. His voice overwhelmed the hymns at church, drowning sopranos and altos with bass. It was hard to find a spot for my voice when I stood next to him. But when he wasn't looking I'd sneak out my tennis racket and pretend to play folksongs like the man I'd seen with a guitar at my uncle's house.

Years later, Fuckit closes her eyes and hums, defying my grandfather. Words arrange themselves into the music, a chorus, a stanza. The unspeakable emotions of Don's rapes find sound. A song about incest, a ballad of surviving. Singing

149

strokes open muscles that were hardened with distrust.

The other voices stop talking in the sound. Notes ride on the exhalation. Stiffness rolls out my fingers until my arms tingle. My feet are firm against the carpet. The music pushes Don away. It says "I have survived in spite of you."

Light from the fire in the Well radiates upward, filling my stomach and bathing my lungs with firelight that turns the blackness to delicate pink. The soft light gathers the grief and anger of YoungerOnes, casting a many-colored aura around my heart. Victorious words and heart rhythm take hold of the room, charging it with hope. In the Well, the voices are centered in circles of gold light. Music travels on the tip of the light, gathering expression from feeling.

My body has no division. The lines that separated my legs from my pelvis, that split my torso from my head, have melted to fluid motion. The sound unplugs my ears, loosening barriers that kept me inside of myself. A song of being broken and enraged. It's hard to sing the word "penis" out loud. In the song I throw his body off of mine, bringing my body back to myself, spreading my life around inside me. My life fits my body, spilling into air, dissolving into vibration. Joining with the voices of other women who sang their stories before me.

◇

"Can you make love to me?" Stephanie asks, reaching out soft arms. I like to feel her skin with my hands, holding and stroking. I wish we could just hold each other and forget about sex.

"I don't want to," Fuckit crosses her arms in front of her chest. It's too hard to be sexual. It restimulates memory. Orgasms make me feel worse.

YoungerOnes hold onto each other, afraid that if I'm sexual, they'll be denied.

Jean says that sexuality, creativity and power are interrelated. I spent most of a day trying to weave the three together. It was an exercise in abstraction; I don't know how to think about sex. It's supposed to be wonderful. It's supposed to be about a deep inner core. It's supposed to be like the sensuous canyons of Georgia O'Keefe's paintings. I don't know how to make sex be that way. I certainly can't imagine feeling powerful while I'm sexual. Sex means that I'm in the hands of someone else, unable to free myself. I just don't understand what's so important about it. Before remembering the incest, sex was a harsh drive that left me feeling hollow and guilty. Maybe there's more, but it's hard to imagine that sex could be worth the struggle.

I wanted Jean to explain the connection, just like I wanted an adult to tell me it was all right to masturbate when I was an adolescent. Jean's reply is that maybe sex, creativity and power don't go together for me.

I wish I remembered what it was like to have new skin, before shame was rubbed all over it. I want to clean the dirty feelings out of me and rejoice in a sexuality that hasn't been torn and defiled. New skin worn numb between callous male fingers. My mother yanking my child hand away from my own crotch. "Dirty. Don't touch yourself there!" I don't know how to get the layers of shame off my body.

I want my body new again. I hate the taste of buried words blurting out incest. I wonder if mouths grow fresh again. What are the limits of rejuvenation? When will it end? Sure Voice says, "Trust the healing, you can learn a better way," but it's hard to believe in what has no precedent.

"You don't like my body," Stephanie says. "You think I'm ugly."

I have mixed feelings about her body, about my body. Bodies are never beautiful. If I love her I have to feel sexual toward her. If I'm not sexual with her she'll hate herself. Sex is always for someone else.

I don't know how to see my body in the mirror. How can I see for myself, instead of what I've been told to see?

"A lot of women have breasts like that," the woman's health care specialist patted my arm, covering their unevenness with tissue paper. Her words made me feel odder, defective instead of normal.

YoungerOne 16 turned pages of *Seventeen* magazine. Girls with sleek golden legs and eyes darkened with skillful applications of mascara. Blond, blue-eyed boys hung on their arms. "This is what girls are supposed to look like. Learn to dress for them and you will have a man." I didn't want a man. I didn't look like that. There was something wrong with me because I didn't look like the girl on that page. I wanted to be safe, looking like that seemed dangerous. But looking like me was not safe either. Who am I if my likeness isn't in magazines or on television?

"I'll never be safe," YoungerOne 11 says. "Jimmy tried to pinch my breasts. Boys came up behind the girls and looked through their shirts to see a bra strap, then they snapped it. The boys whispered about the menstruation movie. Mrs. Maloney said not to tell them about it. But they found out anyway, and chanted Kotex like a dirty word." I feel embarrassed when tampons are advertised on TV. I can't look at the clerk in the store when I buy them.

"You're always the one who has to initiate sex," Stephanie complains. "It's not fair. You always want to be in control." We stand at opposite end of a rope, tugging. I can't turn on the spark that makes me want to reach beyond myself. I fail at controlling it.

I seduced the boy I dated in high school when my parents were gone. I wanted him to fuck me, I took him to my bed. It had to be on my bed. Maybe it would make Don go away. "Spread your legs apart," he said, "wider." It burned. It was over in five minutes and then he said he was going to the YMCA. Everyone leaves. I called Carin, a devoted Christian friend of mine. My heart was beating fast, afraid, guilty. I was desperate to tell someone, as if having chosen sex meant that I could finally talk about it. She said, "How could you!" and hung up on me.

YoungerOne 16 closes her legs more tightly together.

"This body always betrays me. It's dangerous."

My five-year-old body felt partitioned, like something dissected. A head. Shoulders and arms. Legs which began at the knees. The space between wasn't part of my body. It had no language. It had to be covered.

I played doctor with Darrel in the first grade. It was the first time I'd been over at his house. We were on the floor of his closet. He was giving me a check-up with my pants down. The door flew open, his mother said, "What are you doing, stop that right now, it's time to go home, Louise!" Her voice was a telephone wire to my mother, winding words around my throat. Darrel and I never played together again. We sat in opposite corner of the classroom through eleven subsequent grades, ashamed for playing with our bodies. We never talked about it.

I discovered masturbation at twelve when I was at Girl Scout camp. I was swimming in Turtle Lake. I pressed the water between my legs. It's okay, I told myself, I'm not touching myself, it's the water touching me, making that feeling.

"It's a sin to masturbate. I make myself stop doing it," Carin told me. She also told me about an article she read in a Christian magazine. She said a woman climbed into bed with her friend but the other woman pushed her away and said, "Stop in the name of God." I wanted Carin to hold me and stroke my hair. It was a sin to think that. "If you imagine something six times," the minister threatened, "it's the same as if you've done it." Not even my mind was my own.

Sex was a mystery guarded by the adults. Hand. Nose. Wrist. Ankle. A word for every place but the genitals. The genitals were awarded adjectives, "dirty, nasty, obscene, rude." I don't know how to retrieve my sexuality. The mystery remains but I'm supposed to have solved it by now.

"Are you ever going to work on this?" Stephanie asks. "I need to know."

"Sure. I'm doing what I can. It'll get better," Fuckit answers. I feel irritated whenever Stephanie wants to talk about sex. I don't believe it will get better.

◇

Yesterday I felt like a slug wrapped in denim. Last night at the concert, everyone else looked beautiful. I was sure they were thinking that I was ugly. I never know what to wear either. I'm afraid that clothes give sexual messages. My body gets tight. My thighs rub against each other like over-aired innertubes.

My mother dressed me in maternity clothes. She hid her body too, buttoning her blouses to the throat, secreting her bra strap beneath a nylon slip. She rarely wore a swimming suit or shorts. She said she burned easily. Even indoors, her body lacked shape under the layers of her clothing. When I was twenty-two, my mother told me that she never felt sexual, she just liked to be held. She went out with men about seven times in the thirteen years she was divorced. I never saw anyone kissing or holding hands. In my family, bodies and their relationship to sexuality was hidden. Clothing extends the body, enhancing or denying sexuality. Clothes for my mother met the requirements of teaching school; respectable, appropriate and not revealing. Clothes were to create distance between people, not to invite them closer.

"I think we'd feel better if we went swimming," Carrie suggests.

"Nah. I don't want to go swimming. I want to sleep for twenty more minutes, have a cup of freshly ground coffee and read the paper." Fuckit rolls over in bed pulling the flannel sheet over my head.

"Exercise is good for you," Sarah says. "You better go swimming or you'll die from a heart attack. When are you going to start taking care of your body! You're just lazy and fat."

"I am definitely not going swimming or doing anything else that's fucking good for me." Fuckit is now wide-awake. Arguing with Sarah always increases her adrenalin.

"It would feel wonderful," Carrie tells YoungerOnes.

"Moving around in warm water. You used to go swimming—remember how much fun it was?"

"We want to go swimming!" YoungerOnes clamor. "Swimming, take us swimming."

"Ah, you don't really want to go swimming. You'd rather sit and drink coffee like grownups do," Fuckit argues.

"Fuckit!" Carrie glares at her, familiar with her many attempts to persuade YoungerOnes to her point of view. "We will still be able to have a cup of coffee if we leave right now."

"Twenty minutes is my absolute maximum," Fuckit reaches for the coat.

"Five minutes, fifteen more to go," Fuckit watches the clock as I crawl to and fro.

"Kick harder," Sarah admonishes. "Your legs are flabby."

"I like this," YoungerOne 11 says.

"Me too," YoungerOne 8 listens to the sound of bubbles blown in water. "I wish they'd stop yelling at each other though. It's hard to play when Sarah and Fuckit are fighting. I can't pay attention to what I'm doing then. Grandpa used to make me work if he saw me playing. Or eat his candy. He didn't think anything I did was important."

YoungerOnes confer among themselves. "At the count of three," YoungerOne 8 says. "One—two—three—SHUT UP!"

It's the first time YoungerOnes have had their way without crying, moaning or throwing a tantrum. The silence stills my mind. My attention moves between my body and the water. The smooth folding of my legs in kicking, the power of arms pushing and pulling. "Thank you legs, heart, lungs, skin," Carrie smiles. My breath deepens, sinking into my belly, moving my spine.

I feel lighter in my body. My clothes fit. YoungerOnes walk with long exaggerated steps, hopscotching over cracks in the sidewalk. It feels freeing to swing my legs in wide arcs, stretching them out from my pelvis. "YoungerOnes haven't forgotten how to play with our body," Carrie says. "They can teach us."

Maybe I can learn something besides pain from them after all.

◇

As I follow my own growth and participate in workshops, the emphasis of my work has shifted away from giving silent relaxing massages. Increasingly, I journey with my clients as they uncover the cause of tension, pain and numbness in their bodies. In the last several months, much of my work has been with women who are remembering sexual abuse.

Clara is lying on her back on the massage table, covered by a flannel sheet. I bend close to hear her whisper while massaging the muscles along her upper spine. "I have a lump in my throat, I can't swallow," she says. Her legs stiffen as she talks. Her neck is held in a collar of muscles that prevent her from turning her head.

"What does the lump in your throat look like?" I ask, following a line of tension from her jaw into her temples.

"It's a sticky white ball. He put it there... " Clara twists her body away from me, toward the bookcases. She tightens her body further, like children do when they are trying not to feel. Now, the contraction paralyzes her so that she feels unable to escape.

"What keeps the semen in there? Can you spit it out? It doesn't belong in your throat." I know she might not be ready to spit it out. Right now, it's more important to uncover the fears that still make her a victim in her adult life.

"I can't." Her jaw barely moves while she talks. "I see an open mouth screaming behind the ball."

"It's all right to scream here. You can fill this whole room with your loudest voice."

Her mouth opens as if to make sound, but she quickly closes it again. "I can see the child in me screaming. It scares me to see it. I don't want to make that sound." I rest one hand on Clara's stomach while she talks so that she will feel our connection. I can feel anxiety beating beneath her solar plexus, a pulsing under the towel. "He said I would go to jail if I told anyone. It's crazy for that scream to be there. I want to make it go away. I'm hungry. My stomach hurts."

"It's scary to make noise when someone's threatened you. He can't send you to jail." Clara nods slowly, agreeing. "What else happened when you made noise as a kid?" I ask. In addition to the fear of telling, many children are punished for making sound.

"He would hit me with his belt if I tried to get away. He chased me." Silent tears dampen the massage sheet. Clara wipes them away with her hands.

"It's your voice," Fuckit tells Clara. He took it away from you, but it's not his.

"Let's try an experiment." I show Clara a brightly colored beach towel. "This is your voice, filled with color and possibility. But your father still controls this voice. It's hard to make noise without a voice. Let's see what happens if you take your voice back from him by pulling it away from me." I hold as she pulls. I feel her arms decide to hold on, instead of weakening.

"You can't have it," she says. The sound starts as a mumble and grows into sharp strong words. Hugging the towel, Clara looks around my office, making sure her father is not hiding here with his belt.

Sometimes speaking requires many steps.

◇

I look at the floor as if I was saying hello to the carpet instead of Jean. My head won't take my eyes out the window.

"Do you think it's hot in here?" Jean asks as she adjusts the vent with a broomstick.

Her question bounces off the leather feel of my body. Leather that's dead and still worn. Leather has taken the place of my skin.

She lets the silence stand.

I travel without sound from a blurred inspection of her green carpet to the shadowy inner confines of the Well. No one is talking in the Well either, not after last night's memory. I don't want to talk anymore. Each of the voices stands silhouetted and apart from one another, like marionettes frozen on a string.

Fuckit stands, arms folded across her chest, turned away from Carrie. Her legs are thick under black trousers from the men's department at Sears. Her ankles are bound as if Don's belt still encircles them. An overcoat and heavy white shirt conceal her gender. A cigarette dangles from the corner of a growl. Smoke thickens the air around her. A wine bottle in a brown sack leans against her leg. She has not combed her hair.

"Louise, where are you?" I hear Jean's voice in the distance.

The air in the office moves, the Well stays silent.

I study my shoelaces. "You're going to hate me if I tell you," I mutter to the floor.

I feel her lean forward in her chair as if she was going to pick the words up off the ground. She is probably raising her eyebrows.

"I was scared. I didn't mean to. I didn't want him to come to my bed. Sometimes Kevin would rub my crotch through my clothes and that felt good even though I didn't want him to do it... "

"You mentioned that before," Jean says, waiting.

"Don was on top of me, in the morning, just before it got light outside. He touched me hard, squeezing my breasts and bouncing up and down on top of me. His eyes had that faraway look. He covered my face with a pillow but I could still breathe but mostly I held my breath. His bouncing kept building in my body, my mind was so confused—I wasn't thinking anything. My body exploded in a way I'd never felt before. He put his penis in my mouth and filled it up. The feelings of my vagina met the gagging in my mouth in a dirty place in the middle of me. He got off of me, covered me back up with blankets. I pushed my face into pillows with my eyes closed.

"I uh, I had an orgasm." I can not look up. My face is hot. I want to be a dust ball under the couch.

The sixteen-year-old self huddles in the Well. Her body is shaking violently. She is wrapped in a blanket unable to get warm.

I hate looking at her. She makes me sick.

I clomp a fist against the couch. "I hate it. What is wrong with me that I had an orgasm with him! And for years after that I was sexual with men I didn't like. I wanted to use them. I was used to them not seeing who I was. I didn't want to see who they were either. Do disgusting people turn me on? I didn't care about them at all. Now I care about Stephanie but I don't want to be sexual with her. This is so fucked up."

"What about the sixteen-year-old? What about her?" Jean looks to the side of me as if the sixteen-year-old me is next to me on the couch. "Where is your compassion for her?" Jean's eyes are shiny with moisture. She wipes them with a Kleenex.

"Jean cares about you," Carrie tells YoungerOne 16. It's hard for the sixteen-year-old to believe she matters to anyone.

"I shouldn't have let it happen. It is my fault. There must have been something about me that made it happen. It happened over and over again. I was a magnet—I drew them to me." YoungerOne 16 recites the old messages. I take back the shame I'd begun to throw off.

"Let's talk about the orgasm," Jean looks at me. She doesn't seem embarrassed. Her ability to ask me these questions is unnerving. I analyze her expression, searching her face and posture for revulsion. She waits for me to say something. I never know what I'll say beforehand. Words fall out of my mouth.

"It was horrible. I can't masturbate anymore let alone make love. Being aroused is terrifying. I throw up instead of climaxing. I hate my body for feeling sexual at all. I don't want to feel sexual ever. Maybe if I didn't feel sexual none of this would have happened. Now that I think about it, my own masturbation was patterned after Kevin's fondling of me when I had my clothes on. I hate this body!" My armpits are dripping lines of moisture down the sides of my body as I talk.

"Bodies respond to stimulation. We don't have control over them—a lot of the time." Jean folds her fingers under her chin. "In adolescence you grew breasts even though you were afraid of them. Bodies sneeze and cough during solemn moments of silence despite our instructions for quiet."

But this is different than sneezing... I see the sixteen-year-old in the Well out of the corner of my inner eye.

"I didn't want to feel that in my body. I never fantasized about Don or felt sexual toward him. By the time I was in high school I was mostly scared and shy around adult men. I asked one of the male teachers to the father-daughter banquet. I could hardly talk the whole time even though he was nice to me. I felt self-conscious, crawling with the wrong body. This makes me feel scared of my body, out of control of myself. I feel like something's wrong with me that I could be so scared and shocked and still have an orgasm."

Behind the fear is a flash of hard anger. "It's not fair," Fuckit objects. "I'll never have the chance to know what it would have been like to have my own sexuality develop and be under my control. That fucker! It wasn't enough that he had to terrorize me, he took my feelings away from me too. That asshole!"

I pause. No matter how non-judgemental Jean usually is, I keep waiting for her to tell me I'm bad. When I hate myself I think everyone else does too.

"I was terrified about being pregnant when I was in high school," I continue. A girl down the street from my house got pregnant when she was sixteen. It was a scandal, the whole town knew. Mother said how awful it was—that the girl was going to have a hard time now. She said it was the girl's fault, she should have said 'no'. She'd just have to pay for her sins. My mother never even mentioned that a boy was involved." It's hard to make room for the sixteen-year-old to speak. I don't want to feel the feelings that part of my self holds.

I close my eyes and breathe out, trying to still my own

shaking. My arms, legs and jaw are twitching. The closer I get to YoungerOne 16, the more it feels like nothing solid is holding me together.

She's huddled in her blanket rocking. Her eyes look empty as if she's not there behind her face. "I'm sorry about what happened to us," I tell her. "It's not your fault. Please. You don't have to run away from your body anymore. We just responded physically to what was happening. You never should have been put in that position. . . . I know I blamed you for what happened in the way I've hated you. I don't want to do that anymore."

I begin rocking on the couch, holding the end pillow in front of my stomach as a shield against the soft hole that is spilling out my pain.

I have to quiet the other voices in order to hear YoungerOne 16. "I was sure people could tell about Don by looking at me. It got so that I couldn't think very well. I started projects and couldn't finish them. I was coming apart, exploding all the time, but without any noise."

I nod my head in recognition of my present inability to finish what I start—stories, careers and chores. I tried jogging when I attended Stanford. I told myself that I'd run to the end of the block ahead of me. I always stopped to walk before I arrived at my goal. Now I have to stop feeling sexual in my body so I won't have an orgasm.

"I tried to stop masturbating," YoungerOne 16 shrinks inside herself even more, "I fought with myself about it because it was a sin. I just kept feeling evil.

"I knew that if Don could shoot deer which were innocent, then he could shoot me because I already felt guilty. I was afraid he saw my orgasm and that he thought I wanted him to be there but I didn't."

YoungerOne 16's words are laced with tears. The border of the quilt shakes where she clutches it shut. Jean gives me a Kleenex.

"Sometimes I thought I was being punished for talking

back to my mother. I thought Don was trying to keep me in place. I couldn't fight him. I couldn't battle the feelings in my own body. When I heard the doorknob turn, I'd close my eyes and try to pretend nothing was happening. I couldn't move even before he climbed on top of me. My strength, my will and my soul just ran away and left me there wondering why these things kept happening to me. . . . I'm sorry, I'm sorry. I didn't mean to . . . . "

Jean's voice is an anchor from the office, thrown to YoungerOne, "You didn't make it happen. Bodies respond to stimulation. Sixteen-year-olds feel sexual, it's normal." She repeats it several times. YoungerOne 16 doesn't hear her.

"I didn't think of saying 'no,'" YoungerOne whispers, running nervous fingers through her hair. She wants to believe that something about this situation was in her control.

"Do you think that saying 'no' would have stopped him?" Jean's voice is curious, without pressure. She is not interrogating me. The lump of shame softens, the strings tying it in place loosen. Strand by strand, YoungerOne 16 is unwoven from feeling dirty.

"I thought that if I said 'no,' he would punish me harder. No one said 'no' to him. No one said 'no' to any man because they took care of you and provided for you and you were supposed to make life easier for them." She stops, feeling tired.

Fuckit walks over to YoungerOne 16 proudly. "We never said 'yes' to him either. He didn't give a shit about what we thought and felt. The orgasm was a part of us that he stole, just like he took our body and our right to feel safe in our own room. No one thought the feelings of teenagers were important. But the danger was the adults who denied their sexuality while raping us. We were just trying to stay alive around that loony bin. That bastard!"

Sure Voice stands beside YoungerOne 16, stroking her hair. "Without a body," she says, "you could not make music or write poems. You would not feel the earth moving when you walk. The voices would have no home. The body houses the inner and takes you beyond yourself. You are a player in a complex puzzle which changes as you respond to it."

"This body is mine," I look directly into Jean's eyes with my announcement, "I feel so confused about how to get along with it sometimes. It's embarassing to work with other people's bodies and feel so stupid with my own.

"I don't want to hate my ability to feel pleasure. But I don't want to have sex with Stephanie just because I'm supposed to. I feel like I want to hold my own sexuality inside of myself, but I don't know how.

"I'm not going to let Don keep taking it away from me. When I was sixteen, I couldn't fight, couldn't drive away, couldn't comprehend what happened so often... there was no healer then." I look away from Jean, feeling shy. "I don't want to hate myself for what he did to me." My voice is calm and even. Free of weights that closed it into my stomach.

"I believe you," Jean says.

"But I hate him for what he did to me. I hate that we have to go through all this because of what he did," Fuckit says. "Right now, I'd like to kill him."

12 THE FIST

"You're just not hearing me," Mary yells across the phone line.

I don't want to talk about our last session. I just want to veg out for a couple hours with the TV set. I hold the receiver away from my mouth and sigh in the direction of the kitchen.

"You're always pushing me too hard. Sometimes I just want to relax, but you're always making me talk to my body. I don't want to know anymore." Mary's voice is like hail raining through the receiver. "I hate it when you stand by my feet and ask me questions. You should stand by my arms when you talk with me."

I feel Fuckit's irritation and YoungerOnes fear of Mary's anger. My shoulders narrow as if shoelaces were looped through my upper arms.

"We have to stay with this," Carrie says. "We can't just walk away because Mary's angry. I like working with her."

In the last couple of weeks Mary has pounded her friends on pillows in my office, screamed at her boss and buried her lover. Her shoulders stayed tight and hot with the feelings. I asked her what else her anger was telling her since her body didn't soften when she was finished.

"I don't know," she said. "Just give me a massage. I don't want to talk anymore."

When muscles are holding emotion, massage temporarily relieves the tension. My thumbs pressed and vibrated the knot on her shoulder with no effect on the tightness. "Is this sore?" I asked, checking on the ever-increasing deep pressure I'd been applying to the muscle.

"I can hardly feel anything there at all," she said. "Press harder."

Carrie is reviewing our last few sessions while Mary tells me that I don't know what I'm doing on the phone.

"It sounds like you're angry. What happens when I touch other parts of your body away from you arms?" I ask.

"It feels cold, like you've left me. It makes me angry at you."

"Is there anyone else that used to talk to you and touch you without looking at you?" I ask, unsure of whether she'll respond to the question or yell at me for asking it.

"My uncle, when he was beating me. But he doesn't have anything to do with this. I'm mad at you, not at him."

My favorite television show is half over.

"What would you like me to do then?" I ask, feeling desperate for a resolution. YoungerOnes want Mary's anger to go away.

We agree that the sessions will be split between bodywork and massage. I suggest some guided meditation work to increase body awareness. She's not sure about that, we'll talk about it at our next session.

"You don't know enough. You just pretend to help people." Sarah is jumping up and down in the Well, sagging my stomach, pulling my body forward, shrinking my chest.

"I wish I knew the right thing to say to her," Carrie says.

"I do not think you want to steal her learning from her." Sure Voice reminds me of each person's separate quest for understanding. "If you always knew what to do, you would not need to do this kind of work. Being a healer has lessons for you as well as for others."

When my work is going well, I don't think about it. But when I'm struggling with a client, I imagine my entire career crumbling. I wonder if I know enough about getting along with other people to be a healer. Inadequacy colors my perceptions.

I call Sally, another healer. I'm afraid she'll think I'm bad because I made a mistake. I'm afraid of my own anger at Mary.

"Is it okay for Mary to be mad at you?" Sally asks.

"I'm not sure she is mad at me, really. One minute she's angry about not discovering profound truths about herself. She's mad that her shoulder hurts all the time. Then when I work with her shoulder, she's mad because I'm making her work when she just wants to relax."

"What do you want from her?" Sally asks me.

"I want her to find the source of her anger so that she can release it instead of flinging it at everyone else, me included. I guess I'm afraid she'll tell other people that I'm not good at my work."

It's like being afraid of my mother. She called my friends and told them I was crazy. They believed her. They didn't see me.

"What about your anger at her?"

"I needed to tell her I'd call her back at a better time for me. I think that when anyone says I've done something wrong I get defensive. Then I can't hear what they're saying."

"What have you done wrong?"

"I got frustrated giving a massage when her shoulder didn't respond to it. . . . I can't control her timing."

I think about Mary again. I imagine her inner children beaten and raped. She toughens to protect herself from feeling that helplessness. Anger comes to push away the source of pain, but as a child she couldn't get mad at those who were abusing her. So now, the anger comes out in sparks that burn everyone but the perpetrator.

I write in my journal. "The thing I like about being a healer is that Mary and I will meet again and keep trying to reach an understanding. Our journeys are different. I can help her sometimes but I can't heal her, she has to do that herself. Her anger won't destroy me. It sure is teaching me about myself, though." I close the journal and laugh at this journey.

◇

♦*Dream*: I am waiting at the bus stop. Jenny strolls by.

She holds a decapitated man's head dripping blood into a green tupperware salad container like my mother used to use. Jenny thrusts the bowl at me saying, "This is yours." I take the bowl, feeling disgusted. "No. This isn't mine. I didn't do it." People are running after me so I try to escape. Blood from the head trails behind me. I run into a forest and hide the head underneath ferns. I am still yelling, "I didn't do it. It was Jenny, not me." The crowd, a vigilante group of men armed with shovels, moves closer. I wake up. ♦

"Not fair!" My body shouts from under tangled sheets. I search for blankets. "It was just a dream," I tell the inner voices. I reach for B. Bear's soft body, holding it against the aching in my solar plexus.

"Whose head?" Sure Voice asks, warming to the subject of dream analysis when all I want to do is forget it.

"It's five o'clock in the morning!" I tell her. "I don't want to think about it now."

The next morning, I arrive at Stephanie's apartment with a bouquet of yellow roses, feeling cheery. "Did you remember to bring the milk?" she asks, after admiring the flowers.

"You didn't tell me to bring milk." I begin walking backwards.

"Yes I did. On Wednesday, you said you'd stop by the store and pick up some milk. Remember? I said I'm always doing the shopping and you said you'd pick up the milk."

"You know I can't remember anything in the morning! Why didn't you call and remind me?"

"Why should I have to call and remind you," Stephanie responds. "Why didn't you just make a note of it?"

"Because I hate lists. And I hate Saturday morning in the grocery store. All you think about is doing tasks!" My words grow louder with each sentence. "You could spend your whole life doing tasks!"

"I always end up doing chores for both of us," Stephanie says with deliberate calm.

"You never notice what I do contribute." I shove the flowers into a vase. My mind refuses to intervene, words join feeling in fiery escalation. "I'm tired of trying to remember the lists you're always devising for me. And I'm sick of hearing how you're always doing more than me! It doesn't matter what I do—it's never enough for you! I feel like I'm married." Fuckit's the only part of me that I can hear.

Stephanie emits a loud disgusted sigh. "I cannot believe we are going through all this over a half gallon of milk. You're dumping coals all over me for nothing."

"All right, all right." I shake my head, not at all calmed down. "I will go get the goddamned milk!"

I pound the stairs back to the car and slam the door closed. "I am so sick of this crap!" Fuckit mutters with a vengeance. A fool idiot deranged driver crosses me on the right side. "That's illegal, you fool!" I blow the horn. I glare at the clerk in the 7-11 when she asks me if I have anything smaller than a ten dollar bill. "If I had something smaller I would have given it to you." The milk plops down on the seat next to me and tumbles to the floor when I hit the brakes. "Can't anything go right?" I scream to the milk.

"You just can't do anything right," Sarah taunts.

"Louise, Louise," I dimly hear Sure Voice on the other side of the flamed barrier.

"Just leave me alone. Why didn't you remind me about the milk?" I don't want to hear anyone right now.

◆*Memory*. The Saturday morning grapefruit stares me in the face across from my brother's plate of eggs, bacon and toast. I hate grapefruit. Don has already left.

"It's time for you to get your hair cut," my mother begins. "I'll make an appointment with Donna at the beauty shop."

"I don't want my hair cut, I'm growing it out." I am about to add that I can't breathe for three days after the application of lacquer glues each strand into immortality.

"You are too getting your hair cut, young lady. Long

hair makes you look fatter and shorter."

"It's my hair! Just because you want Donna to do your hair doesn't mean I want her to do mine."

My mother picks up the phone. "Donna, Louise needs an appointment. Two o'clock. That will be fine." She puts the phone down.

"Two o'clock," she says to me. "The woodwork in the kitchen needs washing. After breakfast you can clean the shower downstairs, then do the floor and wipe off the woodwork."

"I don't want to clean the house today. I'm going to a movie with Paul. I'm not getting my hair cut."

"You are not going to a movie today. You have work to do around this house. I'll call Paul right now and tell him you have things to do. I spend all week working. . . "

"It's not my fault you work. You're always. . . "

". . . to support you. It hasn't been easy to raise you two kids. . . "

". . . blaming me. Jim never has to clean anthing. . . "

". . . all I ever get from you is arguments. I take you everywhere. . . "

". . . I don't have a choice about getting around, if you'd let me get my learner's permit!"

"I'm just a taxi service for you and you're so ungrateful!"

Voices rising in competition. My mother commands the bellow of a schoolteacher, bringing order to a classroom of thirty-six children. I am a fourteen-year-old.

"How dare you talk back to me!" She orders. "Don't you learn anything in church! Honor your mother. After all I've given you."

I hate you, I hate you, I am thinking.

"Where have I failed, to have a daughter like you? You get going this instant." Her fist is clenched, her face radiates red. The phone is dialed, Paul's number.

I run to my room, slam the door, bury my face in a pillow, dig fingers into palms, lock hatred into a clench of my jaw. I shake with the force I would put into flight if escape was possible. Rage rushes in a closed burning circle within my body. I tear open a candy bar hidden under the bed.

I swallow a chunk of warm sticky carmel and sweet chocolate, shoving the rest into hiding as I hear her footsteps descend the stairs. The door opens without my permission. She does not believe in knocking.

"I called Paul. I told him you have things to do around here. You are grounded for a week, young lady. Now get in there and clean that shower. You do little enough around here as it is. Why don't you take some pride in your home?" ♦

The fire has turned to ash, draining my body. I close my eyes and watch the voices. YoungerOne 14 shivers. "I could never win; it didn't matter what I said to her. She didn't care. I used my rage as a fire wall against her words. I was tired of hearing my mother tell me how worthless I was. How wrong I always was. My self kept getting squeezed into a smaller and smaller space. Nothing was my own. I couldn't stand being hurt by her all the time."

"Keep breathing," Sure Voice encourages, "When you take a full breath you claim your right to live."

"The only one she yelled at was me. Her anger was another family secret." Fuckit gestures toward YoungerOnes. "We took it and took it. It hurt. We didn't have anyone else to get mad at either. It was all right to be mad at her."

Fuckit drops her defiance and for a moment she's unguarded. "Except it wasn't really all right to be mad at anyone. The fact that I was so mad at her just convinced her that I really was bad and crazy. And sometimes when I yelled, I felt crazy like my whole body was going to dissolve into steam. I hoped that if I screamed loud enough I wouldn't have to hear what she said. But she always got her way no matter what."

"You did not want to hear her hurting you," Sure Voice comments.

Fuckit nods. "She said awful things about me. She didn't want to help me. She wanted me to take the blame for everything. Then she'd say she loved me. But I'm no fool. I knew she didn't love me and I don't care. The worst part was that no matter how loud I screamed, YoungerOnes still kind of believed her. But I never believed that old bag. I decided I was never going to be like her! And I told her that too." Fuckit stands up straight and ornery. The incest came at unpredictable times and intervals, but she chipped away at me everyday. There was no time to recover or relax.

"You sounded a little like Mother when you were yelling at Stephanie," YoungerOne 14 says softly.

"But I'm not like her!" Fuckit turns away from YoungerOnes.

"Your Grandfather and Kevin and Don hurt you. You did not get mad at them," Sure Voice reminds her.

Fuckit shakes her head and looks down so Sure Voice won't notice that she's ashamed. "Aw, they weren't even worth getting mad at. Why should I have wasted my breath on those scum bags."

YoungerOnes move around so that they can look at Fuckit. "All right," Fuckit says. "I didn't think I could get mad at them. It was safer not to feel anything about them. I was pretty good at that: I didn't have any feelings at all when Kevin and Grandpa died. But I couldn't stop having feelings about Mother. When she poked, I screamed but she never seemed to hear me."

"It was better to be mad at her than at Grandpa cause he'd hit," YoungerOne 8 says. "Kevin used to threaten to spank me and I knew he could do things a lot worse than that like when he put those toys up my bottom," YoungerOne 11 trails off and looks down when she thinks of Kevin. "By the time Don came along," YoungerOne 16 says, "I thought he was raping me as punishment. If we got mad at him, he would kill us."

In the Pit, a shadow play repeats itself in slow motion. A woman reaches behind herself and grabs handfuls of her past, throwing it at an adolescent girl. The girl reaches into the night and throws handfuls back at the woman. The woman throws the last handful while the night swallows the girl. The night is full of men.

◊

I've just taken a workshop on healing with precious stones. We took turns placing cornelian, rose quartz, aquamarine, bloodstone and amethyst crystals on the chakras, the energy centers of our bodies. I learned that black stones like obsidian are often connected with the subconscious. I thought about the transformation of fiery liquid lava into black rock. When I placed a piece of obsidian at my feet my legs felt strong and rooted. I learned that looking into obsidian brings up hidden memories and provides protection for gentle-hearted people.

I felt great after the workshop. It affirmed my companionship with the ground and with stones in particular. I carry rocks in my pockets and feel their solid slow changes with my fingers. At night, I hold a quartz crystal and feel it pulsing while I listen to soft music on my tape recorder. I imagine the crystal growing deep within the earth. I listen for its stories. It's another way of transforming a time of anxiety into one of gentleness.

I tell Jean about the workshop. "I love rocks. They're special. Each of them has a different quality. I think different ones really do help clean out the incest from my body. I imagine their colors floating through me. The light blue of aquamarine opened my throat. It was easier to swallow for a while. Even the obsidian of the Well is a healing stone, not an enemy.

"Nature heals me. Sometimes when I take walks I hear the spirits of tree talking. When I put my arms around their trunks, I see curtains of green behind my eyes. It makes me feel easy. My shoulders relax." I look at Jean shyly. "My astrologer told me that my rising sign is concerned with spirituality. Sometimes when I'm camping, I feel at home with my spirit."

Jean's frown grows when I mention astrology.

"Well, have you ever had your chart read?" I ask her. I feel shy asking her about herself. I've been taught that it's rude to ask personal questions. I'm nervous about exposing my own feelings about nature and astrology. Some people would call me crazy for believing in that.

"Oh someone told me something about astrology once. I don't believe in that myself."

I scoot farther into the corner of the couch.

"She doesn't believe us," YoungerOnes say. "She probably hasn't believed anything we ever told her. She thinks we're bad."

"She just hasn't got her head on right," Fuckit says. "I was sent here to educate her."

"So do you think I'm making these experiences up?" I risk asking Jean, tentatively. My buttocks hold my legs in place as if I have been cornered by a dangerous animal and might be eaten at any minute.

"I believe that's your experience. When you tell me about astrology, or talking to trees, or spirits... I don't believe in those things myself. The rational 'explained' phenomena are enough for me. So when you talk about non-rational experiences, I imagine that they're a frame around what you're sharing about yourself. I try to understand what you're telling me about you."

I feel YoungerOnes inside of me. "She won't see us anymore because we don't think the same way," they say. "She doesn't believe us."

I don't want Jean to see the tears that follow one another down my cheek. "Do you believe me about the incest?" I ask. I have been learning to trust myself. But what if she's just been humoring me, disbelieving this pain that's so real to me? I strain forward, counting the steps to the door.

"I believe that you were sexually abused. That's not what we're talking about here," she says.

YoungerOnes relax, moving away from the ledge, holding

onto each other.

"But there are other things we will disagree about," she adds. "I like that. I learn about areas that I don't think much about from hearing you."

Fuckit nods importantly.

At the end of the session, I feel closer to Jean even though we don't have the same ideas. Her respect for me encourages me to follow my own growth, even though it may be different from others. Her acceptance eases the wound left by my family's insistence on conformity.

◇

♦*Memory.* I'm seven years old, sitting on the back porch of my cousin's house. My cousins and Jim are on the rope and tire swing, making Tarzan noises as they fly over the wooded hill. I can't play with them because I still have my church clothes on, a white dress with green polka dots. It feels like starch. My mother's visiting my aunt and uncle before we meet my grandparents for lunch at the restaurant.

Princess has brown tiger fur and a splash of white on her belly. She nudges her kitten nose into my dress, making a tiny wet spot. I hold her in my arms even though she hates to be held. A short smooth stick lies next to me. Princess tries to get away.

My body is hollow, lined with red. My head is light as if it was pumped full of air. The stick goes in and out of Princess' bottom. Princess is far away and I am too. It's someone else's hand pushing that stick into Princess' insides.

My older cousin walks up. "Stop that! What are you doing! You're hurting Princess!"

Right then I could feel her fur against my arm and blood coming in dots from the scratches on my hand. The stick drops off the porch into the dirt.

I go sit in the car. I put my hands tight under my legs

so that they won't do anything else when I'm not watching them. My body feels covered with dirt. ♦

YoungerOnes start to cry. My body settles into mud, as if I was in a moist corner of the Well. "I'm sorry, Princess," I whisper over and over again.

When I was thirteen, I was babysitting for my favorite family, the Masons. They had a six-month-old baby. As soon as the parents left, the baby howled. I walked her and tried to sing a lullaby. The crying got louder, turned to screaming. Her face wrinkled with tears, legs kicking in the air. I hit her with my hand. Slapping sounds. She stopped, stunned. When I turned around, Monica, the seven-year-old, was watching me. She moved away from me when I walked closer to her. She went to bed early, without dancing to "Paint Your Wagon" like she always did before.

Later, Mr. Mason said he'd heard that I hit the baby. A cloak of embarrassment moved over my back and stomach, covering my face like a red sweater. When I hit her, I didn't think there was anything wrong with hitting a baby. I hadn't questioned it. But after he communicated his shock, I felt guilty. I didn't want to hurt anyone.

Fuckit sputters around the Well, shaking her fist at the figures in the Pit. Her fist makes a silhouette in the light from the fire. She moves toward Stephanie, using her mouth like my mother. She forgets about caring. With my mother, the words between us were hard like ice with no warmth to melt them. I have always thought that anger had no solution.

The memories of my own abusiveness line the Well like unwanted photographs. I am ashamed of my hitting and hurting, and of my tongue.

Jean says she doesn't think pounding pillows does any good. She's not into that stuff. But sometimes it has helped. Sure Voice says that the experience of incest and the discovery of feeling have always involved my body. Expression, for me, is a bodily act. Now, screams fill the interior of my car, but there's a gap between the sound and how I feel. I'm angry but I don't know how to get it out of my body.

The spiraling heat overwhelms YoungerOnes. "We don't want to hurt anyone," they say. "We don't know what to do." They take food into my mouth and swallow without chewing until my stomach pounds against my jeans. Fuckit smokes cigarettes until my throat feels scratched by cat claws and my voice cracks on words.

The spiral presses against the black obsidian of the Well, making it too hot to hide against.

I draw pictures that castrate the offender. I play my drum till my wrists vibrate. I dance to loud music and shake my fists. I write stories and make myself the heroine. But the rage seems endless.

◇

YoungerOne 16 looks over the ledge at the memories of incest in the Pit. "I don't understand why I had to go through this... or how to move past it."

"What happened to you is what happens in this world. But you are learning healing from knowing your wounds. You will understand growing from facing death." Sure Voice appears next to the fire, an old woman. She has a cane, but she stands sturdy, as if she was planted solidly in dirt long ago. When she talks, the fire leaps, lighting the smudges on YoungerOnes' faces. The belt that Don tied around my ankles circles Fuckit's legs. Carrie's face is etched with newly visible lines of expression.

"We've changed in facing this. We don't say the same things we said before. We aren't crazy," Carrie says. "Aren't crazy," bounces off the moist walls, amplifying.

"This is the helplessness passed on by our family," Carrie places a drab olive green box next to the fire. "This box of helplessness has been passed through generations of our family." The open cover reveals a lead lining.

"We have named what happened to us," YoungerOnes look solemnly toward Sure Voice. They spit sperm from their mouths into the box. As Carrie touches their legs, the bruises from Kevin's bouncing fade.

"Your yelling at YoungerOnes is not what taught them strength," Carrie comments to Sarah.

"Maybe so," Sarah admits in a rare moment of self doubt. "But they were so weak and sniveling. I didn't know how to keep them from doing something stupid and getting hurt more. Yelling they understood."

"There's a lot of things that are crazy, but we're not!" Fuckit points at the Pit. "Incest is crazy. It just hurts people. It makes violence. It's not so different from war or beating people up or throwing sewage into drinking water. It's not going to pollute me any more, that's for sure." She takes the pillow Don covered my face with from YoungerOne 16 and kicks it toward the fire. "I can do what I want to!" She unbuckles the belt and tosses it on top of the pillow.

Sarah puts down the club she has used to bludgeon the voices with accusations of craziness. She looks at Carrie, silent.

Carrie wraps the craziness into a bundle, tying it together with Don's belt. She throws it toward the Pit. The pillow, covered with sperm and bruises, weighted by helplessness and the club, thuds against the floor of the Pit.

The bundle lies unseen, covered by half-light. My mother says, "It looks like you've lost weight, wish I could get this off," while she pats her stomach. She talks to the air, but she believes that I am standing in front of her.

My grandfather bounces little girls on his knee, squeezing them hard, looking for a way up their dresses. Kevin walks with watches, holding them out for sale, saving his obscenity for the ears of eleven-year-olds. Don opens the door to my room. He picks up the bundle without looking at it and tosses it out of his way.

The discarded bundle balances on the ledge, drawing a shadow on the scenes in the pit. A marker between the Well and the Pit.

I do not pick up the craziness. But the lightness of my body turns to a place of panic, a wild throbbing of thoughts in my mind. I feel lost, as if my own feelings and perceptions exist in a void without gravity.

I look into the Pit at Kevin and Grandpa and Don. Incest is not so crazy. For a large part of the population, sexually abusing children is a silent routine. Children growing into lessons of abuse, becoming victims and abusers again, forgetting how to love. In order to call incest crazy, I would have to believe that the world is only a wonderful, just, loving place where people know how to respect each other. I know that isn't true.

The crazy feeling is the denial, the figures pretending that nothing has happened. Denial is a carpet bulging into a hill while the housekeeper says that dirt has not been swept under it.

"Aw shit," Fuckit says. "Don was supposed to trip over the bundle and break his face. He just fucking tossed it aside instead!"

Carrie has been standing motionless by the fire since throwing the craziness to the Pit.

"Carrie," Sure Voice says while closing her fingers around the intricate carving on her cane, "tell them."

"I feel so much stronger," Carrie says, as if talking to herself. Her voice sounds distant. "I see all the voices, traveling in an exotic land, having adventures. We're not in the Well, but outside. There's some kind of a plant with flowers. I can't quite see it. I just know it's there. When I look into the eyes of the voices, I see the fire in them, living, as if it will never go out."

Across the Well, beyond the Pit, a small crack of light appears from a slit in the rocks.

Carrie frowns, shaking her head. She squints toward the opening. "What's that? I thought we had to go out through the top of the Well. But it looks like a door..."

"Aw shit! I don't want to walk in front of the family to get out of here! Why couldn't the door be by this wall? I don't want to climb through that Pit."

"The door is where it is," Sure Voice says, smiling a little at Fuckit's insistence that its location should be different.

"Uh-uh," YoungerOnes say. "We can't go through there. The family's in there. We'd have to walk right in front of them."

"You are not free in here," Sure Voice reminds them. "You will go into the Pit, but you are not traveling alone. The fire burns inside of you. You will be strong enough."

◇

"I'm depressed," I tell Jean. "I get angry and angry and angry. I read the newspaper and yell my head off. There's violence everywhere. Suddenly I stop feeling angry about it; I'm drowning instead, sinking underneath it. It wins and I feel like a pinhead." I shrink down into my corner of the couch.

"You look like a little girl shaking her fist at the world," Jean makes her voice sound wavery like a little kid's.

I raise up tall on the couch in a flash. "I am not! There's a lot of things wrong! It pisses me off that the world is set up in this fucking disgusting manner!"

"I can see that it bothers you." Jean reaches for the clay ball she holds when we talk. "But if you're angry at everything, you end up feeling smaller. You can't use that anger to change anything if you spread it out into little clouds of hot air."

"I get caught in all sorts of extremes. I blow up at minor irritations. I've bitten Stephanie's head off for no reason. I got enraged when one of my officemates left a note about not bringing bicycles into the office. I scribbled a bunch of replies in the office notebook. Then I realized my reply was out of proportion and scratched it out."

"So you're catching yourself dumping the anger where it doesn't belong?"

"Yeah, but only afterwards. A big explosion builds up and my mouth just turns on. I've even been yelling at the six o'clock news. Screaming at the screen."

"Do you feel better then?" Jean asks.

"No."

"Why?" Jean asks with raised eyebrows.

"I just want to kill Don. I can't kill Kevin and Grandpa because they're already dead. But Don's walking around alive, not paying one thing for what he did to me. Walking around like he had a right to rape. I want to get a gun. I want to point it at Don. I want to see him be afraid of me. I want to get him out of this Well and off the face of the earth. I want to hurt him the way he hurt me!"

"So you want to kill him?" Jean raises her eyebrows. "That's your solution? Of course they'll probably lock you up for that, you know."

I feel embarrassed to hear Fuckit echoed back to me. "I don't really believe in killing people. It used to be that I just wanted God to kill him. But now, I don't know. I don't want him to molest other kids. I want him to be afraid of me."

"How will you feel if he's afraid of you?" she asks.

"I'll feel powerful. I'll feel like I'm in control."

"So if you see him shaking because you're holding a gun at his face you'll feel powerful?" Jean leans forward in her chair, watching me.

"Not really," I tell Jean. "Killing him would destroy me too. I know that violence just creates more violence. But I have to do something."

I stop there. A gentle sadness breathes through me, leaving clarity in its wake. "The incest has to stop," I say out loud. Strong words from a powerful place in a still corner of my belly.

"How?" Jean asks. She's stopped moving around in her chair.

"I have to confront him with it. I have to tell him how awful it felt. I have to stop him from doing it again."

"Do you need a gun for that?" she asks.

"No. I need my voice to be strong inside of me. I need my friends to be around I need you to keep helping me."

The opening behind the Pit yawns wider. My family forms a barricade in front of it. The bundle balances on the ledge. I pick it up and look: buttons, sperm, belts tied and bundled into a pillow. I see that it is not a weapon but a statement.

13 THE MIRROR

THE voices have been in an uproar since my decision to confront Don. Terror roams the Well like a ghost, pushing the voices away from the fire.

I can't remember when any family member confronted another. Truth was less important than appearance. My family has no mechanism for facing problems. My mother complained of Don's silences to me but never talked to him about them. Don never told my mother when he wanted her to talk less. He simply picked up the newspaper and folded himself behind it. Occasionally, he'd say, "Oh Carol," in a disapproving tone. When Jim had a problem with our parents he talked to me. When Mother had something she wanted me to know, she told Jim to tell me. Decisions were never made cooperatively.

When I was in college, my mother pressed twenty dollars into my hand and said, "This is our little secret. We won't tell Don about it. He thinks I shouldn't give you any more money. But I want you to have this."

Silences. My mother found the envelope of letters Don's mother wrote to him at his job. She hadn't wanted my mother to see them. My mother talked to me but not to Don or his mother, carrying her suspicions year after year.

When I close my eyes, I see YoungerOnes crouching behind Fuckit, speaking fears. "We can't tell them about the incest. It will kill them. Mother will go crazy and have to be institutionalized. Don will kill us with a gun. Jim will hate us."

I have a cranky aunt who alternates between complaining about the inadequacy of family gatherings and asserting her own superiority in such matters. "Oh, you're not using that bowl are you?" she said as my mother emptied mashed potatoes into a green bowl. "I have a nicer bowl that that. You should have told me, I would have brought it." My mother muttered to me about this aunt's rudeness, while smiling and acting cordial toward her. It is more important to be nice than to be sincere.

"I know what's going to happen," Fuckit announces with her hands on her hips. "If we tell them about the incest, they'll say I'm the villain because I talked about it. They'll blame me for causing trouble, just like they always have. They'll never take responsibility for it. They're fucking hopeless."

"It's always felt dangerous to talk about how we feel," YoungerOne 16 says. "Sometimes I don't even know how I'm feeling. We've lost friends because we couldn't say what was bothering us. We were used to thinking it was all our fault."

I wonder if I really have to confront my family. They'll probably disinherit me and I'll never have enough money to buy a house or land. I'll end up paying for Don's perversions. My mother will tell people I knew in Bryce that I'm crazy. She'll have me committed.

"I don't have to do this," I declare with conviction to the apartment walls. The Ruth Bernard poster of a nude woman, half-hidden by the knee drawn in front of her, stares back. A heavy feeling follows my words, as if I'm trapped in an old box.

If I don't confront them, I'll be living their lie. I imagine going to my parent's house on holidays, hiding my feelings behind a mask that I never allow to slip. How could I avoid wondering if Don was raping someone else? Can I continue to be co-conspirator in the myth that all is well in this family, letting the silence bind another generation of cousins and nieces and nephews into abuse, suicide, self-hatred and violence?

The past formed the foundation for each step I've taken, a layer of secrets and denial. Confronting my family brings the past to the present. I have to know I can face them.

If I never confront them, Fuckit will continue reacting against my mother and Don instead of growing past them.

She'll direct her anger against their beliefs instead of using it to stand up for me. Making decisions to smoke because they hate smoking, to waste time because they believe in work. Fighting with myself because I never won with my parents. Fuckit would keep rebelling because I never said "no" to their most significant violation of me.

But what do I say? How do I go about being honest? I don't know how to be with someone without conforming—unless Fuckit's anger is triggered. Even with Stephanie, I watch TV when I'd rather be taking a walk. I can't write when she's in the same room with me—it's as if I feel her presence looking over my shoulder. I'm afraid of hurting her feelings when I tell her I'm not all right. When I do tell her, her face closes and she seems to leave. Then I feel guilty. It's easier to pretend that everything is fine. I don't know how to disagree without separating.

Twenty years ago, a relative of mine married one of his employees, Katy. My Aunt Linda decided that Katy was marrying her brother-in-law for his inheritance. My mother defended Aunt Linda because they were friends. Linda and Katy haven't talked with each other for years, nor do they attend the same gatherings. The accusations have become a feud. My mother said she was on Linda's side, as if there was only one truth, as if sides must be taken. The land my uncles inherited jointly is in continual dispute because of the unspoken suspicions. I hear my brother and cousin repeat the judgements of Linda and my mother. There has never been talk of reconciliation or meeting. In my family, the women wage war between themselves. The men fight through omission, holding the final say. The loser, like Katy, can be tossed out.

I enrolled in an assertiveness training class seven years ago, hoping to find the solution for excruciating periods of feeling like my tongue was tied around my tonsils. I met with the group four times and managed to say "hello" at the beginning. I was afraid the group leader could read my mind because she was a healer. I'd never met one before. The other six women in the group practiced asking their bosses for raises and telling their boyfriends that they didn't want to go to the football game on Saturday. I wasn't in a relationship at the time and my boss at the restaurant would never pay more than minimum wage. I didn't say one word beyond the introductions for the eight hours that we met. I couldn't let the group know that my shyness was a terror of their rejection if I said the wrong words. I haven't had much practice revealing myself.

It was only after my feelings surfaced in my sessions with Jean and Kate that I realized I have preferences. My friends hurt my feelings sometimes. Until now, my response was to withdraw.

Even meetings with the healers with whom I share office space leave me reaching for the door and the privacy of a cigarette. I obsess about what I've said. "I shouldn't have said I didn't want Zelda to join the office group. Everyone thinks I'm a horrible person now." I rehearse the scene over and over again, finding words which eluded me, deleting the ones that make me feel vulnerable. In the back of my mind, YoungerOnes chant, "We've said the wrong thing. We're going to get in trouble." At first saying the "wrong thing" was talking about the incest. But over time, the "wrong thing" became any disagreement. Saying the "wrong thing" included asking for what I wanted from another person. The admonition "Don't tell" convinced me that words were dangerous. But words are also power.

I am challenged to be honest with my clients in response to their feelings. "That sounds painful," "I feel angry when you do that," "I don't understand what you're saying. Could you explain it to me again?" My work as a healer pushes me to speak my own feelings. Bit by bit I learn to work through conflict.

"It's harder than I thought to just be who we are in front of other people," Carrie writes in her journal. "It's scary to be truthful and to risk someone else's truth. But it feels clean inside when we aren't pretending."

◇

"So if I tell them about the incest, then everything will get better?" YoungerOnes ask.

"Yeah." YoungerOne 10 says. "If we tell Don how horrible his rape of us was, he'll feel sorry. He'll say he did it and it's bothered him a lot and he's glad we brought it up so he can get it off his conscience. He'll come see Jean with us and he'll hear how much we hurt. It'll make us feel a lot better when he says it's his fault, that we didn't make him do it."

"He'll see his own healer," YoungerOne 6 says, "and he'll never hurt any children again."

"Mother will listen to us too," YoungerOne 10 says. "It'll be the first time she'll ever have heard us. She and Carrie will talk to each other and Mother won't treat us like we're crazy cause she'll see we're really neat."

"Maybe she'll get help too," YoungerOne 11 adds hopefully. "She doesn't like herself very well either. Maybe she'll see her own healer."

"Maybe Grandpa made her eat his candy like me," YoungerOne 5 suggests. "She'll be glad that we started talking about this."

"I miss Jim." YoungerOne 13 looks sad thinking of him. "He never understood why I hated the family so much and why I ran away from home. If he knows what happened, he'll understand and love me again. I'm his big sister. He'll come visit and we'll go out on the town with Fuckit. He'll make sure his kids don't get hurt like we did."

I want to believe YoungerOnes even though I know that the majority of offenders confronted with sexual abuse deny it.

Jean says not to expect people to act differently from the way they usually act. Confronting the incest will shatter my family's web of silence. But whenever there's a loss, even a loss of silence, there is denial, pretending that nothing has really changed. Clinging to pieces of a raft while maintaining that the ship still floats. This is the most probable outcome. I do not want to believe it.

Sure Voice says, "You can not make them change, no matter what you do. When you speak, it must be for yourself."

◇

Fuckit slams my apartment door with satisfaction, I take long pavement-pounding strides. The storm wind moves leaves against streetlights. "I don't want to!" Fuckit says inside of me. "I don't want to have to keep spending time doing this. I'm twenty-nine years old and I can't seem to escape being sixteen—or five, for that matter. There's always another thing to do with this incest business. And I'm the one who has to spend the time doing it. Don isn't sitting around worrying about me. As far as he's concerned I don't even exist. He may not even remember! This is too fucking hard."

Behind me, I hear measured footsteps, long and fast. "I'll probably get raped now," I think with a mixture of fatalism and hopelessness.

"I am not going to cross to the other side of the street you jerk," Fuckit yells at the footsteps. "There ought to be a curfew law for men. Keep the rapists off the street." He turns down the side street.

"So if I confront them, Sure Voice, how's it going to change anything? Will it make me immune to the ever present hazard of assault for merely walking down the sidewalk? Will my family seek out their own healers? Will violence reduce itself in the least because I did this thing?" I ask.

"It's not going to do any good," Fuckit answers.

"Nothing is going to change," YoungerOne 14 whispers.

I know these phrases by heart.

♦*Memory*. This is the first time I've taken the city bus. I'm running away from home. I boarded in front of the high school. I got off a block from the juvenile detention center at the courthouse. The counter makes me feel like a dwarf, catching me mid-chest. I feel smaller than fourteen. "I can't live at home," I whisper while the rest of my voice puddles at the base of my throat. My knees wobble back and forth. A woman puts me in a cell, locked with two sets of bars and two skeleton keys. The detention center was originally the adult jail. Sitting on the toilet makes me ashamed because the matron could walk by and look in.

The judge who knows my mother comes by to tell me how shocked he was that I would leave my home because my mother's such a wonderful person. "What do you think you're doing to your poor mother?" he asks in judicial tones that condemn instead of question. I can't think so I just say, "I can't live there anymore." My voice betrays me, winding out on a thin string sliding through the holes between my teeth. I roll my hands tight so he can't see my fear. If he knows how weak my legs are he'll just push me down the hallway and into my mother's car. He keeps calling me "Carol's daughter," like I don't have a name of my own.

I like the first foster family. Mrs. Harding is my Girl Scout leader. It seems like she cares about me. She rocks me in her lap and stays up nights with me. I don't want her to leave me alone. I cry a lot but I don't tell her about Kevin. I can't talk about it. I don't know the words for what he does. I can't think of anything except that my mother yells at me a lot. The judge thought it was all right for her to yell at me. Nobody asks about anything else. But at the Harding's nobody yells at me. It's the first time I realize that families aren't all the same. I'm the sixth kid here. Mrs. Harding tells me that seven always seemed the wrong number for her family, but eight is even. I can't believe she likes having me around.

My mother calls here. "After all I've done for you," she says. "Grandma's down sick in bed and she'll probably die because of you doing this. What are people going to think? You better pack your bags, young lady, because I'm coming to get you right now!" Then silence. Mrs. Harding calls a counselor who calls my mother and tells her it would be better not to come get me. But my mother never says she won't come. My suitcase stands in the hall. I sob and pray, "Don't come. Please don't let her come." She doesn't. But each week she calls and my uncles call and Jim calls. They all tell me to go home again, don't I realize what I'm doing to my mother. Jim says he never wants to be like me. No one asks why I left. Kevin calls to say he'll give me a good spanking and haul me back home in his car. I wait afraid. No one comes but they are always here. I stay up all night pacing the circular driveway around the house.

My mother tells the superintendant of schools that Mrs. Harding shouldn't substitute teach in the district because she is breaking up a family by keeping me at her house. Mrs. Harding loses her job. I am a liability. The counselor at the mental health center asks me few questions. Our sessions are largely silent. Sometimes she buys me a hamburger. I cry some but the words are stashed away.

The judge says I am too happy staying with the Hardings so I should move somewhere else. I am put in another foster home. He says that if I am too happy I won't want to go back home.

My foster brother comes in at night and grabs and bites my breasts. Mrs. Carr, the foster mother, tells me not to wear my bra to bed, that it's bad for me. She searches through my clothes and my diaries. She listens to my telephone calls on an extension. Their dachshund chews my shoes and slippers and I get yelled at for leaving them out. Every morning they ask when I will be going home.

I make a record there because the Carrs are related to a man with recording equipment. The songs are all about love and peace. It's scary to sing in front of them.

I keep getting good grades. I climb into textbooks and travel away on ideas that have nothing to do with myself.

I go home, because I can't decide whether the foster home is better than my home. I am sick of visits from un-

cles and threats from my mother. I don't really believe it'll
be better, but there's nothing to do but surrender. ♦

"But I didn't know that the 'wonderful' man my mother
had married when I was gone would have another side. If I had
known about him I probably would have killed myself because
there wasn't anything left to try," YoungerOne 14 says softly.

"So," Sure Voice looks at the pictures and pauses.

"If I confront them, I'll just have to go through all of that
again. Someone I love will be hurt and I'll get punished. It
might even be worse than being raped by Don." YoungerOne
14 feels exhausted.

"What are you afraid of losing this time?" Sure Voice asks
softly. "Friends, career, family?"

"I guess I've already lost the family. I can't even imagine
missing them," Carrie answers, draping an arm around
YoungerOne 14's shoulders.

Sure Voice talks loud enough to be heard by all the voices.
"They can not hurt you anymore. They can not reach into
your life and strangle it. Your friends would no longer believe
your mother. You can talk now. And you can walk away. They
can not send you to reform school or talk to your teachers. You
are past that, but you will never know that until you act on
what you have learned. All the shame that has been planted inside of you is ready to be weeded. It dangles from the rocks of
the Well, waiting to drop. Waiting to be returned to the
sources of it."

◇

I have put off writing the letter to Don. I rehearse, searching for words that go beyond the flames of "I hate you" and
"Go to hell."

Inside me, YoungerOnes are seated as far from the Pit as
possible. Fuckit stands on the ledge, throwing rocks at the figures in the Pit. "I'll scare them away," she says.

"That's not going to work," Carrie says. "They're not
moving one iota no matter how many of those stones you

throw. They don't even notice."

"It's good enough," Sarah says. "Let's just throw rocks. You'll never be able to talk to them. You'll die. They'll kill you. They'll die. You'll chicken out. You're lying.

"If you stick your neck out it'll get chopped off. That's just how the world works. There's nothing outside this old Well anyway." Sarah appears to be growing taller as she talks.

"We'll never know what's outside the Well if we don't leave it." Carrie looks at Sarah's hard, weathered face. Sarah's neck recedes into her shoulders like a turtle escaping into a shell. "Look Sarah, we'll need you to proofread the letter so that our feelings are presented clearly. You are coming with us. We can't leave you behind."

Sarah stomps away grumbling. Fuckit crosses her arms and glares at the pens and blank pages.

Sure Voice breathes on Fuckit's back causing a wind to blow her closer to the desk. Fuckit digs her heels into the carpet and pretends to contemplate her wardrobe. The tension in my body increases with the conflict and fear of the voices. "We can't do this without you," Carrie urges while comforting Younger-Ones. "This is your chance to say how you feel about it. This is the first time that you can say anything you want and everything that needs to be said."

"They won't listen," Fuckit insists, "Never have, never will. I can see it now. Mother screaming, 'How could you do this to us,' as if I had raped myself."

Carrie looks at Fuckit angrily, out of patience. "If we're just doing this to make them listen, then we're sunk. Because it's more than likely they won't. But I'm tired of doing things for them. Molested for them, silenced for them, loyal to a system that's diseased and destructive. I'm doing this for us. I want out of this Well. I'm tired of being afraid of saying the wrong thing. I'm tired of joining in family gatherings that are silent about what is going on. I'm sick of seeing Don and Grandpa and Kevin as grown-up monsters while I'm a weak powerless infant. I'm tired of taking things I don't like, paralyzed about speaking up. And I'm tired of YoungerOne's pleas for someone else to stop the abuse. We are too old for another mother. If we want to heal, we have to act healed. We have to do the thing that has always scared us the most."

Fuckit moves to take the chair. She ceremoniously uncaps the pen. "Everything has to be so damn hard," she mumbles. "Don," she begins. The sentences form without pause, moving from one to another without torment as if the words have been waiting. At the end Fuckit wails.

◇

A week later, it is only the yellow note pad that reminds me of my resolve. "What if it's not true? What if I've made it up?" A tight worry wraps itself into my middle. "What if I can't do this?" lurks under each doubt, testing me. The letter needs typing, but I am afraid to reread it. Afraid to remember my commitment.

"I'm going backwards," I tell Sure Voice. "The YoungerOnes only know what they've experienced. I forget why I'm doing this. I'm not courageous. Don has terrorized me for so long that I'm half afraid I'll drop dead just seeing him." The Well is full of fresh air. Don's shadow crosses the opening.

"You have what you need but you forget it. You are not used to trusting yourself." Sure Voice's words come from the ground under the fire pit. I imagine poking through the ashes with a stick. The stick strikes stone. I find a green emerald which casts the light of fresh leaves into my palm as I pick it up. "Emerald brings good fortune to travelers," Sure Voice says. "Life that has survived fire." Even Fuckit is silent watching pictures form inside the stone: a child hurt, a child betrayed, a child enraged, a child growing anyway. Surviving.

Next to the emerald is a red garnet. Red like blood until I pick it up and see light shining from it. "Garnets are made of courage," Sure Voice continues. "Courage is not possible without fear."

Beneath those is a loose slab of obsidian. Unlike the rocks

which form the walls of the Well, this is polished. A shiny black triangle of volcanic glass that reflects a clear image. I stare into the black reflective mirror, looking into my twenty-nine-year-old face. "This rock holds both the past and the future," Sure Voice says. "It will remind you of where you have been. There is always somewhere new to explore; this mirror holds those mysteries also. The past leads to the future." Looking into the obsidian mirror I see the faces of my friends circling me as YoungerOnes moved through tears and rage and terror. I watch as my friends change; I see new faces and faces I've watched grow older. I see myself in Kate's office with unnamed fears and then in Jean's office, understanding them. The pictures slide through my remembering, through conversations with friends who did not walk away from me. I am bending over the massage table, working, hearing other women who were abused. Taking courage with them. The pictures move again, to writing, singing, dancing barefoot. Finally the pictures cede to an ancient woman with a changing face.

"I am always here," Sure Voice says.

"I can," I say out loud. I look into the mirror of obsidian. I hold the stones in my hand. They pulse in the rhythm of my changing.

14 THE HAND

♦MEMORY. I am two. I have a new brother. I hate him. My grandmother holds him all day. I wish she'd hold me. "Be quiet, Jim's asleep. Be gentle, he's only a baby. Such a cute baby," she says.

My father is invisible like air. Gone. "Where's Daddy, Daddy, Daddy?" I keep trying to find him.

"You don't have a daddy," Mommy says.

"Yes I do!"

"We live here now. With your Grandpa and Grandma."

"I want Daddy!"

"Quit screaming. Go outside and help Grandpa. I don't know what I'm going to do with you."

How do I go outside? Where's the door? This is the wrong house. Where's my room? My house doesn't have stairs. The ground is far away. Help. There's no one to help me. I'm lost in this house.

Standing on the porch, crying. Jim came and Daddy left. "Bad girl, you make too much noise," Daddy said. I was bad and he left.

Mommy squeezes too tight and cries into my clothes. "You and Jim are all I've got." I wiggle away from her. I want to throw things like Daddy does. Then I have to go outside. Mommy picks up Jim instead. She stops crying when she holds him. She gets soft like she used to be sometimes.

"Someday, when Jim gets older," my neighbor, Mrs. Dunn, told me, "you'll have someone to play with."♦

Jim's hand holding mine. I remember when he tottered, not sure of his feet, and I pulled him up again. "It's okay," I said to the tears from his fall, "I'll help you." I looked both ways for us at street corners. I knew about crossing streets, school, fractions, and staying within the lines with crayons before he did. I was an older "guide," but I wasn't one of "them," the distrusted grownups. I pretend I am holding his hand now.

Now I just miss him. He's the first one in my family that I'm going to tell about the incest. The incest was a family secret. Jim's the only person in my family that I remember loving. Maybe he remembers something, maybe Kevin hurt him too.

"You take care of Jim," my grandmother told me. I felt important having someone in my charge. She didn't mention that he would grow taller than me. Or that he'd casually call women "chick" or "babe." For the longest time he seemed to need my counsel, which varied in quality. Sometimes I was kind and full of wanting to love someone. Other times, I was the bossy older sister, desperate for control. We fought with teeth and hands, but somehow returned to warmth. I thought I would always be the leader and he would follow, looking up to me.

Together, we hid Mother's spanking yardstick behind the dresser. When she couldn't find it, we escaped, running from the room, gleeful at our triumph. Unfortunately, the yardstick was replaced by a paddle the size of a breadboard, dotted with holes. In a spanking, air caught against wood. The impact sounded like exploding bombs. Jim and I stole dimes and pennies for dizzying trips to the corner store on bicycles, shoveling forbidden sugar into our mouths. We invented a contest. Jim was Trailways and I was Greyhound. We rocked our heads on pillows and counted out loud until we fell asleep, pretending to travel far away. One count for each beat of our heads moving across pillows. Each count meant we had traveled a mile. Jim rocked his head and sang himself to sleep through high school. I stopped counting before he did.

I don't remember precisely when our alliance was shattered, or if it was just chipped away in small bites as Jim got treated differently from myself. I smiled obediently and kissed the cheeks of all the relatives. Jim was allowed more dignity. It was all right for him to wrinkle his nose at kisses and declare them "mushy." Trucks and dolls divided us. Jim's pants shed circles of earth on the floor next to my grandmother's old-fashioned wringer. I wasn't supposed to get dirty. Jim made whirring noises in his mouth, I poured delicate cups of tea into tiny cups and passed imaginary cookies. I burrowed into books while Jim played basketball with my cousins. When we played together I chose school because I was the teacher. He liked playing house and grocery store better because he was in charge, the father, the storekeeper.

"You take good care of your mother now. You're the man of the family," Uncle George told Jim when he was six years old. Jim must have heard that a thousand times. Standing in a miniature suit on Sunday shaking hands with the minister. "Take care of your mother. You're the man." Jim developed a dark solemn face.

I grew into secrets that turned heavy inside. On the outside I was cheerful and quiet. I remember telling him, "Don't be afraid. I will die for you." He vowed to die for me, too. But he never told me not to be afraid. I never told him I was.

I don't know if we've ever been afraid of the same things. The man who is my brother lives next door to my parents with his wife. Never really leaving our mother. Woven into the lives of uncles and cousins, eating dinner regularly with the "folks," going hunting, fishing and farming with Don. Running mutual errands. There are more strings from him to them than between him and me.

"A man is so good for your brother," my aunt told me. "He's really growing into a man now," she said as Don taught Jim how to shoot guns and kill goats and deer. Jim began to walk like Don, dangling a toothpick at the corner of his mouth.

It was a shock to return as an exchange student to Australia and find him handsome. He was a cheerleader. He had skin that browned in a single afternoon. He was thin and popular. He acted free and relaxed. Jealousy was hating Jim for having what I wanted.

But he continued to come to me for advice. I was the older sister when he needed to battle the adults, or when he couldn't talk to them. When he was a freshman in high school, he began dating. "She wants me to. . . sleep with her," he said, "I don't know what to do." His question scared me. "Do it," I told him. If he was sexual with her, then I wouldn't be the only sinner. It didn't occur to me to ask him how he felt or what he wanted. I feel guilty about the ways I didn't help him.

The strings between us are stapled to my heart and belly. I want to pull them and draw him closer to me. I want to say, "I have missed you. I know what has come between us now, I'll tell you." I want to know who he is, what he feels and dreams. I want to hold hands again. I want to hear him say, "I believe you. I understand now. I wondered why you were always so unhappy."

As much as I'd like to separate Jim from mother and Don, I know that my family is like a net. I'm afraid that when I cut the strings, everyone will fall away from me. With Jean's help I decided to talk with Jim first. But when I think about confronting him, my mind leapfrogs to meeting with Don and seeing my mother.

I thought I'd gotten used to the memories; that I'd finished with the pain and rage of them. But as I get closer to talking with Jim, I feel Don's body heavy on me again. YoungerOnes wake me with anxiety. Sarah says, "You've made everything up," over and over again.

"We didn't make these feelings up," YoungerOnes say defiantly.

"Look at our life, Sarah. Look at YoungerOnes—that's the proof. When we started remembering the incest, we began changing. Our behavior, our fear, our shame, our self-hating all made sense. We can't live with this secret anymore."

"You're too scared to do this," Sarah reminds YoungerOnes of their fears. "You'll die."

"Sarah you really are a fucking ogre sometimes." Fuckit sticks her tongue out at her. She kneels by YoungerOnes. "We have a superb plan. We have Stephanie, Jean, Paul, Dennis, Joan, Gretch, the healers at the office. A whole fucking mob of people who believe us."

"Now," Fuckit begins as YoungerOnes look at her affectionately. "I'm going to teach you some magic words so that you don't get so scared all the time. Repeat after me: 'I'm so mean, you better run through the flames of hell, with cans of gasoline tied round your waist, before you mess with me!'"

YoungerOnes stumble over the words a bit, but soon they're strutting around the ledge and chanting so loud that Sarah is drowned out altogether.

◇

I look at the phone again. Stephanie is cooking chicken for our dinner. When I'm ready to call Jim she'll sit beside me and hold my hand. I'm going to ask him to come up and talk with me. I am going to tell him about the incest—about Kevin and Grandpa and Don. I want him to know that I didn't want to abandon him when I ran away from home. I was running from Kevin.

It is 6:00 Sunday night. I imagine him and Cindy in their kitchen, eating at the same table that Jim and I once shared. Stephanie's hand is warm and solid, fitting between my fingers. She returns my squeeze. I have love already. I'm not alone. I am not jumping off a cliff into an uncertain net.

Jim answers the phone, "Hello sis. What are you doing up there?" He always makes the hundred miles between us sound farther.

"Well, um I'm okay. I want to know if you can come up and see me. I have something to tell you about."

I hear him conferring with Cindy. "We still have your

birthday present here," he says, "we didn't get around to mailing it."

Stephanie gives him directions to her apartment where
we'll meet. The line between Jim and me is broken, leaving a
week of waiting, planning, stomach-racking anxiety. I take my
hand back from Stephanie, holding myself. The phone call is
one event in a chain. I am not sure what comes after this or if
there will even be life after the chain has run its course. I want
to trust my brother to be my brother. But I don't trust the
dynamics of my family.

Carrie keeps reassuring YoungerOnes, "I won't let you get
hurt."

Fuckit paces a lot. We have taken a hundred walks in a
week. Sucked hundreds of cigarettes. Carrie has poured nightly
cups of valerian root tea and gobbled extra doses of Vitamin B.

I've cried and yelled in Brenda's office, finally allowing my
shoulders to fall from my ears. . . at least for a couple of hours.

The days are full of memories repeating themselves. Don's
body on top of me. My body becomes a board, still and flat. At
work, half of my mind is rehearsing. What I will say if he
says. . . if she says. . . Will I be able to talk at all?

I meditate, chasing the voices into silence, hearing only
breath entering and leaving my nose. But then Don's iced eyes
are next to my forehead, boring into my mind.

I count the hours until my appointment with Jean. I want
to sit in her office all week, protected from the other motions
I'm committed to carrying through. I want Jean to give me an
injection that guarantees my ability to do this.

When the day I see Jean finally arrives the hour passes like
a minute. I don't want to leave and wait some more. I am not
sleeping well. I have dreams of chasing Don only to find that
he's chasing me. Jim yells at us to "stop it." I look for Jim but
he has disappeared.

Jean reminds me of my courage. I have already survived
the worst. Jean pretends that she is Jim. She rejects me, saying,

"I don't believe you, you're crazy, you made this up." I know I'm not making it up. I don't lose that knowing. "This is what happened," I tell her, "Don raped me."

Jean changes her lines as Jim, saying "Yes, I believe you. Yes, I'll stand by you."

I don't know how to allow his support. I am used to rejection. I'm afraid to practice him believing me, because if he rejects me Sunday, it will hurt more.

What if the memories go back to hiding in my body? What if the evidence is stolen by my fear?

It's like waiting for finals to end. Studying, while wishing the answers had already been recorded. Hours spent counting on the hours after the test has been passed. I worry about talking to Don. I don't think beyond that.

◊

I meditate and practice again and again what I will tell Jim. This morning Stephanie held me tight. I didn't want her to leave.

I pick up a small emerald and see fragments of the past moving through it. I affirm my survival. I imagine myself clothed in the living color of the forest. I scotch tape a red garnet to my belly. I rest my hands against it. Fuckit says, "I wish we didn't have to do this," one more time. In the obsidian mirror I see myself separated from my brother by a chasm. As much as I long for Jim's hand, the only way it will possibly return is by telling him. Otherwise we will just keep pretending until we don't know each other at all. Sure Voice says, "I am here."

"We're here," voices announce as the doorbell rings. Jim and Cindy arrive with a birthday package containing a matching set of towels. The initial chatting makes my feet itch. Pressure builds in my calves. Speak or flee.

"I wanted to tell you about something. It's hard to talk about it. But I'd like you to hear me through before we talk," I start.

"Okay," Jim nods and wrinkles his brow in concentration, drawing eyebrows together. I have deepening lines in the same spot. Cindy moves closer to him. I sit on the witness stand waiting for judgement.

"You remember when I was a kid and tried to kill myself?"

Jim nods, frowning.

"I was really miserable. I was being sexually abused by Kevin. He did a lot of horrible things to me—I'm not going to tell you the details. But he called me obscene words and shoved things up my anus among other things." I am protective of Jim, afraid to tell him exactly what happened.

"Before that Grandpa molested me. It started when I was five and went on until we moved to the little house next door to them. He stuck his penis in my mouth and told me it was Grandpa's candy. I was scared and confused. He told me I was Grandpa's little girl. I knew that if I told I'd get in big trouble. It felt bad and it seemed like my body was getting frozen. I knew I couldn't say 'no' to Grandpa." Jim shakes his head agreeing, frowning, silent.

I cross, uncross, recross my legs. I put the coffee cup down with shaking hands aware that the table edge seems miles away. I'm afraid of dropping the cup, staining the carpet, falling apart.

"When we moved next door I thought things would be different but then there was Kevin. He'd come over before you and Mother got out of school. You were in sports, she was in meetings.

"I remember talking to you on the phone when I was living with the Hardings. Now I realize it must have seemed like I was abandoning you when I ran away but I wasn't. I was trying to leave Kevin—and to leave Mother because she kept saying I was crazy. But Kevin called when I was at the Hardings and kept telling me he was going to come and spank some sense into me and haul me home."

When I look at Jim, he looks down at the floor. Cindy looks away. I feel deserted.

"This isn't easy," I say, panicking.

Jim shakes his head, agreeing.

"There's more." I take a deep breath. "It's about Don. After we moved to the new house he'd come in early in the morning before he went hunting. Sometimes he'd bring his gun in with him. He'd roll me over when I was sleeping and put a pillow over my mouth. He'd lift up my nightgown and. He um." How can I tell him what Don did? It's hard to find words. The room seems unreal. "He molested me too." Words fall out. I am looking down. The clock sounds time.

"I'm going to talk to him about it," my voice suddenly sounds firm, decided. "I can't keep this inside me anymore. I wanted to tell you. Partly because of my relationship to you. And partly because it might shake things up in Bryce."

"I can see it," Jim says. His forehead is split into wrinkles.

"Do you believe me?"

"I believe you," he says and looks me straight in the eye. My chest begins to soften and melt. The fear tingles when it leaves through my fingers.

"Well," Cindy says, "I believe you about your grandfather. I mean, old men and all. My grandfather used 'play around' with me. They're just old. And I didn't know Kevin."

"Kevin was weird," Jim says. "I never liked him. It seemed like there was something strange about him."

"I always thought that you liked him. . . . Did he ever hurt you?" I ask.

"Not that I remember. But Uncle George was always with us when we went fishing."

"But I can't imagine Don doing that," Cindy adds. "He's always been nice to me."

"I don't know," Jim says. "We really don't know anything about Don. He keeps to himself."

"I was thinking that you might know more about him. Does he ever tell you anything?" I search for clues to validate my memory.

"No," Jim says. "We just talk about the cows and sports.

He's pretty quiet."

"You know one thing about incest offenders is that they're often unobtrusive. You can't tell by looking at them. They're not dirty old men."

"Yeah. I can see that," Jim rubs his chin.

"I've written Don a letter that I'm going to have him read when I talk to him. Do you want to read it?"

"No. No. That's okay." Jim nods. Then he says, predictably, "Well, the one I'm worried about is Mother."

"I want to talk to her too. I've blamed her for the incest, I think. But I also have things I want to clear up with her." It's easier to talk about her.

"This is going to upset her. She may need a lot of help from you. You'll have to be right there by the phone waiting for her to call." Jim leans forward, taking her into his fortress so that distress won't kill her. He commands his male voice, the one that takes charge.

"We're always afraid Mother will self-destruct if we tell her the truth," I say. "She has a way of not seeing what she doesn't want to see no matter what happens. We're always supposed to consider her weak and helpless. I think that she thinks of herself that way. But I don't think she is." The old anger singes my words.

"You know Louise, your mother has changed on a lot of things since I've known her, but she's never changed regarding you," Cindy says. The statement flashes by like a subliminal advertisement. Lost in the relief of YoungerOnes and the jubilance of Fuckit.

"He believes us. He believes us. We haven't died yet." A low, almost unheard chorus wants to go back to those comforting words and not have them pass so quickly.

"I think she knew about the incest, but she didn't want to know so she pretended that it wasn't happening. She told me once how uneasy she felt about Kevin. So she always made sure we were around when she was with him. She wanted us to protect her from him."

"It's funny," Jim is leaning back again, his defense temporarily abandoned. "I remember when her friend, Carl, was arrested in the bathroom with another man for lewd acts. Mother didn't believe he did it even though he was caught in the act."

The key turns in the door, Stephanie arrives home. I wonder—if they do deal with the incest, how will they react when I tell them I'm a lesbian? I push the future away. I stop from rushing into her arms. Instead, I introduce my friend, Stephanie.

"How are you doing with all of this stuff?" She looks at them, waiting.

"Well it's hard. It's a lot. But I can see it happening." Jim answers.

"Do you understand what Louise is saying?" Stephanie asks.

"Yes," Jim nods.

"It's kind of hard to take in," Stephanie suggests.

"But I understand more now," Jim says. He looks at his watch. "We have to meet Brian for dinner. We'll talk more later. Thanks for telling us."

"I hope we see more of you now," Stephanie tells them at the door.

"Yes, I'm sure we will," Jim says and gives me a tall hug. We are grownups, we hug instead of holding hands.

He believed me! He believed me! I am elated, ecstatic. In the Well, I imagine Jim and I walking toward each other. I separate him from Don and Mother. YoungerOnes draw pictures of brothers and sisters playing. Fuckit's saying, "All right! All right!" Carrie's grinning. Sarah's almost smiling. I anticipate dinners full of reminiscing. I imagine I am the brave colorful aunt to his future children.

15   THE PIT

THE phone call. Don answers. I am startled by the familiarity of his voice. I imagine him at the other end. A toothpick to the side of his mouth. A flannel shirt, faded jeans.

Carrie pushes rehearsed words through the receiver. "Don, this is Louise, I need to talk to you about something, how about Wednesday night at a restaurant up here, this is the address, see you then." Click. Another breath.

My mind stops, a white sheet of empty paper. Floating. I stand and bend to touch the carpet, burying my fingertips between the pile. I can't really believe I'm going to accuse Don of raping me. Years of wanting to tell someone else who would stop him for me. Someone else with authority, who would make my family listen on my behalf. "We want a mother," YoungerOnes still say, "We want someone else to fight for us." I don't know if I can do this for myself.

He's coming because I asked him to come. Why don't I feel powerful? He didn't ask why I want to talk with him, as if this was normal. What is he thinking? What does he remember? I reassure myself, he has no reason to bring a gun. But the memories have guns in them.

We'll meet in a restaurant. Stephanie and Paul will be close, protecting me. I imagine them lunging into the aisle from their booth, stopping an assault. "Don't be melodramatic," Sarah ridicules. YoungerOne 16 turns to Sarah, drawing herself to her full height, "Don't underestimate him!" she spits at Sarah's feet. Carrie touches YoungerOne 16 reassuringly as she shrinks from the unfamiliarity of her own conviction. "He won't be in our house," Carrie says calmly, "We'll never be behind a closed door with him again."

With my mind's eye, I see the voices crossing the Pit, an unlikely band of pilgrims walking slowly over the thick mud. Each step through the viscous ooze renews the fear of being stuck in the helplessness of old memories. YoungerOnes carry the parcel of craziness, hugging the pillows wrapped by Don's belt. The closer they get to Don, the smaller they feel. He is a grown man, they are children. "We don't trust him, how can we tell him how we felt?" YoungerOne 16 trips. "What if I'm not strong enough?" she whispers to Carrie.

"Maybe we're wrong," YoungerOne 13 says. She looks at Don and my mother as they stand across the Pit. They look too ordinary. I feel a familiar stabbing pain in my vagina. "He's getting us."

Sarah blocks Carrie's efforts to comfort them. "See how much safer it was on that ledge? The ground was familiar and solid. We shouldn't be here. You deserve to get hurt for walking through dangerous places." When I look closely I can see Sarah's knees shaking. She turns to YoungerOnes. "If you confront him, he'll call you bad. You are bad," she threatens, pointing at them.

"Fuckit!" YoungerOne 5 yells, "Tell her I'm not bad."

Carrie touches Sarah lightly on the shoulder. "Is it bad to be afraid?" she asks.

Sarah looks at the mud. "What if we do get out of here? What then? You might think you don't need me anymore. But I'm important. I'm better than Fuckit! We have to eat well, get exercise, write, have discipline and get things done. Without me, everything would fall apart. It's easy to make my voice carry in this old Well, it echoes. I'm used to YoungerOnes being afraid of me. Who knows what will happen out there! It could be worse!" Sarah's wrinkles tighten into hard ridges between her eyebrows.

"I'm sure there will be a place for you," Carrie placates. 'But we could move through here easier if you'd quit scaring YoungerOnes. Confronting Don is hard enough already."

Fuckit carries coals from the fire in a small box on a string. When the voices first descended into the Pit, Fuckit roared at Don, "You bastard. How dare you do that to me? You asshole! I'll cut off your precious penis! I'll punch your face out! I'll poke your eyes in! I don't fucking care what you have to say. You don't get the last word any more." For a while I felt strong in my anger. But as we've moved closer to our arranged meeting time, Fuckit's anger has thinned. "Maybe we could run out of the Pit without talking to him," she suggests as his face becomes distinct, bringing memories of lying powerless and exposed beneath him. Remembering when the strength of my body left me to passivity and silence.

"That won't work," Carrie rolls her eyes at Fuckit. "Besides, why should we always have to run from him?"

Fuckit stops to draw courage from the fire she carries. "How dare you do that to us! We're not going to let it pass without yelling about how wrong it was. I'm so mean... "

Carrie holds the letter and the emerald, the garnet and the mirror of obsidian. She rehearses what I will say.

I role-played the confrontation with Jean. She played Don, denying the incest, saying "I didn't do that. You're crazy." I repeated what I knew, "I remember you raping me. It was during hunting season. Come see Jean with me and we'll talk more about this." When Jean read my letter there were tears in her eyes. Maybe my words will move him. Maybe he'll understand what he's done to me.

"I wish Jean was going to be there with us," YoungerOnes said after the session. "She could protect us."

"She'll call us afterwards," Carrie reminds them. "And we'll see her the next day. We can trust our self, like Jean says. We need to know that something terrible won't happen to us if we speak. We're taking what we learned with Jean with us. We are important!"

I exhale loudly, and concentrate on my legs. "Think solid ground," I say over and over to myself.

YoungerOnes still clutch my wishes. If I am only good

enough I can make him change. If I'm good enough, Grandpa will stop feeding me his candy. If I'm good enough, Don will stop punishing me. It's hard to stop believing in false power.

I know he'll probably deny it. It didn't seem so awful when I practiced it with Jean. But it wasn't real. I can't imagine saying this and not being heard.

"People do not believe what they refuse to see," Sure Voice says. "You can not open the eyes of another unless their eyes are ready to open. You will say what you have seen. This meeting is for you."

I've come too far to continue the deceptions. This is part of my journey out of the past.

◊

I have reservations at a restaurant with large private booths. Paul and Stephanie will sit out of Don's sight but within mine. The decisions were made without models. I debate their wisdom at the last minute, reassuring myself with logical thoughts. I chose the restaurant because it is public, not a room with closed doors. I chose to meet him alone instead of with Jean because of my need to stand up for myself. I need to show YoungerOnes that I can defend us. I chose to have Paul and Stephanie come as allies to debrief with when it is over. I know that they'll still love me even if I can't go through with it.

I arrange my seat, marking my place with my daypack. My stomach shakes violently, defying my attempts at deep breathing. I smoke my thirty-fifth cigarette. Standing on the sidewalk, watching for him. What if he gets lost? What if he doesn't show up? Did I tell him this Wednesday? I agonized over what to wear. The tent dresses I wore to hide myself in high school didn't keep him away. Tonight I dressed for my own comfort, slacks and a light sweater. I wear silver jewelry, with amethyst. My clothes didn't make him rape me.

He reaches the corner by the restaurant. He's dressed up—

a new plaid shirt and pants with an ornate belt buckle. He smiles and waves when he sees me. Only now do I understand that he's come to play Father. He thinks I have called him to ask for advice or blessing. He has not come to be questioned because that has never happened to him before.

For the first time since I was a small child, I long intensely for a father. Wishing that he was coming to give me his advice, wishing I had known a man as counselor and ally and caregiver instead of as rapist.

He comes closer, grinning. I feel guilty now for calling him here. Bad about pulling him out of Bryce where his meals are made for him and his scarce words are obeyed. Afraid he will not be able to sit in a restaurant with cloth napkins and waiters even though I know he's been in nice restaurants before. Afraid the city will swallow him. Afraid he will be too weak to hear what he's done and will melt away. No one tells him how they feel.

We meet at the door. "You found it," I say, wondering if my legs will hold me up the distance to the table. I pretend I own the restaurant. "Right this way," I say officiously.

"There was a little traffic, getting out around 5:00 or so," he comments.

It's hard for me to chat. I can't think of what to say. The waiter hands us a menu. I command the words to stop swimming. I refuse a drink. I order a spinach salad for which I have no appetite. He orders veal, the slaughter of young calves. The waiter leaves.

"Um," I struggle to start.

I hold the rock I tucked in my pocket. The one with the lines on it. The rock that reminds me of years spent hating myself.

"This is hard," I look him in the eye. I've never met his eyes in conversation. His eyes look back without saying anything.

"I wrote you this letter. I'd like you to read it first and then we can talk about it." I hand him the letter.

He doesn't take it. "I left my reading glasses at home," he says.

"Aw shit!" Fuckit says inside the Well. "That jerk! I cannot believe this is happening!"

"Well, I'll have to read it to you then," I say calmly, "I'd like to finish reading it before we talk about it."

My hand shakes the words as I read. From a corner of my eye I look past Don and catch a glimpse of Paul's sleeve. I draw a breath up from the ground and imagine myself surrounded by light.

"Don,

"I am giving you this letter because I have things that are important for me to say to you. It is about my relationship to you. I am your stepdaughter. You as an adult and a parent were responsible for my welfare, my protection and my environment.

"But when I think of you as my parent, as my stepfather, I remember you coming into my room early in the morning, taking off your pants, rolling me over, and raping me. I remember your hunting rifle on the other bed."

My voice is shaking. The police should be here saying this to him. But they won't be here. Or they would look at this rock of a man and shake their heads and walk away. I am his stepdaughter and he raped me. "Prove it," they would say, "show us stained underwear within twenty-four hours."

I read on, controlling my voice, briefly touching my anger at the wasted years of feeling dirty and bad. I see YoungerOne 16 sitting on the edge of the bed. I watch her walking like a zombie, day after day. I see her giving up, too tired of fighting the blows that adolescence did not prevent. Feeling like a five-year-old at sixteen and twenty-eight. How much I've hated myself. I read for the sixteen-year-old, for myself.

"I have relived the fear, the terror, the revulsion, the horror and the helplessness of those times. For every time that you used me, I have many times over been haunted with the humiliation and the worthlessness that I felt when you violated my trust in you.

"I have carried the weight of those incidents around for many years. And I'm not going to carry them in secret or silence anymore.

"I remember sitting on the edge of my bed after you left. Sixteen years old. My mouth hurt and my insides ached. I felt too raw to cry or to talk. There was no one to help me. I took showers and tried to wash you down the drain. I stuck my thumb down my throat and tried to throw you up. I got dressed and went for a walk. I felt so old. I felt like I had no control over my body or my life. I decided there was no safety, no love and no one to trust. I caught the bus and went to high school. I walked around in a state of numbness. Inside of me something shut down. I hated my body for being a girl. I took twenty-four aspirin for the headache that would not go away. I hated myself for being your victim. I thought that there must truly be something wrong with me because that happened to me.

"But now I know that there was nothing wrong with me. But there was something very wrong with what you did. You were the adult, the parent. It was wrong for you to violate me like that, wrong for you to rape me, to be sexual with me. Your actions were without respect for me, without respect for me as a separate individual person, for my feelings, for my relationship to you, or for my age. You were the adult. It was your responsibility to respect and protect me. It is especially painful that when Mother married you, she said that you would 'protect us.' It hurts that you didn't. It hurts my body and my feelings and my spirit and my sense of what to expect from people that I trust.

"I do not know if I can put the effects of your rapes of me into words that tell the magnitude of the grief and the anger that I feel toward you."

It seems that I have been reading forever, the word rape cutting the air. My voice goes on. The scream inside is hidden. My muscles are too shaky to throw the letter at him.

"It has marked my life beyond the incidents. The most important thing that the incest took from me was my self-confidence, my belief that I was a person and a woman and that that was good. Instead, I felt like your hole. I have gone through several bad relationships, fantasized continually about killing myself, and distrusted anyone who cared about me. I set out to destroy my body in as many ways as possible. I have had a long time of self-hating. I have had years of that putrid fear that never leaves. Years of being afraid even while in my own room. Years of being unable to speak my feelings. Years of pretending that the most devastating and horrifying events of my existence did not happen.

"I resent paying the price for your wrongness. But nonetheless, I have paid. And I'm writing this letter to tell you that I am not going to pay anymore.

"I have been in therapy for four years. I began therapy because I was suicidal and constantly depressed. I did not know what it felt like to be happy, to feel alive, or to feel like I was worth the same basic respect as another human being. I did not know what it felt like to trust and to love another person. Therapy has been a lot of hard work. To look at my memories of your violation of me and to feel the incredible amount of rage, horror, fear and pain—has taken more courage than I knew myself to be capable of having."

I stop, holding my courage to me, looking quickly past the paper to Don's face. It is without expression.

"But this letter—and this meeting—take the most courage of all because for thirteen years I have been terrorized by memories of you and full of shame because of what you did to me. But now I am angry, because you had no right to rip your way into my body. You had no right to trample my sexuality. It has left a horrible scar which festered and infected me for a long time.

"I will never trust you.

"I intend to heal from you, because I am a valuable person and I do deserve respect.

"You could help me heal by admitting that the rapes—the incest—were your responsibility. At minimum, I feel that you owe me an apology.

"The cost of professional help averages one hundred and forty dollars a month for four years. I believe that it's part of the debt that you owe me, whether you choose to pay it or not.

"I do not know if I can forgive you. I know that I cannot forgive you unless you seek professional help and come to terms with your sexual offenses... both so that you deal with your rapes of me and so that you never ever repeat a sexual act with any child.

"And even with that, I do not know if I can forgive you. I am too angry at the consequences of your violations of me. I know that I will never forget about it. Nor will I be silent about it ever again."

It's over. For a minute I expect my voice to hang in the air with words that will never go away.

"Why, Louise," Don says, "anyone who would do such a thing would be bad."

My words land on the ground with a thud.

"I never did that, Louise. Why I would never do such a thing." His eyes still look blank. I can see myself reflected in them.

"I remember you molesting me. I remember you coming into my room early in the mornings during hunting season." I look him in the eye. I have nothing else to say.

He looks at his plate and cuts a piece of meat. "Why, your mother and I have had a very happy marriage, Louise."

"I'm going to talk to Mother too. I have some things I want to say to her about my relationship with her." Why is he talking about Mother? I'm talking about me.

"How would you feel if you were in my place?" he says.

But what about my place? What about me? My words should mark the air. Instead, I'm watching them dissolve as if they hadn't been spoken.

"This is what I remember happening. Do you remember

coming into my room and being sexual with me?" I'm tired of caring about how he feels. That is not why we're here.

For a moment his eyes look different—as if he has seen something. A shutter unfolds and he seems to remember. He moves his hand slightly as if to brush it away.

"I'd swear on a stack of Bibles I didn't do that. The only time I was in your room was when your cat got killed."

"I don't remember you being there then," I say. "This is not about the cat, this is about being sexually used by you."

"Well someone else may have done that but it wasn't me. You must have me mixed up with someone else."

Does this mean he knows about Kevin and Grandpa? Is that what gave him permission to come into my room without fearing my reaction? Or did he become someone else when he grunted and treated me like an animal? I can't find a way to say this out loud. I want to hear him say that he did it. I want a confession, not a trial.

"I never stay overnight at home anymore. I leave after a few hours. I'm scared to be there."

"Well what about the summer you stayed at home? I didn't do anything then did I?" he challenges.

The summer between my freshmen and sophomore years when I came home to work and save money. Still scared to leave home, but anxious being there.

"No. Not then. It happened when I was in high school."

"But not then." He sounds almost proud of himself that he didn't do anything then. But that wasn't during hunting season either. He continues to say he did nothing.

"But I remember it being you. It has massively affected my life. I felt like I wanted to die." This has cost my life.

"But your mother and I gave you everything. You were an exchange student."

"But I wasn't safe. You used me in the most disrespectful way." My voice is shaking, bordering tears and violence. My palms are thick with sweating, unable to grip the salad fork even if I could bring myself to eat. I look him in the eye again.

"I didn't do it," he says again.

Standoff. Part of me wants to say, "Oh it's nothing, it's okay, you didn't do it." Allowing his voice the final word on any disputed subject as it has always been. My mother bows to his voice. There were no arguments, no debates with Don. He has held unquestioned power.

But it's not okay this time. I won't go back to pretending. I won't betray myself. I will not call myself a liar when I have reclaimed honesty. But the sheer sound of my voice is not going to get us any farther this evening.

"Well, I would like you to see my therapist with me then. I have no reason that I know of to make this up. But if I am making it up I certainly want to know that."

"I'm not seeing him again without Jean, that's for damn sure," Fuckit declares.

"I'll do that," he says, "but I didn't do it."

"I remember you doing it," I look him in the eye. "Maybe if you have more time you'll remember it too. . . . I expect to hear from you within a week."

He rises to go, leaving the letter in a white folded pile on the tablecloth. "You'd better take this too," I hand it up to him. He presses the bill next to my letter in his hand. He walks out without looking backward.

◇

I slide into the booth next to Stephanie. I don't feel strong, courageous or whole. I feel like I've been kicked in the stomach. I wonder if I'm a lunatic.

"What did he say?" Paul and Stephanie ask eagerly. Stephanie takes my hand. I can hardly feel her.

"He said he didn't do it," I say.

"Exactly what did he say?" she insists. "Now's a good time to understand what happened."

"Okay. I wanted him to validate me. Goddamn it! I would have liked it better if he'd admitted doing it while denying that it had any effect on me." I feel like a dead rose. I thought that saying it to him would make me feel better. Instead I feel old.

"He reminds me of a little kid whose hand's been caught in a cookie jar," Paul says. "The first thing he has to say is 'it wasn't me.'"

"Well he sure said that. About eight times," Fuckit mutters. She feels battered by the denial.

"It was so weird. I did this to tell him how I felt about it and he never acknowledged my feeling or pain. . . . It felt like he didn't care about me at all."

"He was busy defending himself. He didn't want to look at it," Paul says.

Stephanie pulls out a slip of paper and takes notes as I tell her about the exchange. We go over each sentence. I begin to see the through the facade of his denial, like a wall which has cracked to show the undercoat.

"If he admits the incest, then that makes him bad," Stephanie says. "He can't separate what he's done from who he is."

"No one in my family distinguishes between behavior and being," I tell Stephanie, remembering my sessions with Jean.

"Even with that, there are some things here that indicate he knows and remembers," Stephanie squeezes my hand again, "At one point he's saying it must have been someone else. He's not denying that it happened to you."

"And then he talks about being in your room," Paul adds, "trying to make up some other reason for being there."

"You know, my kitten was killed when he accidentally lowered the garage door on her. The summer I was at my parent's house between my freshman and sophomore years. I remember my mother telling me about it but I don't remember Don coming to my room.

"It was eerie the way he said that he didn't do anything to me when I was in college. Almost like saying he'd done something before and changed his ways, restrained himself."

"Well you weren't dependent on him then either," Stephanie says. "He wouldn't have the same kind of control

over you when you were home for the summer and supporting yourself."

"Yeah. That makes sense. I even worked at night then. I knew I didn't want to be home."

"So how are you feeling?" Stephanie puts her arm around my shoulder.

"You did it," Paul says, patient.

"I feel shaky and spaced out," I tell them. "My hands and feet are tingling. I can't stop shaking. It was hard to hear him say 'I didn't do that.' I've been taught to believe him.

"But at least he said he'd see Jean with me. Maybe if he has more time—and there's someone else there, he'll admit it."

"I wish he'd have the nightmares about it that I've had," Fuckit says. "I feel passed over and invisible, as if we were talking about cheating at a hand of bridge instead of about rape."

◇

Paul, Stephanie, Dennis and Grace sit in the kitchen as I smoke cigarettes. I knew I wanted my friends to be with me after confronting Don. I keep looking at them, grateful for their presence. Grace has known me through my whole process of remembering. I look at Paul and remember how much of my history he represents. I have known him since high school. We lived in the same dorm at college and even shared a house. I remind myself that he believes me. He cares about me. He is family to me in a way my family has never been. Paul brings a bottle of champagne from the refrigerator and toasts: "Courage."

I don't feel courageous right now. It's hard to think. The voices utter bits of phrases. "He said he didn't... " "The cat... " "My mother... " "Not dead. Are we dead?" "What comes next?" "I don't know."

"Just drink champagne," Fuckit says. "Enough is enough."

I have nothing else to say to Don. But there are still many words I would like to hear from him.

My body hasn't stopped shaking, tremors up-end my stomach and spill down my legs. I am wrapped in a blanket. I can't get warm. Assaulted by denial. Still surprised that my words were not enough to move him. Yet not surprised, he acted like he always does.

The phone rings. It's my brother, spitting fire through the lines that connect us.

I'm numb.

"What are you doing!" he demands. "Don got home and called me over. How could you write such a letter to him? How dare you say those things! I didn't think your letter would be like that!"

"But I asked you if you wanted to read it."

"Well I didn't know it was going to be like that! I go over there and he's waving that letter all around and tells me to read it. Now I don't know what he'll do. Cindy's worried that he'll shoot us. . . . And he's saying he didn't do it."

"Of course he's saying that. Most offenders deny it initially." I warned him. Why is he yelling at me?

"Well maybe he didn't do it. I just don't know. And he's not so sure he's going up there to see your therapist. Maybe he should take one of his own along just in case. Probably he shouldn't see anyone you've been seeing at all."

The floor leaves my feet. I am pacing in air, watching my brother pulled back into the shadows of the Pit. "Goddamn it Jim, you said you believed me. So now when he gets home you rush to his side and comfort him. Thanks a lot, brother." I scream into the phone, struck by slaps of unexpected betrayal. Tunneling into the anger against Don, my rage at not being heard mixed with my rage at rape. I gather it into my voice and throw it at Jim. Arguing as I have argued only with my mother. Screaming at him, ignoring the hands of Stephanie trying to slow me down, not slowed by Paul's frantic head shaking. I am too exhausted to continue measuring my words.

"Why did you have to tell me in the first place?" Jim is saying. "Why did you have to come in and mess up my life?

Don didn't bother me. What do you think this is going to do to Mother? You better be damn sure that you're available to her night and day, hand on the phone whenever she wants to talk."

"Don't tell me what I have to do, Jim. I'm tired of you trying to take care of Mother. She can take care of herself, goddamn it. It's not fair. I told you what would happen and now you're saying you don't believe me."

"Well, he's pretty upset. He's really angry. He says they gave you everything and now you turn around and do this."

"I told you why I had to do this, Jim. I can't carry it around within myself anymore. That letter was true. I had to say that to Don." I try to arrange my feelings into concise logical words.

"Well you didn't have to say it like you did. Using the word rape—come on, Louise."

"But it was rape. And it was incest. I'm not going to call it something else."

"Well he says he didn't do it and now I don't know who to believe. But he's not going to just see you and that therapist. Come on, you can't expect him to do that. She's probably brainwashed you. She'll be against him."

"The purpose of seeing Jean is to have some discussion about this and to hear each other. I've been really hurt here but no one, including you, seems to care one iota about that. It's true that it's none of your business but it is because it concerns the family." My voice is a wire grating against metal. Inside, the unspoken plea, "Come back Jim, don't leave me again."

"You're always stirring up trouble," he says. "Why couldn't you just let things be?"

All the adrenalin simultaneously empties. Swallowed by another standoff. Coming to consciousness with the phone tight against my ear and a trail of paces between the living room and the kitchen.

"I don't think it's going to help to talk more now. I'm angry at Don and I'm pissed at you."

"I'll call again tomorrow," he says.

I look at Paul and Stephanie and Grace and Dennis. I feel ashamed of my public outpouring. "He's not sure he believes me," I tell them. "It feels like nothing I say or went through matters."

"You got a little carried away with him," Paul comments.

"I know. I was furious. I wanted him to hear me. Maybe it'll be better when I talk to him tomorrow. If he calls me back. Don may not even see Jean with me."

"This isn't easy," Stephanie says, "but you're doing it."

I hug my friends. Stephanie says, "I love you." I hold her, not wanting to let go. Paul says, "It'll be okay. You're still here." Grace rubs my shoulders.

Being seen with my feelings hanging out makes me feel shy. But my friends stay with me. My bonds with them are stronger than those with my family. My friends and I chose each other. We aren't forced to be together. I may have lost Don and Jim, but I haven't lost the people who really know me.

The voices stand together in a circle. Fuckit even has an arm around Carrie's shoulder. They rock back and forth surrounded by friends. I sleep without dreams or nightmares.

16 THE CORD

THE next day. An hour of cigarettes and black coffee. Slowly turning the pages of the morning paper, reading everything, even the recipes. Words turning to paragraphs: war, famine, fashion, etiquette. Words slipping past my mind without impression. The hour stretches into a second one, my body is forming to the chair at the dining room table. It's like coming home after a vacation. Where do I go now, what do I think about? The maps have been used and folded backwards.

Inside of me, YoungerOnes have collapsed into a heap next to the opening in the Pit. They hold each other, pretending to be asleep.

Carrie sits next to them, resting a hand against Younger-One 16's face. Daylight pools in a patch on Carrie's shoulder. She stares into space, exhausted, thinking of nothing.

"Sure Voice?" I whisper out loud. My ears refuse to listen for her answer. Confronting Don wore them out.

Sarah leans into the obsidian of the Well, untouched by the fresh air coming from beyond the Pit. Occasionally she mutters. "Fat lot of good that whole business did." She is sinking in mud.

Only Fuckit is active, pacing in front of the opening. "We are not going to think about a fucking thing today!" she announces. She looks at the inertia surrounding her, grinning widely at the sight of Sarah stuck in mud. "Hey! I'm in charge here!" She grabs my coat and car keys, careful not to look toward the family figures gathered at the opening.

The phone rings before I reach the door. It's Jim, keeping his promise to call me. His voice fluctuates in temperature from warm tea to ice cubes.

"I'm sorry I got so angry at you last night," I begin. I hold my feelings in a tight chest wad, resisting the urge to pull him close again.

"I got a bit heated too," he admits.

"I realized that I was really angry at Don. Then when you said you didn't know if you believed me, I felt betrayed. I don't like yelling at you. I don't want to do it anymore." Please say that you believe me again. Say that you understand what I'm doing. YoungerOnes open one eye and look at my inner picture of Jim. Will my brother help me cross the street to safety? Isn't it his turn?

His voice freezes instead. "Well, I'm just not looking forward to when Mother gets home from her vacation. This could kill her." I imagine the tanned skin wrinkling above his eyebrows.

"Jim, this isn't going to kill her." Does he really believe that the woman who birthed him will die from words?

"Well," he says. "Cindy called a professional she heard about to ask if Don would start shooting at us. She told her he probably wouldn't. She also said she wasn't suprised that you're angry."

"I never said he'd start to kill you," I say feeling weary. Is he blaming Don's guns on me? I am strangling the receiver with my hand.

"Mother gets home tomorrow, you know," Jim says.

"Do you think Don will tell her?"

"I don't know," he says.

"They don't usually talk to each other.

"Well Don's pretty mad," Jim says. "The poor guy. He might tell her. You've really put us in a bind down here."

"Poor guy? Shit!" Fuckit regrets not shooting Don after all.

"I didn't intend to put you in a bind. You don't have to get in the middle of this." I can feel the argument of last night beginning to repeat itself.

"You have shaken up my life!" He raises his voice, heating it. "I worry about Mother."

I want to say, "But what about me? Do you believe me, are you concerned about what I'm talking about here, about being raped? Will it always be an abstraction for you? I never should have left out the details. Aren't you afraid for the children you and Cindy will raise right next door to him?"

I want to ask, "Who are you, Jim? What do you see when you look back? Don't you feel robbed that you were a man before you were a child? Don't you get angry about the lies we were raised with?"

He says, "I have to go now. I'm sure we'll be in touch later."

I say, "Take care of yourself, Jim. Thanks for calling."

The phone clicks into place with finality, without connection. Our conversation in Stephanie's apartment is unreal. Promises and allegiances that melt against daylight.

Fuckit flees the house. My wooden legs leave no impression on the grass in the park. The trees have lost color. The branches are naked, unmoving.

I take my shoes off in the cold late October ground and wait for my soles to grow roots. All I feel is hardness, a chill creeping up past my ankles forming an ice circle around my knees. I put my socks back on. I don't know what anything means. I have spent my courage. I am hollow.

I'm sick of the Well, exhausted in the preparations for leaving. A confused heroine who tried to slay a beast. The beast turned into a middle-aged man who denied that he'd ever been a monster. Flashing stabs of guilt: what if I have destroyed Don, what if he flips out? How can Jim fear his guns and believe in him at the same time? I thought the confrontation would probably end in denial but I didn't really believe that it would.

I want someone to take my hand and guide me. Why did I think this would make me feel powerful?

I would like to forget and pretend that nothing matters.

◇

The only one in my family I haven't talked to yet is my mother. The desire for a mother has haunted me into adulthood. I've hated myself for wanting a love that could make me safe. When I gave up on my mother, I formed desperate attachments with older women, feeling perpetually like a child in relationship to them. I waited for their betrayal, I withdrew at any criticism.

I hear YoungerOnes wishing inside of me, "Mother will apologize. She'll take my side this time. She'll see us. We are important to her."

But the men have always been most important, regardless of what they did. I hated her for what they did to me. Just like psychology made mothers responsible for the abusive acts of men whether they're mass murderers or incest offenders. I feel guilty for blaming her. Guilty for hating her. Feminists aren't supposed to hate women.

"Wait a fucking minute!" Fuckit protests. "She knew about the incest. She didn't sexually abuse us but she didn't fucking stop it either."

Memories. My grandfather violating me while my mother is in the adjoining room. Kevin on top of me. She sends me into the basement. Years later she tells me, "I was afraid of Kevin. He didn't get along very well with adults. I never went anywhere with him alone, I always took you kids with me for protection." She never talked about protecting me. She thought dressing me in maternity clothes would help but it only made me ugly.

Did she hear Don's footsteps going downstairs when he left her bed in the morning? Didn't she wonder about his past? Why did she need to know the hard sentences in my diaries and the treasures hidden in my dresser drawer, while she didn't require the most basic information from the man she married?

"But she's so weak," YoungerOnes say protectively. I see my mother's hands clasped uselessly in front of her solar plexus, unable to defend herself. Unwilling to defend me. Or unable?

"She didn't like us!" Fuckit says. "She wanted to hurt me with her words. She wanted me to be crazy and bad. Bitch! She wrote me a letter when I was seeing Kate. In the middle of it she wrote, 'I have often wished you were dead.'"

"All of her threats to punish us! All her blaming. It's not just that she knew about the incest. It's that she carried the invasions further so that nowhere was safe. She was cruel. I'm not going to forgive her even if Jean says that I have to forgive her in order to forgive myself."

"My mother's going to teach here," I proudly announced to Miss Dairyman, who was on playground duty. I thought it would make me special to have my mother at school. I didn't understand that being a teacher's kid meant that I would always be known as her daughter, never as myself. I didn't forsee her presence as a trap. I didn't understand that my teacher's perceptions of me would be increasingly based upon my mother's definition of my behavior. Ultimately my grade school teachers became a part of my mother's support system. She seemed to make a special effort to befriend my teachers, all the way through high school. When they told me what a wonderful mother I had, I just looked at them silently and wondered why they couldn't see how bad I felt.

Her eyes were everywhere, judging me, stealing the words from my diaries, examining my friends. "Don't talk about this family," she warned me. "Don't tell anyone what goes on in this house!" But she talked about me and the problems she had with me. She said that I had a "poor attitude" and "communist ideas." "Louise is crazy," she told my teachers. "I don't know what to do with her, I've given her everything."

YoungerOne 14 shakes her head. "When I ran away, the court made me go to a mental health center. After I went back home, the counselor said Mother and I should come in together. Mother said, 'We don't need any more of that nonsense! People will get the wrong idea.'

"Getting help would have been admitting something was wrong. We wouldn't be the 'perfect family' anymore. Appearance was more important than me."

"She took fucking everything," Fuckit spits in the mud, "Nothing was mine—not feelings, or ideas, or friends, or favorite teachers." A barrage of continual accusation, at home, reaching into my school life and my relationships with others.

"She's had a hard life," Sarah says. I can't argue with that either. It triggers the old conflict—my mother as powerless, my mother as vicious.

A cord stretches from my belly, from the place where we were connected, daughter to mother. A cord that remains unbroken. A cord that feels like a chain.

◇

"What do you want from your mother now?" Jean asks.

I shake my head thinking of the unspoken ground between my mother and me. "Sometimes I still want to save her. I want to tell her about feminism and healing. I start thinking that I know how to help her. I lecture her in my head. I tell her, 'I've learned that I'm not bad. I know you were taught that you aren't important because you're a woman. It's not true. I'll help you, follow me.'"

YoungerOnes squirm uncomfortably. "She'll use us up. She'll want us to take care of her instead of growing strong herself."

"What she did is not okay!" Fuckit screams. "I don't give a fuck about how she deals with herself. She's a grown woman for godsakes! I want her to hear what happened. I want her to say she fucked up! I want her to admit that she did something wrong instead of blaming it on me!"

Carries smiles sadly at Fuckit. "All we can do is tell her what was true for us. If I could have anything, I'd want to know what was really going on with her when we were growing up."

"So if you were going to tell her what you wanted from

her, what would you say?" Jean sits back in her chair. She's been insistent about me coming to terms with my mother. Sometimes Fuckit wonders if that's because Jean's a mother and mothers stick together.

"I want her to quit fucking up my relationship with Stephanie!" Fuckit announces.

"What?" Jean asks, surprised, "Your mother hasn't called Stephanie or been involved at all there."

"But I act like my mother with Stephanie sometimes. Other times Stephanie reminds me of my mother and then I say things that I don't mean to Stephanie. If it wasn't for my mother, I'd have an easier time being in this relationship," Fuckit announces.

"That isn't your mother's stuff," Jean says emphatically. "How you get along with Stephanie is your responsibility."

"Why do I always have to work on everything? My mother never will! I feel like I have her goddamn pain as well as my own!" Fuckit fumes.

"So what would you tell your mother?" Sometimes Jean can be disgustingly focused.

"I'd tell her that we're past being mother and daughter," Carrie speaks. "Those were roles that never allowed us to see each other. But we are both women. I want to tell her how I felt about my life with her. I want to ask her why she allowed Kevin around me when she was afraid to be with him herself. Why did she threaten to put me in reform school? What did she know about Don? Why did she say she'd kill me if I tried to kill myself? Why didn't she stick up for me? Because we're both women, I want to understand her. I have to tell her how betrayed by her I feel and that I'm angry. That betrayal gets snagged when other women in my life disappoint me, as if I'm living that wound over and over again.

"I don't know how I'll feel about her after that. Maybe nothing will be left then and we'll never see each other. But I'll feel completed with her. Or perhaps we will surprise each other and begin a new relationship.

"I want her to know that I'm not asking her to leave Don, because that's her decision, not mine. I'd suggest that they get help. I'd want to tell her that I believe in her ability to face what I have to tell her."

I'm going to ask my mother to see Jean with me. I know I'll need Jean's help in hearing her. I'm used to fighting her off with fiery words that leap from the edge of my tongue. I'll talk to her about the incest, as well as about the dynamics between us. For a minute, it's scary to think of Jean, my mother and I in the same room. "What if she takes Jean away or convinces her that we're crazy?" YoungerOnes whisper.

"This is Jean," Carrie reminds them. "If she thought we were crazy, she'd tell us herself." It's funny how I've come to trust her honesty.

In the Pit, the figure of my mother blocks the opening, just as she blocked the door when I tried to leave home at sixteen. Ropes tie her to Don, Jim and myself. Behind her, I see generations of my family enshrined in storybook myths of perfection. In the Pit, my mother doesn't look at me. Instead, she bows her head before the myth and closes her eyes.

◇

I check the mailbox at my office before going upstairs to receive a massage from Brenda. My mother's familiar grade school perfect penmanship crosses the envelope in even loops. The envelope is thin, almost weightless. It was mailed yesterday, the same day she arrived home from her trip. Today is Halloween, the day of the dead.

My name stares at me in blue ink. I don't want to know what she has to say. My stomach squeezes tender nerves in my belly. My heart picks up speed, beating too quickly, as if it's trying to fly out of my chest but can't escape. I will not open the letter by myself.

Brenda sits next to me on the couch while I read it. It says, "Louise, I don't want to hear any more or see you again, Carol."

I look for more, I look between the lines, I turn the nearly blank page over in my strong hands. I read the significance of a signature saying "Carol" instead of "Mother." She has never used her first name with me before.

Yesterday, I thought I was past feeling, drained by anticipation and anxiety, exhausted from traveling the last inches toward the opening of the Well.

Long coarse screams of "No, No, No" sound like the moaning of a wounded animal. My arms grab the air as if I could yank my mother's sentence off the page and throw her words back at her. "She didn't even talk to me! She just heard Don. I don't even know what he told her! Damn. Damn her!" My body is a volcano exhaling red earth guts in fire and liquid.

Brenda has me lie on a foam mat. The floor shakes under my heels and fists. My mouth stretches open like a carved pumpkin. Roaring. "No. She took away my chance to talk to her!"

The rage is long, as if each cell must scream.

"We must be invisible," YoungerOnes say inside of me. They pinch themselves. "Are we here?" What will make her see me? "I will look miserable, I'll do good in school, I'll write songs, I'll try to kill myself, I'll get fat, I'll run away. . . . Nothing works. I grow up. I'll be honest. I'll just tell her. She won't let me. I'm easier to throw away. I really don't matter to her." YoungerOnes stop screaming. They've run out of things to say.

"How could she not talk with me?" Tears come out with burning words. I pick up the letter, the familiar handwriting. I want to disbelieve it. My body is in a vise, pressing into the pain and tears, snapping the cord between my mother and I without breaking it cleanly. "How could I matter so little?"

Brenda massages my feet. The weeping is quiet. My mother has slammed and locked the door between us. She has always controlled the doors.

"Breathe, Louise. How are you?" Brenda asks. I open my eyes. I am not a child who has no one with her. Brenda holds my hand for a minute.

I start to laugh. "My mother responded in the same way that she always has. Listening to Don. Not hearing me. I didn't think she'd do that again. I thought I could make her ears open to me. I always overestimate her."

Brenda gently massages my chest and stomach, smoothing the frayed edges of cord left by the outward rush of feeling.

"In a way I feel validated. At least she's clearly saying she won't hear me instead of just ignoring me and pretending everything's fine. This makes me glad I didn't try to tell her when I was a child. It was safer for me to keep the secret then. Maybe she'll have to think about it anyway, maybe someday.

"I can't make her know me if she doesn't want to. Maybe she can't. She has so much invested in pretending. Now she's through with me. She really doesn't want to know."

"She hasn't killed you," Brenda says.

"When my grandmother couldn't take care of herself, my mother hired a woman named Maggie to stay with her during the day—to cook her meals, give her medication and make sure that my grandmother was cared for. My mother thought Maggie was wonderful.

"My grandmother began to say that Maggie was trying to kill her. My grandmother never said anything like that about anyone. My mother said, 'Maggie's always so nice to me. Grandma must be losing her mind.' Whenever my grandma told my mother about Maggie, my mother would tell her that it wasn't true, that she shouldn't say such things.

"Grandma got a lot sicker and finally my mother took her to the doctor. The doctor said, "What's happened to all her medicine? She's getting four times her prescribed dosage of insulin." When they returned to my grandmother's house, her wedding ring, pearl necklace and watch were gone. So was Maggie.

"I asked my mother if she'd called the police.

"'Oh no,' she said and looked surprised.

"'But this person could hurt someone else. She almost

killed Grandma.'

"'That's none of our business,' my mother said.

"If my mother hadn't heard the doctor confirm what my grandmother knew from the beginning, my grandmother would have been poisoned."

Now Don says unknown things about me. My mother will listen to him, trusting the words of men.

◇

"Mother," Carrie writes in her journal. She crosses it out and starts again. "Carol, You have a choice of whether to read this letter." YoungerOnes write their pain, asking the old questions, "Why? Why?" Fuckit stomps her rage into the words, "As usual, you haven't heard me. You always wanted to know where you failed in raising someone like me. You don't really want to know. I'm glad I don't have anything else to do with you."

Sarah says, "Send the letters. Don't send the letters. You should have done the whole thing differently."

My family has excommunicated troublesome members before. A distant uncle who committed suicide. A great aunt who went "crazy." Protecting the myth of perfect family. My mother continues the generations of betrayal.

"You cannot make her hear you," Sure Voice says. "As you journey outside the Well, you will understand more. You know your anger and your grief. You have seen how the structure of your family allowed incest to continue from offender to offender without challenge. You have told Don what needed to be said. The incest is no longer a secret growing inside of you like poison."

I pick up the crystal quartz next to my bed and turn it over in candlelight. Silver threads are suspended near the top like birds. When Grace gave me the crystal for Christmas she said that the wings were messages. At the bottom, wisps of white are suspended like clouds in a glass sky. The crystal pulses and warms my hand, solid and smooth under my fingers. My breath moves in and out like the wind, then in the rhythm of waves. Life enters and fills, life leaves and empties.

Next to the crystal is the grey stone crossed with black lines. The stone that reminded me of what I'd forgotten. I held this rock tightly when I confronted Don. It seems odd that the rock has not changed, strange that it is not covered with sweat and nightmares and blood.

I reach toward it but Fuckit stops my hand. "I don't want to pick it up any more," she says.

"This rock has been a friend," Carrie says firmly. She puts a hand on Fuckit's shoulder while she picks up the rock.

"These lines remind me of our ties. A line from you, Fuckit, to me, to YoungerOnes, to Sarah and to the center, to Louise who speaks."

"Where is Sure Voice?" YoungerOne 10 asks.

"She just makes us do everything the hard way anyway," Fuckit mutters. "The confrontation was scary and hard and he denied it anyway and now I feel like shit!"

"She helped us, Fuckit," YoungerOne 10 says softly. "I knew she was there—somewhere—the whole time. I didn't know how to hear her back then, but there was something that kept you fighting. . . and dreaming. All this hurt. . . . " She points at the other voices. "And we're still here. We never fully believed that we were a piece of garbage that could be tossed from grandfather to uncle to stepfather. Sure Voice always knew we weren't worthless."

"Why, the rock is a part of me, of course," Sure Voice says.

The lines bring the parts of me together, sewn in solid rock. These lines aren't like the threads that held me to my family and bound me to the Well. Despite all that has happened to me, I did not shatter.

The voices circle and cross, tangle and unwind around her.

◊

Two weeks pass. I never hear from Don. I knew that the

letter from my mother meant that he would not see Jean with me. Jim doesn't call me or respond to the card I sent him. I keep checking the mailbox, unwilling to believe that words from my mother won't peek out. But it's always empty.

17 THE DUST

EVER since I confronted Don about the incest, I've felt disoriented. It's like floating in a void or stumbling around the Mad House at a carnival. I thought that confronting Don about the incest would change me. I do feel changed, but I don't feel strong and confident like I'd hoped. Instead I feel lost and without guidance. I am a hundred pieces searching for center or wholeness.

The opening in the Pit is a ragged hole in the obsidian wall. Next to the exit, the figures of Jim, my mother and Don have collapsed, like balloons withered by a pin. After my mother's letter, the mud floor of the Pit began lurching, tilting with the roll of quaking earth. Familiar black walls began to moan and shatter.

The sensations in my body have changed. Fear is no longer a tight fist in my solar plexus. The taut line that divided my belly from my chest has snapped. My breath fills the whole of me, expanding my torso and reaching into my pelvis. It's easier to reach my feelings, but I'm not sure what they're telling me. Gradually I realize that I am through talking to Don. I have nothing else to accomplish with him. Now the Well is falling apart without its secrets. I feel tentative as the rock breaks into boulders and an avalanche of pebbles. My stomach flutters, unsettled by dissolution of rock, anxious as the inner bin of stored secrets crumbles. I have a hole in my belly where the rocks of the Well held the echoes of past pain. I used to believe that if I held onto these rocks, my essence couldn't be sucked out by invaders. I used the pain to remind me that I was alive. Now there's nothing to hold onto.

"Hey, the walls are moving! It's time to get out of here!"
Fuckit doesn't even look down at the pile of deflated family figures she jumps over on her way out of the Well.

Sarah rushes out ahead of Carrie, shouting, "Doomsday.
You've had it. You'll never get out of here alive."

Carrie holds the obsidian mirror and the hand of
YoungerOne 16 while each YoungerOne holds the hand of her
next younger sister. Carrie pulls them out from the falling
walls and yells ahead for Fuckit. Behind them, the Well collapses.

The outside air is Dust. Millions of particles, some held in
suspense, others settling soundlessly like brown snow.

YoungerOne 16 trips, pulling all the YoungerOnes with
her into a heap. Her hand slips from Carrie's.

"YoungerOnes! YoungerOnes!" Carrie calls, unable to see
her own hand through the curtain of dirt. "Where are you?"
The Dust holds her voice against her mouth.

I feel as if the familiar is falling apart. The voices scatter
without a plan to hold them together. I am chased once more
by the memories, though they don't feel as close as they once
were. My fear speaks through the Dust; a muted aching that
makes me want to hold onto something. I thought that after
the confrontation I'd attend to my future. Instead I feel scattered and confused. I'm not afraid of being killed now, but I
don't know how to be alive. I'm used to being a victim. I feel
like a snail without a shell. I wander within the familiar mind
messages, "Don't let anyone know who you are." "Stop
projects before they're finished so that no one else can inter-
rupt you." "Don't be happy or something bad will happen."
"It's not safe to stay at home." "Don't feel sexual." How do I
change a hundred decisions when I don't know what else to do?

Sure Voice speaks softly to Carrie. "You have come far and
learned much. You know how to survive. You have already
learned new ways. Do you think you will stop growing because
the scenery has changed?"

"What scenery?" Carrie's tears turn to mud. "I know the

voices have been honest and courageous. I know I can fight off invaders. But I don't know where I'm going. I don't know how to measure what I've done. Everything's changed and it doesn't feel good."

"What you have lost leaves an aching," Sure Voice tells her.

I cry for the loss of the Well, even though I fought so hard to free myself from it. Now, being outside of the Well reminds me of what I don't know.

◇

Jean's bookcases flash magic titles: *Anger, Emotions, Getting Free, For Your Own Good.* I wish there was a book called *Now What.*

The framed poster says, "All you have to do is Breathe, Breathe, Breathe." I want to scream at Jean, "I am breathing. I've been breathing. But what else. What now?"

"Since the confrontation, I feel splintered, as if my personality broke into separate pieces that can't communicate with each other," I tell Jean, as I take my traditional place on the sofa in her office. "It's like wandering in a Dust storm, groping for direction.

"Sarah yells all the time. No matter what I do, she throws Dust at me. When I eat, Sarah recites calories and tells me I'm fat, fat, fat. And I've got to quit smoking. I wake up in the middle of the night, afraid I've got cancer or emphysema. When she's not reforming me, she's reliving the confrontation. 'If only you'd said something different at a different time, then everything would be fine.' Fuckit refuses all suggestions of activity and complains of boredom. She wants nothing to do with the incest and keeps saying, 'It's over.'"

"Let's work on your critic," Jean suggests, "since that voice is waking you up in the middle of the night."

I've held out a goldfish bowl of problems and Jean has drawn one. I want to know how to build an instant bridge between the behavior from the Well and new ways of being. Inside, YoungerOnes feel isolated. They wish Jean would work with them instead.

Jean ruffles through the mountains of books and articles on her desk, searching for a piece of blank paper.

"You should be productive like Jean is," Sarah yells. "Just look at all the work she does - healing, writing, speaking, organizing, leading. While you're in this duststorm. You're a failure."

"So what is this critical voice saying?" Jean asks.

"Well. . . right now, she's comparing me unfavorably to you." I look away, avoiding the assumption that I know anything about Jean. I'm ashamed to admit that I want to be like her, as if that would take something away from her. "Besides that, the critic has been saying that I shouldn't have used the word 'rape' in the confrontation. Then she says I should get on with it. 'When are you going to make those phone calls? When are you going to quit smoking? When are you going to lose weight? You shouldn't have taken a walk then, you're supposed to be writing.' And then if I'm writing, she says, 'When are you going to get more exercise?'" When I imitate Sarah's voice, my face turns tight and worried.

"The more Sarah yells, the harder Fuckit squirms, so I end up going out somewhere for coffee or Scotch. Or to a movie or even shopping. Then Sarah makes me feel guilty. And YoungerOnes are afraid we'll die for not doing what we're supposed to do. . . . I am not getting along very well with myself."

"I will show you a trick," Jean begins. "It's simple, but you have to do it or it won't work."

"Anything," I say, though I can hear Sarah saying, 'Nothing is simple.' The pressure on my right shoulder increases, spreading into my neck. Sarah sits on my shoulder yelling into my ear. "When you brought out that pen and paper," I tell Jean, "my critic started yelling, 'I won't go, I won't go.'"

Jean raises her eyebrows in surprise and turns her swivel chair toward me. "We're not getting rid of your critic," she says. My face falls because I was hoping this was going to be a really good trick—one that would make Sarah disappear altogether.

"We're just going to get your critic to tell the truth," Jean explains.

"I am telling the truth." Sarah digs into my trapezius, sending shooting pains into my shoulder. "If you'd just do what I say... "

"Ouch!" I stop to consider Sarah. "Sarah wants me to be in control of everything, but I end up feeling powerless because of her impossible expectations."

"That part of you tells you her judgements instead of accurately assessing the situation. A lot of what I hear you saying is about the past or the future." Jean writes 'shouldn't have said rape' in one column. "Now," she says, "what is making your critic say that in the first place? What's really happening?"

"Don denied that he did it. My family isn't speaking to me."

Jean writes "loss of family" opposite Sarah's blaming. "A part of you likes to think you could control the world if only you'd done something differently. But how could you make Don confess? The law has prosecutors and judges in solemn courtrooms. If that setting can't make people confess, why do you think you can?"

Sarah sputters but can't think of a retort.

"So, when your critic is yelling, first you need to record what she's telling you. Then find an objective statement about the situation. It is possible to reeducate your critic."

"Don didn't take responsibility for the incest," I tell Sarah. The pressure in my shoulder eases. "I may or may not quit smoking." The pain leaves my neck.

At home, I make a sheet like Jean suggested, with Sarah's subjective statements on one side and my objective responses on the other.

"You're fat," Sarah says.

"I ate a piece of chocolate for breakfast," I remind Sarah of the new way.

Sarah's unusual silence amplifies the sound of the Dust. Without endless tasks to divert me, I refocus on my own process. I feel like a wooden wheel with broken spokes, creaking as I turn.

◊

Stephanie and I have decorated the Christmas tree with our collective ornaments. Two months after my mother's rejection I still search the mailbox, shaking open advertising circulars in case a card is stuck between the pages. It's hard to believe that a card from my mother or Jim won't appear.

"I don't care. It's no different," Fuckit growls, denying loss. The Dust has thinned to a dry drizzle around her. She dangles above ground, her shirt caught on the limb of a nearly invisible tree. She swings her fist at the nothingness of air. She bounces like a marionette when she tries to stomp her feet.

"Fuckit!" Sure Voice calls.

"I don't want to talk to you now, you old ghost. Just leave me alone. I used to know how to be and now I don't. I just swing back and forth without an escape or a target, caught on this fucking branch. I can't even yell at Sarah because Carrie whispers the 'truth' to her before I can get mad." Fuckit twists away from Sure Voice's arm on her wrist.

"Is it hard to be without your family at Christmas?" Sure Voice gently changes the subject.

"Naw! I don't miss them a bit—except for those graham cracker Christmas cookies.

"I never fit in anyway. But that's okay. I am who I am. If I could just get down from here." Fuckit squirms, then emits a dramatic sigh. "Sometimes I wonder what Mother said about me in her annual xeroxed Christmas letter. Something like, 'We are sorry to announce that our daughter died in a car wreck on her way home from church.' Or maybe she's invented a fantasy daughter and given her my name. Maybe she's even married me off for her friends. She's good at lying."

Fuckit punches a memory, hitting herself accidentally. "Shit!"

"Do you have to fight against someone in order to be yourself?" Sure Voice asks.

"Everything would be okay if I could just move. I'm hanging in air as if I was on some circus ride that got stuck." Fuckit looks down, avoiding Sure Voice's questions.

Her voice softens, "I'll tell you a secret, Sure Voice, but you've got to promise on your best honor not to tell Carrie. . . . "

"Do you still have to make me promise, Fuckit?"

"It wouldn't hurt," Fuckit says seriously. Then, glancing at Sure Voice, "It'd be better if you crossed your heart a couple times and spit on my palm," she grins mischievously.

"You and Carrie will work things out with yourselves," Sure Voice tells her.

"Carrie always makes me feel like I'm not good enough next to her. Then I feel like I'm supposed to be how she is. But I just want to be who I am—a little wild and ornery and charming." Fuckit grins.

"Now suddenly I'm a used up rebel and I'm afraid I'll get tossed overboard or that I'll have to be sweet and nice and good. I can't be those things."

"I want you to be who you are," Sure Voice pats Fuckit's shoulder warmly. "You have so much life in you. Could you use some of that energy to learn from those you admire instead of fighting those you dislike?"

Fuckit digs a cigarette out of her pack. "I don't want to lose who I am." She kicks the air in a renewed attempt at freeing herself. "Hey," she says, failing at escape, "Get me down from here. You're supposed to help with things like this."

"You never want to be where you are, do you?" Sure Voice shakes her head quizzically.

My back feels rigid—it reminds me of waiting for an unkind hand to pull my shoulder, forcing me to do something that I don't want to do.

Under the Christmas tree, Stephanie piles presents

wrapped in Garfields and fantasy lands.

Inside of me, Fuckit wiggles. "I don't want those. If I take them, I end up owing her."

Don gave me a car once, a Volkswagen bug when I graduated from college. It feels bad to think of that car. I shouldn't have taken it. Don probably thought he was paying for my voice. Mobility in exchange for freedom. "Your mother and I gave you everything," Don said at our meeting.

"So I'd better not accept anything. I'm fucking fine the way I am," Fuckit spits flecks of dirt. "Whoever designed this growth stuff was a fucking lunatic! I did everything you said to do, Sure Voice. Where's my reward?"

"If I helped you down, Fuckit, you might fear that you owed me your uniqueness. I would not want that." Sure Voice pats Fuckit's hand and vanishes into the Dust.

◇

My friend Judy and I celebrate the holiday in a fancy restaurant with linen tablecloths and two sets of glasses. We exchange presents and laughter. I am relaxing into warm good cheer. Suddenly a man who looks like Don is seated behind us. I squelch the impulse to shrink beneathe the table. I see Don's penis again. A familiar glob grows in my throat.

It's embarrassing to be reminded of the incest when I don't expect it. I can't let Judy know. I can't tell her how lost and confused I feel. She has been supportive of me around the incest for a long time. I'm ashamed that I'm not whole yet. I worry that my friends think I'm a jerk.

But I won't sit here and allow a bald head to imtimidate me. I have grown past being threatened—even by my own fear.

I look again in his direction on the way to the bathroom, reassuring YoungerOnes that it's not Don. I close the bathroom stall and push out from my chest with both arms. "Get off me you bastard!" I say to him. "I won't allow you to take my breath away again."

I imagine that I am a tree, rooted deeply, with leaves blown by wind. A tree in summertime that has already survived the frost.

Lately, a lot of people tell me that I'm looking good. I didn't know what they were talking about. But on my way out of the bathroom, the mirror catches a light in my eye. My eyes aren't dull as they used to be. My body is filling with life, even in the Dust.

◇

It's been four months since the confrontation and I still feel lost. When I close my eyes I hear Carrie. "I can't see anything yet," she whispers, wiping her eyes. She holds the polished obsidian mirror in front of her face but the only image is the rain of Dust. It feels like the future has evaporated.

"I used to be able to see past my doubts," Carrie says. "I saw the voices climbing, looking strong and resourceful. We were surrounded by friends. The visions felt so right to me. I imagined saying anything I wanted without fear of someone else's response. I was so sure that leaving the Well would bring freedom." The Dust settles like a mantle on Carrie's shoulders while she cries.

For a moment, the confines of the Well seem desirable to me. Then Carrie laughs, "I guess I needed a lesson on emptiness before moving on." She chuckles again, "Now I'm talking out loud to myself and sounding like Sure Voice to boot! It's a good thing Fuckit isn't listening.

"There is a time not to try," she decides, while reassuring herself that nothing lasts forever. She settles cross-legged between Dust drifts and closes her eyes. She feels the breath enter and leave her body. Thinking stops and she surrenders to the touch of falling Dust. I stop searching to find peace with my self.

◇

YoungerOnes leak through my eyes as I sit across from Jean. "We wish she'd been our mother," they say. "We wish she'd be our mother now."

"Sometimes I feel needy toward you," I sneak a glance at Jean and then look out the window. When I first started seeing Jean she told me she'd never be my friend. Fuckit stuck out her tongue and said, "I don't want you for a friend, so there!" But YoungerOnes aren't looking for friendship. They just can't seem to stop wanting someone else to take care of them.

"Sometimes I wish you'd hold me. I wish you'd call and ask how I'm doing. I feel stupid telling you this. I don't want to feel this way about you." I hate this feeling. The need is an ache in my stomach, stretching up to my chest. A hand of grasping fingers that never gets enough touch. The feeling varies with how secure YoungerOnes feel at the time. I've never admitted it before though. I'm afraid Jean will push her chair back against the wall, away from me. She'll say, "This is our last session. You should see someone else now."

She doesn't say anything about my confession. "For the next session," she says, "think about how you're like your mother. Write a list of what you have in common."

A falling sensation twists my stomach. YoungerOnes open their mouths and make sucking motions. Grasping for connections. I clamp my jaw tight, controlling the muscles in my body. "Don't show it," I tell myself. "Don't let Jean know you wanted her to say that it's okay to feel this way about her."

"I don't want to be like my mother," I hear myself say. "I don't even like her. There are other women I'd rather be like."

My breathing tightens. I watch the clock saying two minutes till this is over. As the session ends, I want to punish her for suggesting that I'm like my mother. But mostly I want to make her suffer for not saying it's okay to need her. YoungerOnes hide in Dust. The Dust is real.

I cry in the bathroom. "Well, she didn't send us away," YoungerOnes say. "I just wanted her to say that we matter," YoungerOne 10 says, "It hurt when she didn't."

"I think she likes us anyway," YoungerOne 13 says, drying tears with the back of her sleeve. "I'm not going to do that assignment about our mother though."

After my session with Jean, I donate clothes, stuffed animals and ragged paperbacks to the Goodwill. As I'm leaving, I back my van into a Chevy. The owner appears from Pay 'N Save. He has a custom bumper. "Hard to tell how much damage this might be," he says.

"It's not fair." "I can't handle this, it's too hard." "I don't have enough money to pay my insurance deductible." "Why did this have to happen to us?" YoungerOnes begin their familiar litany, sinking under helplessness.

"Being safe is not the same as having all things go your way," Sure Voice reminds YoungerOnes.

Fear follows, then rage at the Goodwill for planting their donation box in a dangerous parking lot. Bouncing from mood to mood and voice to voice.

When the voices have finished, I am left with a stream of giggles. Since the Well left my belly in the earthquake, there's no container to hold the feelings. They follow one another spontaneously, relaying messages as they leave my body.

◇

Inside of me, Carrie stands and stretches from her meditation on Dust. She sees children when she looks in the obsidian mirror.

"I will take you to them," Sure Voice offers.

Carrie finds YoungerOnes in a shivering tight group in a shallow cave of packed earth.

"We thought you were just going to leave us here to die, Carrie," YoungerOnes accuse, holding the pain. They back away, afraid to accept her and then have to suffer her leaving again. "And Louise just keeps working and seeing Stephanie. She hardly pays any attention to us."

"Aw c'mon," Carrie says, with affection. "We've just been sorting out what we don't need anymore before we go any farther. And I can see that you aren't dead at all. You survived just fine."

"We know how to survive," YoungerOne 10 says proudly, "We want to do more than that."

"We need to be protected," YoungerOne 13 says accusingly, "even if we don't need a mother all the time. Like the other night when we went to the lake to play the drums. A jeep with two men circled us while we sat in the van. We just sat there while they yelled at us. We were too frightened to move."

"There was a can of hairspray right next to you," Carrie says. "We were prepared to protect ourselves. We just have to remember that we can cause change. You've had more practice hiding than in defending yourself. But we have big arms and legs, car keys and a loud grown-up voice. Look at what we've done already. We knocked the Well down."

"So what's next?" YoungerOnes ask, apparently reassured.

"I've got some ideas," Carrie says. "You thought of some of them a long time ago, but you were too afraid to do them. Some writing and singing, learning more about healing. Maybe even some teaching. I think we could learn how to get along with Sarah and Fuckit a little better. We have a lot to learn about intimacy too, I think."

"I don't know," YoungerOne 7 says dubiously. "I don't know how to do any of that stuff—especially with other people."

"You were not born knowing how to walk," Sure Voice says. "You learned when it was time. Your family taught you to be quiet and hide. Now you are learning to be who you are. You choose what you want to learn. You can make as much noise as you wish."

◊

I am the only person at the lake on a Thursday afternoon in late January. I have come to acknowledge my losses with a ritual. I have come to affirm my healing.

I gather dead leaves and heavy rocks. I place my collection

on the wet grass and walk clockwise around it. Dirt clings to my fingers. I walk a circle around the incest. Circling the memory of remembering what I had forgotten. I walk for the time without memory, the time I felt dead and dirty.

I walk for the tears and for the anger that shook my body hard and left me soft in its releasing. My feet mark the times I met my despair and feared that the misery was bottomless. I walk the lies I believed as a child.

I walk the decision to meet Don and to break the silence. I walk slow with the betrayal of my brother. I walk stomping with anger at Don's denial. Clear, stinging pictures. I circle the cord snapped by my mother. My feet beat a path in the grass.

I walk my possession of memory. I affirm my growth with firm steps. I walk aware of my body's shifting balance in walking. I walk embracing the cycles of my woman's body, feeling the curve of my hips and the roundness of my breasts.

I walk for all I haven't learned yet.

I sit in the circle's middle and breathe, surrounded by the distant and the near past. Water meets the rocks along the shore in rhythm. My breath is drawn down low in my body, into my pelvis, moving my torso in long strokes. I draw in my own life on the inspiration. Exhaling, I expel what no longer feeds me.

I part the falling earth inside myself and touch YoungerOne's tight dirty hands. I put my child fantasies of family into a thick oblong rock. I chant goodbye and throw it. The water applauds, leaping up in a dance as the rock sinks. More rocks, holding secrets and terror, self-hatred and denial. Paired with leaves eaten by insects, spotted with disease. The leaves float for a short while and then drown. Just as the beliefs they represent came to the surface and now are abandoned. I say goodbye to the powerlessness I felt as a child.

I throw three thick, misshapen rocks. My arm stretches far, flinging away the bodies of Don, Kevin and Grandpa. The voices listen from their places in the amber dust. I stroke Fuckit's flailing arms. I brush Sarah's worried forehead. I grin into Carrie's deep eyes.

My hands find rhythm with the mallets of my drum, hitting wood in changing pattern. The beat echoes across the lake, amplified between grass and open sky. I play a song for the voices; gentle rhythms for my children, fancy double rolls for Fuckit, a low beat for Sarah. As I play for Carrie, I watch a robin fly free across the sky. For her, a heartbeat, light and strong on the wood.

The trees across the lake are green silhouettes of alder. I look at my reflection for a long time. It wrinkles when the wind blows, but does not fade. I have not lost everything.

◇

It's been eight months since I confronted my family. The voices have been coming back together inside me. Fuckit joined Carrie and YoungerOnes after a long-neglected visit to the dentist. I had stopped going when the dentist's fingers and drills began reminding me of penises. Sitting in the dental chair meant choking and being afraid to close my eyes. But this time, Fuckit claimed my mouth as my own. I imagined healing the wounds instead of fighting the dentist. Fuckit could move again.

Last night when Sarah joined the other voices, the wind blew the last of the Dust away. This morning, the voices are gathered in an excited circle. They stand in a large open space with rich plowed dirt covering their ankles. Above them, a Tree branch the size of a telephone pole waves new bunches of colossal, freshly opened leaves.

"We're here!" Carrie says, "We made it!" She grins and hugs the YoungerOnes joyously.

"What on earth is she talking about now?" Fuckit asks, somewhat disgruntled that Carrie didn't tell her about this part. "Sometimes I wonder about Carrie's state of mind what with all those visions and weird dreams."

18   The Climb

I woke with plans for the future. I'm looking forward to the possibilities of being an adult. For the first time, I don't feel haunted by old mysteries. The raw places in my heart are mending. My arms, grown strong from pushing off the bodies which pinned me down, want to reach forward and embrace new experience. My body has been feeling lighter and full of movement, as if a cycle of discovery and healing has been completed. I feel ready to take new risks.

When I close my eyes, the image I see is in startling contrast to the blackness of the Well and the drab brown Dust. A Tree fills my mind's eye, as fantastic as the Tree of Life embroideries imported from Mexico, but real, as if I too could climb into the clouds. I feel my desire for expansion as the Tree pushes outward, feeding from my breasts, returning breath to the air sacs that hang within my lungs. Its trunk grows deep into my belly, sending roots through my legs, into ground. The branches press upward, winding through unexplored areas of my mind, reaching to the sunlight over my head. I imagine that if I climbed this Tree, I would have adventure and perspective.

The limbs curl and twist into ladders and perches. The limbs branch into sturdy twigs, with flat oblong leaves that span seasonal change, as if the past and future, as well as the present, were always with me. On its north side, a single leaf drops with a sigh to the ground, feeding the soil which grows the Tree, reminding me that all experiences shape my growth.

When I think about all the things I'd like to do, the Tree seems vibrant with color. I see dancing flowers, flowers with secret tunnels inside them, others shaped like breasts, hands and vulvas. The flowers hint at dreams, unanswered questions and creativity. Limbs tipped with buds protect new growth of uncertain color and texture, holding the dreams not yet dreamed. The Tree reminds me of the awe I felt as a massage student considering the mysteries within the skin.

The Tree holds the cycles of who I am and reaches beyond that to my connection with others, reminding me that I also exist in relationship. In the distance I see other people climbing the thousand long-muscled limbs of this Tree. I feel ready to try meeting them, instead of hiding from them.

Emotions open inside of me as Carrie tries to take in the vast kaleidoscope before her. "Some of the dreams are closer to being real," Carrie says. "But there's so much I don't know. I don't know how to trust our creativity or how to move from inside our self to outside. The Well closed our senses. As much as I've longed to be here, I know how to be captive better than how to be free."

I feel myself caught between having a vision and overwhelmed at the thought of proceeding. I am used to surviving and getting through, not to planning for the future. After years of hiding my true feelings, I'm still tentative with other people, not sure how to be open.

Sure Voice chuckles inside the massive trunk. Tiny vibrations tickle the limbs while she talks. "This is the Tree of Everything that Happens," she explains, "As you climb this Tree, you will see that all the flowers, seeds, limbs and leaves on this Tree have a purpose. The destination is not as important as the quality of your journey."

"But what about the clutter on some of those limbs? I think we should save this tree!" Sarah points her finger at the trunk.

"You do not need to prove your self. You were born good," Sure Voice says firmly, looking at Sarah. "At times you will clear debris. But the Tree does not need saving. She grows as you take care of her. You will see."

Sarah looks dubious. "I thought they were supposed to be

healed. But the voices still do bad things, like smoking."

"Healing is a process of knowing yourself with love. The voices will grow out of destructive habits because they will naturally choose other ways," Sure Voice says gently. "You will learn which flowers heal, which ones challenge and stimulate, and which ones intrigue you but leave you feeling empty inside. As for what you do with your time, it is as Jean says: the key is to trust yourself and listen for your time. You are here to learn. Doing is only a vehicle for learning."

"I'm on the committee for the women's cultural festival," Karen is telling me on the phone. "I know you're a writer and you mentioned songwriting too. I was hoping you'd submit some of your work."

"Thanks for calling me," I respond with Fuckit's enthusiasm. "I did see a leaflet about that the other day—I have some songs that I'd like to sing."

Fuckit imagines crowds gathered to watch her stand beside the sky blue trumpet flower on the fifth limb, a half mile across the tree. "What a great flower, huh folks?" She imagines the thunderous roar of an admiring audience.

YoungerOne 10 frowns. "They might not all applaud like that," she warns Fuckit. "What if they throw things instead?"

Sure Voice fixed my eyes on this leaflet a week ago. I dutifully stole it from the bulletin board and conveniently lost it in the chaos of my daypack. I suspect I relegated the whole event to the Siberian recesses of my memory as I've done in the past. Then I could regret the missed opportunity safely after the deadline.

But talking with Karen seemed to stir the flowers on the tree into a riot of exciting color, like the first winds of autumn. For a minute I could imagine standing in front of others and sharing the songs born in the private inner womb of sound. Now, hanging up the phone, my teeth send tight clicking sounds into my skull and the ground feels cold under my tennis shoes. The chill blows up from my feet, freezing my breath, gripping my torso like long male fingers.

◆*Memory*. "Can you sing us a song, Louise?" Uncle Todd bends till his large nose is inches from my six-year-old face. He looks like one of the sunflowers that the wind blows over in his yard. His breath smells like coffee and pancakes.

I sing at Sunday school and church sometimes, but I don't remember any of those songs. Uncle Todd and Aunt Josie, Mommy, Uncle Jack and Aunt Linda, Grandpa and Grandma are sitting in my grandparent's living room after church.

"Come on," Uncle Todd encourages and I remember Mommy showing me a picture of him in a sailor suit in front of a flat microphone and she said he sang on the radio once. The grownups are smiling at me and not yelling so I start making up a song and jumping around with one hand at the back of my neck. Sometimes when I jump around Mommy yells, "You got the sillies, calm down and don't get carried away!"

Thinking of that picture of Uncle Todd makes me brave though and I start singing, "I don't like Grandpa's candy cause it tastes icky, Grandpa's candy makes me sicky," but the grownups aren't watching me, they're talking to each other like they're on a different planet, a taller one with none of my music on it. Except for Grandpa, he says, "That's enough now, Weezy." His hand swallows my shoulders. It feels like the ceiling's fallen down and trapped me there. Then I just want to be a kitten and crawl up under the springs of the big chair like Tiger does.◆

I rock with B. Bear while YoungerOne 6 tells this story, nurturing my self through old wounds. I keep thinking I'm through with the incest, that I can continue without stopping to allow for it. Inside of me, YoungerOne 6 curls into a smooth cranny of the Tree. The other voices surround her protectively. Old fear unravels from a ball in my throat, streaming through my mouth in wounded sound, breaking through locked places in the tips of my fingers.

"Our songs are important," Carrie reminds YoungerOnes. "We can be open and vulnerable sometimes. Other times we can explore the crannies and crevices of the Tree.

"But we have that song about incest that Fuckit wrote. And other songs that come from our feelings, love songs and growing songs that we all wrote together... " YoungerOne 10 says. "We were treated like we didn't have feelings by Grandpa. We pretended to be what he wanted on the outside. So we kept our true self tucked away. We can't lie with our songs. If we don't lie someone might hurt us."

"I won't let us get hurt," Fuckit says, flexing her biceps.

"Sometimes it hurts not to be liked," Carrie gently reminds Fuckit, knowing that Fuckit sometimes wants approval more than the joy of self-expression.

I have known my voice in the privacy of my room, strong and lovely—a melody played by the instrument of my body. Other days my voice creaks and strains, stained by fear and worry. The effort of freeing my voice from the pillows and penises of my past continues step by step.

"If I sing, will it be good?" YoungerOne 10 asks Sure Voice.

Sure Voice smiles, "Singing is a bridge from your inner self to the outer whole, like a limb connecting the trunk to the flower."

Sure Voice never promises that everything will go well.

◇

I thought that the vacation would bring Stephanie and me closer. If we could only play, I thought, everything would be better. Instead, the trip to the Southwest has been a fiasco of mechanical failure, dishonest mechanics and discord between Stephanie and me. The fractures in our relationship widen to gaping holes that I don't know how to mend.

I'm not even sure I want to be in a lover relationship. The

flowers urge me to write, sing, study healing and build a family of friends. When I close my eyes and look into the obsidian mirror, I don't see Stephanie.

But ending this relationship seems like a failure of effort. I'm only now realizing that we've spent the last two years concerned with my process of healing from the incest. Stephanie assumes that now I'll turn my attention toward being lovers. I keep thinking that one day I'll understand how to do that and I'll feel more toward her. But when? Am I just afraid of intimacy?

As the circumstances of our trip deteriorate, we both withdraw and then emerge, slicing each other with the sharp edge of our tempers. We apologize. It's hard to deal with my van repeatedly blowing engines. We're in a dark, air-conditioned motel room, sanitized, smelling like Ajax. A motel room charged on Stephanie's credit card. Stephanie faces me, propped across the bed on pillows, brown eyes alternating wet and fierce. She wants to know if we're going to be sexual, if I'm ever going to work on it. I have heard all these questions before.

What do I owe Stephanie for listening to the horror of my past? Is this vacation a symptom of our breaking apart? Do I have to be sexual if I don't want to be? I can't seem to care about her without betraying myself.

My sexuality is changing. In the last couple of months, rich sexual feelings spin through my body, weaving new sensations of depth and touch. The feelings aren't stuck in my abdomen, but move all the way through me like a scented breath. My thighs and buttocks tingle when I move with myself. I smile instead of cry after I masturbate now because my body feels good. Looser instead of more tensed. Making love to myself is like exploring the dark fertile soil that roots the Tree inside me.

But I don't want to share it with Stephanie. I want to hug my sexuality to myself. Recently, I've even been sexually attracted to other women. I don't know what it means when their hug is suddenly electric. I've always separated being sexual from love. Is that what I'm doing now? Or is the love I feel for Stephanie not sexual?

I promise Stephanie that I'll work on it. I tell her I still want to be in the relationship. I remember our wrestling, adventures, conversations and laughter. When I think of Stephanie going away, I feel a hole in my chest. I don't know if the flowers are really calling me to myself. Maybe I'm reacting to the incest. Maybe I'm confusing Stephanie with my mother. I just want to go home and recover from this vacation.

◊

Stephanie and I have just had one of those arguments that makes both of us feel horrible. I come home to be alone and to understand my anger. Inside, I see Carrie looking at an image of my mother in the obsidian mirror. It's been over two years since her letter. Right now I'd rather watch television, eat chocolate or go out and have a drink than think about her. But our relationship still touches my friendships and my sense of my self. I vaguely remember Jean's question, "How are you like your mother?" A question that I refused to consider. But on some days I look in the mirror and see the lines of my mother's face on my own.

She had many faces—cruel and frightened, masklike and vulnerable, vengeful and battered. The thought of being like her is terrifying. Yet the threads of invisible umbilical cord still ache with wanting connection. Even though I speak to express my own convictions, I'm still trying to convince her. I imagine shaking my mother by the shoulders, saying, "Listen to me!" Then I recoil with shock, remembering her hands on my child shoulders while I sucked my ears away from her voice. "Listen to me, young lady!" she screamed over and over again. In memory, hatred pours over me from her eyes. But now I see that she was seeing the bad girl that she felt she'd been. I became the part of herself that she hated. She blamed me for my pain just as she'd blamed herself for her divorce, never challenging the beliefs about family and religion that she'd been raised with. She taught me how to be a victim, how to be betrayed. But it wasn't a bludgeon consciously designed to humiliate me, it was what she believed.

"I'm tired of understanding you," Fuckit yells at her.

The roar of my adolescent rage at her refusal to hear or see searches for form. My fury laughs at pillow pounding and anger exercises. "I will speak," it hisses, enraged at the memory of my mother violating my diaries and turning my own words against me.

The beginning of a poem. An outburst of lines. Then fumbling with typewriter keys. Fuckit screams, "Damn her. Damn her!" at the ferocious orange dragon flower of inspiration. A thick goo shuts the opening in the flower like a gag tied across a mouth. "Mother has sabatoged this typewriter!" Fuckit maintains. She considers shoving the machine out the window in a grand dramatic gesture.

Carrie hands Fuckit a pen. Feeling finds lines. "The womb is never paid for." Fuckit forgets to light a cigarette until I'm nearly finished. The rage at my mother empties into line and meter. My body looses clenched fists as the words travel from inside myself to the paper. Thoughts appear before they are considered, weaving a subconscious design. My body is filled with light which flows unrestrained.

"You aren't a writer!" a loud voice bellows from the limb above Fuckit and Carrie. I hear my relatives laughing when I say I want to be a writer in response to their question of career. They didn't ask what I would write about.

"It's Sarah," YoungerOnes recognize her shoes through the thick leaves. My shoulders relax. Voices from above remind me of God. As usual, it's only Sarah imitating Him.

My fury roars again, blasting through the binding of old judgement to speak the poem. Words turn the pain of past hatred to affirmation, snagging the elusive truth of feeling. YoungerOnes lead to the center of emotion, taking the courage of Fuckit and the wisdom of Carrie. Carrie translates visions into speech, ignoring the obstacles. I feel ecstacy in rereading the lines, tasting them aloud by candlelight in the kitchen until my voice scratches to a stop, begging for rest.

"Wait a minute!" Sarah objects, "You can't say that about your mother! We're supposed to be celebrating women," Sarah insists earnestly. "We should invent a better mother or think of something good about this one. This is an unfeminist poem. We can't ever let anyone read it!"

"This is a true poem," Sure Voice says firmly. "Creativity can turn anger into vision.

"There is also another mother," Sure Voice looks at Sarah, then at YoungerOnes. "You walk upon her body. Her breasts grow your food. Her spirit is Nature. If you listen, you can hear her words carried by the wind. She says, 'You are my daughter. You live with me.' She spreads a cape of ferns, primroses and daisies around your shoulders. Your wounds suck healing salve from her cape. She is patient. She turns anger into poetry and grief into song. She is an alchemist of ages, wiser with each passing. She does not demand conformity. This mother is always tending and teaching you."

◇

♦*Dream*: I am sitting in the living room of my mother's house, reading in the rocking chair. I'm enjoying the story so much that I don't notice that someone else has entered the room.

My grandfather stands in front of me pushing his penis to my mouth saying, "Grandpa's candy. Suck Grandpa's candy."

I push past him saying, "No. No."

I go out the front door but Kevin's station wagon is blocking my car and I can't leave. ♦

"You have not finished with them," Sure Voice says.

Although I confronted Don, I never dealt with Grandpa or Kevin, because they were dead. Old cords still bind me to them. It has become important to have clean endings so that I am not pursued by ghosts.

The branch the voices have been climbing smells like rotting flesh. The limb itself is covered by slug trails. My stomach cramps. My mouth and throat are stopped by mucus. A sickly yellow flower shaped like a penis undulates over the top of YoungerOnes' head, shaking the limb beneath them.

"I am God," the flower says. Green leaves age and fall from the tree as it speaks. "You're mine. I can do anything I want with you."

"No. No you can't," YoungerOnes' knuckles whiten. "We don't believe you anymore."

"You taught us badly," Carrie begins. "You taught us that everything you did was good, but that we were evil. You taught us that playing was dangerous, that our body was filthy, and that we were worthless. Because of you we thought that work had to hurt us. You're disgusting."

The flower shrinks and withers, blown piece by piece into the wind.

Until now, the anger at my grandfather has been diffuse, a red mist that burned without searing. It was hard to be mad at an old man. The image of my grandfather as God and lord was tempered by my mother and grandmother whispering about my grandfather's "tantrums" in the kitchen. I learned that challenging my grandfather would destroy him just as God could not tolerate other Gods. "Men are just like little boys," my mother said. "It's better to let them win." Men were supposed to "protect and provide." But like a child, my grandfather was never held responsible for his actions. When I told my sister-in-law about him, she replied, "Oh, old men do that. My grandfather 'played around' with me too." As if age gives a license for abuse. As if abuse were "play."

I write a letter to my grandfather. I stand as an adult, next to YoungerOne 5. I write how horrible it felt to be caged between his hands, how near death it felt to have my breath blocked by his penis. I write about my body now, growing strong, full of enough strength to push him away from me.

In the morning, I take a shower and wash Grandpa out of

my body. I dig a hole in the park with a stick. I put a Snicker's bar in the hole. I've always hated Snicker's candy bars. I read the letter out loud as if my grandfather was here. I'm not scared this time. I spit into the hole. I step hard on the earth, pressing the letter and the candy into the ground.

I remember my confrontation of Don two years ago; the linen tablecloth and high booths of the restaurant framing my last memory of him. I don't feel the guilt I experienced for months after the confrontation, when I imagined him stooped low by my accusations, plowing his fields in torment. Instead, I sing my anger at his denial and his guns and at the culture that supports it. I remember looking him in the eye and saying the secret out loud. And telling him that I wouldn't allow his abuse of me, or be silent, any longer.

◊

Fuckit walks past the disintegrating flower of my grand-father, to a black flower with rows of sharp teeth. It reminds me of Kevin. YoungerOnes 11, 12 and 13 throw twigs at it. It's easy to be mad at him.

"You took my body as I was changing to a woman," YoungerOne 13 screams. "I like my breasts now. They're mine. I'd poke your eyes out."

"I've brought Kevin with me," I tell Jean. "I need to finish with him. I don't want to do it alone. I want a witness to this exorcism."

"What do you want me to do?" she asks.

"I just want you to hear me do it."

I pretend he's sitting on the chair in the corner. I wish it had nails sticking up from the cushions.

"How does Kevin feel about this?" Jean asks.

"He feels nervous because he's never been to a healer. But he's arrogant. He's sure that he can convince you that he hasn't done anything wrong, just like he convinced my mother.

"But I know what you did," I point at Kevin. "I hate you for putting toys up my anus. For making me eat shit. For putting your hands in my crotch in your car. I hate you for lying on top of me and calling me names. As if I was the filthy one instead of you. I hate you for dying before I could tell you this to your face!"

My voice has changed from shaking to firm hot anger. "I know now that you didn't pick me because I was awful, but because I was there, convenient.

"But my legs are strong enough to push you off now. My voice is strong enough to bring help on my screams. I am protected now. I give you back your lies. I bury your shit on your body. 'Incest' does not tell the awful things you did to me. But I will name them out loud, in public. I have felt your hands crawl on me for years. Sex became a vile thing through you. But I am not vile or dirty like those names you called me.

"I am fine without your watches. Now I don't have to count the minutes until it's over."

I feel Jean's presence supporting me. "What does he say?" she asks.

"Nothing. He's dead. He died with his secrets and his reasons. I'm glad he's dead."

I imagine his tombstone. I send him back to it. I cry with relief. Jean hands me a Kleenex. We share a smile about all that has passed between us in this room.

◇

"All right! We're going to perform!" Fuckit struts around the room with the acceptance letter from the women's cultural celebration. She practices bowing to applause.

"Uh huh," YoungerOnes say, wide-eyed. "They might not like us. Singing is like showing our insides. We always mess up in front of others." They inch backward on the limb. It looks like a long way to the ground. They imagine falling with a splat.

After all this work on myself, it still gives me anxiety attacks to imagine people looking at me. The anonymous audience becomes hostile judges who want me to fail. My own doubts sound credible in Sarah's inner voice, "So what do you know that's worth saying out loud? It's not like you're Joan Baez or Meg Christian."

I sing at the women's coffeehouse for practice. My voice seems to float outside of my body, eluding key and rhythm. My fear sneers at me from my solar plexus, causing the lyrics to seem small and sentimental. The audience shifts in their chairs. From the stage, their grins appear glued to their faces. I continue, but I've lost faith in the music: hopelessness curdles the melody. The cultural celebration is a week away. I hide inside myself. But when I look into the black inner mirror, I see myself singing.

Sharon offers to help me. We meet regularly to support our mutual creative processes. I've been inspired by her understanding of the relationship between her painting and her growth. I am shy at first—I've never sung in front of her. But she acts as if it's a normal interaction. She fills a bucket with water and suggests that I stand in it to help me feel my feet. If I can stay grounded, my voice won't float outside of my body. Sharon positions a full-length mirror in front of me. "Try looking at yourself as you sing," she suggests, "It's just you."

I see clear eyes, brown hair, a medium-round, strong woman. A learning woman. A woman who falls down and gets up again.

The terror doesn't evaporate completely. I hold the support of Sharon, Stephanie and Jean close while I wait my turn. I hear Jean's words advising me to "sing bad." "I'm good at being bad," Fuckit exclaimed, freed from expectations of perfection. I hear Jean's closing words, "Just enjoy yourself." The singing is for me too.

Looking out from a raised platform, through microphones and wires at an audience of diverse women, stopping for songs in the middle of whatever complex feelings and thoughts they brought with them this day. I offer what I know to now, but what they do with it is beyond my reach. My arms swing long and loose. My whole body is bathed in a field of golden light and pure sound; it is like standing in a shower of glitter. My voice reaches into corners, amplified. My spine is a ladder lifting me taller. A broad, stretching grin fits my face naturally, without pretending. I had fun. I didn't need other people to tell me I was all right. After years of checking myself against the faces of my family, I feel freedom. I am expanded like a hot air balloon, a multi-colored wind-strong fabric sailing next to birds. A sense of myself without closing off from others. Rare moments.

◇

I agreed to see Ann, a healer, with Stephanie. I was afraid that Stephanie and Ann would decide that I was a horrible person. Instead, Stephanie and I have spent the last month airing grievances. Stephanie complains that I don't spend enough time with her and that I'm not sexual. She thinks that I don't hear her. I end up moving farther away from her on the couch where we've divided our territory with a box of Kleenex. I imagine judgement in the tightness of the healer's lips when I say I feel squeezed, robbed of my self.

The voices have been debating my relationship with Stephanie for months. "How dare you leave her now, after all Stephanie's gone through with you. Months of YoungerOne's babbling and Fuckit's rage," Sarah says.

Carrie has argued that we should try to work things out, that we need to learn how to love. But it's finally clear that our present relationship doesn't feel loving.

Stephanie and I sit stiffly apart from each other in Ann's office. "I've decided I don't want to be in the relationship anymore." My voice shakes like string blown in wind. "I really want to be friends. I want to keep coming here and work out the issues between us so that we don't have to lose each other. I don't want to lose you." Water beads in the lines on my hands.

"It's not fair!" Stephanie shouts, crying. "I helped you

through so much. Why don't you work on your issues about intimacy, instead of just dumping me?" Fire joins water in her voice.

I don't know whether to duel or to run. YoungerOnes desperately want everything to be smooth and painless. In the past, they said, "Maybe it will get better." But it hasn't. I try to soothe the wound, "Stephanie, I'm not dumping you. I'm just not getting what I need. I need time to know myself and my creativity." How do I get past this pain? "I know I've made a lot of mistakes. . . "

"Yeah. I'm angry at your mistakes. We should have been coming here a long time ago for help. Maybe we could have saved the relationship then!"

"I don't think it would have made a difference. It needs to be a priority, but in my heart, it isn't. I want my body to myself, I can't keep feeling like I should be sharing it with you."

"Yeah. Now that you've worked through your old stuff you want out. I thought you'd want to be sexual again. I kept telling you it was important to me. When did you know you didn't want to be sexual with me? When did you know you wanted out?"

"I was confused about what was the incest and what was between us."

Guilt is a cold skeleton that whispers, "You should have done something different." But what? I've walked away from relationships before, severing my feelings, pretending that the other person never mattered to me. Just as I felt "nothing" toward my grandfather, Don and Kevin. Or I'd build differences into an angry separation like I did with my mother, abandoning friends to accumulated unspoken discomfort. Treating roommates callously instead of with an open discussion of feeling. This time, I delayed breaking up—hoping we would come to an agreement, not wanting to repeat my own pattern of walking away without looking back. This way doesn't feel good either.

Maybe I should have ended this relationship as soon as I

began remembering the incest. Stephanie gave more to me than she wanted, while saying that my issues were more important than hers. I didn't pay enough attention to what was happening between us, nor did I know myself well enough to articulate what didn't feel right. I wish she was breaking up with me instead. But deep inside of me I know I can't be in this relationship anymore. Breaking up has been a gradual understanding, not a cataclysmic realization.

"I kept thinking that I'd give you comfort and affection, then you'd get better and do the same for me," Stephanie says, appealing for Ann's agreement.

But I didn't agree to pay her back. I didn't know that's what she wanted. What does reciprocity mean? I think about women who support their husbands through medical school. When he finishes, he leaves her. Is that what I've done? But it doesn't seem right to base a relationship on obligation either. Sharon told me a story once, about a neighbor who helped her when she really needed it. "I'm afraid I won't be able to repay you," Sharon told her. "Oh, you'll give something to someone else when they need it, that's how it works." It seems to me the circle of giving is bigger than two. I can't repay Stephanie in kind, but I have given to others from what she gave me.

"Stephanie, I want to be supportive of you. I want to know you. But I don't want to be lovers. I can't. We want different things." My voice crosses between shaking and yelling, wanted her to understand, wanting all the pain to stop.

"You get everything you want. Now you're deciding our future. You're in charge of everything," Stephanie accuses. "I'm still in love with you. When did you stop loving me? What did I do wrong?"

"I still love you. But I'm not 'in love' with you. I'm sorry." Why couldn't we have reached the same conclusion? Why is it so difficult to like each other in the same way, in the same amount instead of expectations and needs forming at cross-purposes.

Later it seems strange that one sentence could rearrange

my life. The flowers I thought were calling me from the Tree look hopelessly far away and less exciting than I remember. I see tears in the inner obsidian mirror. I rock in the rocking chair that Stephanie gave me and cry, remembering the soft comfort of Stephanie's arms.

"I kept telling her that our needs weren't more important than hers," Fuckit says. "I felt uncomfortable when she took care of us. I felt like she wanted something. . . "

"But we wanted to be important," YoungerOnes confess.

"We couldn't know then what we know now," Carrie says. "We just have to be honest. She had choices too. She could have changed the relationship. We both have responsibility. It was hard for both of us to talk about our feelings. Maybe we were too afraid of hurting each other. . . . I wish I'd known how to be a lot more honest a lot earlier."

But shouldn't I want a relationship more than anything else? Isn't that normal? Shouldn't that be more important to me than creativity or chasing visions? Is it selfish to use my time for art? Isn't it wrong to want to meet more people instead of staying where I am? Right now I feel horrible. I already miss Stephanie and it's only been a couple of hours. It feels like when the Well fell apart—the ground tilts and the rules I grew up with don't apply any more.

"You sought healing so that you could fully be yourself," Sure Voice says. "It is not always easy to be faithful to your path. But you have learned to go where you need to go."

◊

Laughter. Greetings. The aroma of herb teas. I am settled in an armchair between Deborah and Selene. We begin in the quiet sound of a dozen scratching pens, starting class by writing without lifting pen from paper for ten minutes. The day tumbles from my arms as I move toward my center and away from the roles I have played. Words come from image and emotion, sculpting meaning from impression, speaking mysteries that reveal me to myself.

Within this room, Coreen shared lines from a poem about her mother's dying. In this room, words have become powerful like crystals, amplified by our collective polishing. We gather as women writing and learning. We study our craft. We read the women who have written before us and beside us. When I look up, I see a smile tugging the corner of Selene's lips as her eyes dance back over her words. I've been coming to these writing classes for six months. I almost didn't make it here at all.

♦*Memory*. "I'm scared to go in there," YoungerOnes huddle behind a waxy pink flower. My heart is beating heavily in my stomach.

"We could skip tonight. We could skip this quarter," Fuckit suggests.

Carrie gently pulls YoungerOnes from hiding. "We don't have to stay. This is an experiment."

Six women sit on couches and floor pillows. Four more arrive later. I smile tenatively and say hello to an Angela and a Kelly. As usual, I can't think of anything to say after that, even though this is a writer's group and as a writer I should have something to say to other writers.

We're instructed to reveal our names and something about ourselves in clockwise order. My heartbeat is a drum pounding against my inner ear. Names blur into the nervous sips of tea. I'm at the far end of the circle. The entire group of intelligent, creative, attractive, powerful women stare at me en masse. My voice comes out in stiff puffs. I mention incest and the book while wishing that everyone would look somewhere else. At the end I don't know whether I've been talking thirty seconds or five minutes.

"Will something bad happen?" YoungerOnes ask. It's still hard to say the word incest in a "matter-of-fact" tone. But Charlotte passes out the syllabus. No one seems to be staring at me with frowns or whispering bad things. ♦
I've had more practice hiding my words than speaking

them. Groups hold an ancient terror for me, like the family gatherings of my childhood. Then, the test was fitting in with the squad of cousins, being compared by virtue of clothing, poise and godliness. Dark secrets and creative tendencies were not acceptable. School reinforced the narrow aisle of approved behavior. I get caught on the old hooks.

"My poem's not as good as Selene's," YoungerOnes whisper anxiously. The children inside me struggle to define themselves using others as the yardstick.

"You can't write," Sarah sneers, projecting her judgement onto an innocent class member who I imagine doesn't like me. YoungerOnes cringe in fearful anticipation.

"I don't give a fuck what anyone says!" Fuckit interjects. I am reminded that I am myself. None of us can write the words of another.

"We are each gifted with our own stories," Carrie reminds the voices. "Together our stories form a mosaic that speaks of women's lives. We are all breaking silence."

Our trust grows as we share rhythm and words. We speak poems of mother-love and mother-rage, of child-pain and children dying. Poetry celebrating lovers and affirming separation. Stanzas of blood and ritual. As we speak our pain, we affirm our healing. In naming our captors we free ourselves. Together we make a new language that embraces ecstacy, with words large enough to encompass the diversity of our lives.

Carrie collects the feedback from the group about my poem. She catches it in a wooden bowl. In my family, criticsm meant that I was bad. Parents held the only truth. I didn't understand then that they spoke from the narrowness of their own beliefs. YoungerOnes swallowed their judgement even when it didn't seem right. Now Carrie sifts through the bowl of suggestions for different words, shorter sentences and the "mmmm" of a good line. I choose suggestions that shine the words, tossing away the ones that don't seem right to me.

I imagine us all holding our bowls and our poetry. My vision grows as I see what I could not see alone. In my family, the father held power at the expense of everyone else. Here, I learn that we can all be powerful. Speaking uplifts all of us. I learn that respect is at the expense of no one. I see beauty in what makes us different as well as what brings us together.

19   THE GIFT

THE sky thickens with clouds promising to lash my kitchen windows with the tail of winter. The wind shakes the chimes in restrained bouts. The newspaper is spread open on the table in front of me, documenting war, rape and child abuse. A jumble of unnamed feelings presses against my ribs. I settle deeper into the kitchen chair, a discontented lump sucking up lethargy like a cat on a heating vent.

"I thought that when we grew up, we'd be safe," YoungerOne 10 says. "I know we're not in that Well anymore. But when I remember all those things happening to us, I know that other bad things could happen too. We could be raped or get run over or be in a nuclear war. It's hard to keep going when I think about what might happen." As she speaks, I feel the tension and longing in my chest magnify. I breathe into the sensation, feeling it as deeply as possible. In the past, my fears spiraled into a consuming panic until I learned to meet the fear and listen.

As I've healed, YoungerOnes have grown. YoungerOne 16 doesn't hide under the round of her back. She tests the world and finds hope in it. She believes in radical change with the energy of the young. I skip across dance floors making faces and laughing. I have no secrets in hiding. I don't have to worry about the sounds or movements that spill out from me. YoungerOnes have taught me play.

Often, Carrie's touch nurtures the parts of me that are tired or wounded. Other times, Fuckit's pep talks will turn fear to fire and the voices will rush ahead. Even Sarah has been known to offer the perfect bit of practical advice at exactly the right moment. As the parts of me learn to work together with love for my self, I am able to take greater risks and explore deeper feelings. But I have not left fear behind.

Carrie leans against the Tree, touching spine to trunk, imagining her toes curled through the roots, reminding me of the earth which supports and teaches me. I consider my healing journey and its consequences. In some ways, my change has been as dramatic as the loud orange flowers which roar from the limb of the Tree like dragons. The voices stand tall, affirming life, choosing caring over self-destruction and healing over denial. When I was fourteen, I vowed I would die before I reached thirty. Now, at thirty-three, I feel more alive than I felt at fourteen. I make decisions I didn't even know were possible five years ago. But some steps are slow. The solidness of trusting the self takes time to develop, like rings growing outward one a year inside the trunk of this Tree. Today, reading the newspaper, I'm overwhelmed by the need for healing which stretches beyond my self.

Carrie closes her eyes and runs fingers through her short dark hair. I rest my forehead on my fingers, soothing the lines left by trying to figure everything out. Thoughts empty from my mind, blowing loose through the sky like clouds. I feel moist sap joining tree with ground. I feel my blood run like the sap, joining me with all that lives.

"As you heal, you help to heal all else," Sure Voice says inside of me. "You are a part of everything. Healing begins in parts. It stretches beyond your self when you speak of what you have seen." Sure Voice sits in the middle of the treehouse floor, ringed by YoungerOnes' child faces, Fuckit's tall defiance, Sarah's tight frown and Carrie's clear eyes. Sure Voice is a sturdy woman with an air of regal antiquity. She is a light swelling the center of my chest. When I listen to her I'm not afraid. When she talks, her words become part of my body.

"When you were small," she begins in her story voice, "I was within you, but you did not know me. Your family told you that all that was holy was called God. They said that God was not a part of you, but lived in the sky. So you looked outside of your self for saving. That was not the way for you.

"You have had help from others, but you must live from inside your self, following your vision. Then you can join with the vision of others without losing your own unique part."

The other voices nod. "But I know that already," YoungerOne 10 says.

"Yet you do not feel safe?" Sure Voice asks pointedly.

YoungerOne 10 blushes and then recovers. "But bad things could happen," she says earnestly.

"Tell me what could happen that you could not learn from? Has the incest only taken from you?" Her questions stand firm in the circle.

I watch, an observer of the voices. Through the incest, I learned that vision can create a new landscape. I don't know the future, but I suspect I won't feel as lost as I felt before I knew the voices. My feelings may be mysterious for a while, but they have never failed to reveal a message, a reason. When I know where the feeling comes from, I can see what's possible.

I have come to trust my journey. It lives within me just as each plant is propelled by an inward force to grow and be itself. The incest is a tragedy. But in searching for healing, I found myself in a way I'm not sure I would have discovered without this challenge. I don't need to separate myself from other people in order to be safe.

YoungerOne 10 still looks dubious. "It's been hard though," she objects.

"Yes," Sure Voice says. "It is like climbing this Tree. Some limbs are easy to reach and wide enough to walk. Others make you stretch and crawl." She pauses and looks softly at YoungerOne 10 for a minute. "Child, have you been without help?"

My memory begins to show me almost forgotten faces who were all a part of my healing. I see women who cared for me at exactly the right moments. Laura, a next door neighbor to my youngest selves. I see her kneeling in front of me, searching my eyes, making the effort of warming me with grown-up attention. I see a fourth grade teacher who told me I was "special." A long line of English teachers and Girl Scout leaders who encouraged me to be creative. I see Mrs. Harding rocking me in her arms after I ran away from home. I see May in Australia with her pottery, teaching me that talk could soften the hard places inside. Now I see that my heart has been touched many times. This touching kept it from being sealed shut, reminding YoungerOnes that there was more than rape and cruelty in the hearts of others. At the time, my pain was so great that their caring seemed like a spare rain which barely covered the bottom of a vast empty bucket. But today I see how the hands of these women shaped the part of me called Carrie. Hands that passed hope and visions of a different future to me. Hands that join with mine in healing others.

"Kate and Jean encouraged your inner growth," Sure Voice says. "They supported your process rather than imposing themselves upon you. They encouraged you to trust your self. That is the task of a healer."

Jean and Kate taught me that being an adult means having power. They helped me to hold the offenders responsible for the incest. Learning that freed me so that I could take responsibility for my self. I think of the intensity of Jean's eyes and of the times she challenged me. Jean let me be both afraid and strong. Kate taught me to listen to the children inside of me.

My friends are family in a way that my biological family never was. Their growth encourages me; we learn from watching each other learn. We strive for relationships where we are both powerful, and sometimes we wrestle over our autonomy. The strong women in my life stop to cry. Sometimes we speak through our tears and frustration, other times we speak through rage. We dance in ecstacy. We are laughing more often. As a child, I learned that strength was the denial of feeling. Now I see that feeling is the key to self-honesty. Within feeling is found the passion for change. "It requires more courage to be moved by emotion than it takes to deny pain,"

Sure Voice says.

Healing from incest is not an easy journey. I think about the women I've worked with and the courage I've witnessed in them. Increasing numbers of women are talking about their experience with incest and about their unique healing journeys. The amount of sexual abuse is horrifying. . . . But Younger-Ones know now that I'm not alone, that I did not make the incest happen.

As I hear other women share their experiences of incest, I hear their horror and pain, but I am amazed by our remarkable strength and creativity in surviving and in healing. I hear women reclaiming their inner children, honoring their feelings and rediscovering the desire to grow and love. I see women moving out of isolation to support each other in groups, to take the risks of telling and to search for healers who empower them. I know women who have grown wiser in their journeys; who have broken the patterns of generations in their lifetime. Around me, as women speak about the violence in their families, they are creating a new awareness that is changing how we create families now. Violence within the family is not so different from the violence that haunts our lives in a wider sense. As we confront the denial of our personal pain, we also face the denial of our collective planetary wounds.

◇

Inside of me, Sarah squirms uncomfortably as I acknowledge my inner voices. Sure Voice looks meaningfully at her and then smiles, as if some message has passed unspoken between them. Sarah whispers into Carrie's ear and leaves the circle.

"You will always carry memories and scars," Sure Voice tells YoungerOnes. "Healing is a lifetime of cleaning wounds and stitching them closed with the threads of creative understanding. As you continue to climb this Tree and move beyond it, you will see how healing reaches beyond your own body.

You will meet fear many times. Fear will continue to teach you courage."

"So exactly who are you?" Fuckit asks Sure Voice. "And how old are you anyway?"

"I never tell my age," Sure Voice says, "people make too many assumptions on the basis of that. I am very simple really. I am a part of you, but I am more than who you are. I have walked behind you and I know the places ahead."

"I think you're a cross between a 'higher self' and a 'human growth cheerleader,'" Fuckit says. "'There is a way up this tree, rah, rah. You can do it. Do not forget to smell the flowers. Rah, rah. Look Louise look. See. See.'" Fuckit twirls a flower as a pom-pom while YoungerOnes giggle.

"Ahem." Sarah's voice is muffled by the large collection of flowers and seeds she's holding in her arms.

"You got them," Carrie says knowingly.

"I don't fucking believe my eyes," Fuckit rubs her forehead with mock vigor. "Sarah—with flowers? And they're not dead?"

"Fuckit," Sarah says through her teeth and then stops abruptly, counting to ten while Carrie squeezes her shoulder.

Carrie whispers into Sarah's ear. My shoulders fall as Sarah relaxes. "I have something to give you all. . . " she begins.

Fuckit starts to sputter and turn away.

"Give her a chance, Fuckit," Carrie urges. "She's not going to make you do anything."

"I um," Sarah pauses. It's hard to imagine her at a loss for words. "I've been thinking about the Well and its Pit. And about the Dust, and this Tree." Sarah looks down and takes a deep breath. Carrie keeps her arm around her shoulder. "I'm sorry that I hurt us sometimes. I know that none of you like me very much because I yell a lot and I'm always telling you what to do.

"I started yelling at YoungerOnes a long time before Fuckit

and Carrie were part of the voices. I had to grow up and take care of us, even though we were still little kids. So many adults said we were bad that I believed them. I didn't even want to associate with the rest of you. I pretended that I was separate. I figured that if I made us perfect, the incest would stop. I thought that if we were good enough, we'd be safe and people would love us."

"Instead, you made us hate our self," YoungerOnes tell her.

"I thought grownups took care of kids by yelling and denying that kids have feelings... But I like you. I believe in you... so I brought you these seeds."

Sarah hands YoungerOnes seeds shaped like tear drops. "I used to tell you not to cry, but I was wrong."

As Sarah and Carrie talk to YoungerOnes, I feel a tenderness toward myself. The resilience of my child selves gives me hope for change and a belief in survival. Their grief, my grief, led me through the Well, washing memory clean.

"I brought you some flowers to play with, too." Sarah hands YoungerOnes a mixed bouquet of orange dragon flowers, blue heart flowers that sparkle with glitter and a fluffly round white flower. A group of tiny question flowers are scattered through the bunch, rusty buds that open into curious shapes.

"You mean we can play and you won't yell at us?" YoungerOnes rearrange the blossoms with a great deal of sniffing, tasting and examination of color. They hold them to the sun, peering closely to see the cells catch fire. They move the flowers into shade, watching the blues deepen. "You're not going to yell anymore?" they ask with disbelief. "What are you going to do if you're not being mean to us?" "Does that mean you're not going to tell us what to do anymore?"

"Now wait a minute, I have plans that I think you should... "

"Maybe," Carrie interrupts swiftly, "YoungerOnes could just play right now... "

"She's never going to fucking lay off us!" Fuckit says in a tight voice.

"I have skills to contribute too, Fuckit." Sarah walks toward her holding a large milky white flower which reveals fine colored threads in the light, like an opal. "If it wasn't for me, your songs would never have gotten any better. I shudder to think of your poetry without my critical intervention. You just don't want to have anything to do with me."

"All right! It's true. I don't like you. You remind me of my family. You don't know how to have fun. You're always fucking comparing me to other people and calling me a failure."

I see the part of me that longs to perform and take risks, stopped by a critical voice. Sometimes it feels like the enthusiasm will blow apart inside of me, held in because of Sarah's threats.

"None of us is perfect!" Carrie steps between them. "But I've seen you two collaborate creatively. Fuckit, sometimes you need a nudge to get where you're going. Sarah is still learning how to respect you. She overreacts because she doesn't want us to be hurt from reactions to your flamboyance."

"This is for you, Fuckit," Sarah holds out the flower. It makes music as the wind stirs its petals. Fine deep blues and frosty reds dance in watercolor designs with the shifting light of the sun.

Fuckit stares at it, stopped despite her pledged animosity.

"This doesn't mean that we're friends," Sarah begins.

"Good."

Sarah snorts but then interrupts her established pattern of retort. "I'm only going to tell you this once, Fuckit, so you better listen. I'm glad you're one of the voices. Your rebellious nature helped us survive the abuse as well as the journey to this Tree. You taught me that I was angry at the abuse, not at the voices. You speak out, like me. I admire your spontaneity. . . even though it's impractical."

Fuckit takes the flower. "I learn from you, too," she says softly while looking at the limb. She struts around with the flower for a minute, admiring the changing colors, singing a tune to the wind song.

"Hey, Sarah," Fuckit raises her eyebrows and grins. "Have you ever thought about being a stage manager? You know, you could handle all those nasty details like phone calls, practice, rehearsal."

"I've been thinking that if you'd only... "

"Sarah," Carrie warns.

"These are for you," Sarah shoves a large bundle toward Carrie and turns away.

Carrie walks around to face her. She diplomatically doesn't comment on the small puddles in Sarah's tired eyes.

"Sure Voice helped me find the flowers for you. She said that the yellow ones give hope, the purple buttons give strength and the spreading white scroll flower tells of endless dreams and vision... I know you'll learn how to use them." Sarah hesitates. "I wouldn't have known that it was possible to heal without you. I didn't believe anything would ever change until you challenged me."

Carrie and Sarah hug, a tall young woman with lines around her eyes and a stooped greying women with deep worry marks in her forhead.

"We both have plans for the future," Carrie smiles. As Carrie looks into Sarah's face, Sarah's tight mouth softens. "I'm sure we'll be climbing together for a long time," Carrie says.

Incest split my mind from my body. The different parts of my self took on attributes of the abuse: victim, abuser, fighter and healer. As I heal, the divisions in my self mend. The diverse aspects of my personality join together in deepening cooperation, creating a new whole instead of a collection of competing parts. I grow in my ability to affirm the qualities of each voice, drawing them into a unified sense of my self, trusting an ongoing inner wisdom.

"Over here!" Sure Voice calls from a distant limb.

"Well I'm ready to go. Let's move the fuck on!" Fuckit begins to climb. "I'm never staying in one place again for twenty-three years, that's for sure. Besides, I want to get a closer look at that lavender trumpet flower. It's going to teach me how to make a lot of noise!"

"Your shoes. . . " Sarah calls.

"I've been having those dreams again," Carrie tells Fuckit.

"Just a minute," YoungerOnes say, fingering a question flower. "We haven't figured everything out yet. What if we fall off that limb? There's a group under that trumpet flower—what if they don't like us? Are we going to make any new friends? What about our sexual feelings?"

Fuckit laces up her climbing boots and takes a small YoungerOne hand while Carrie reaches for another. "What the fuck!" Fuckit says while YoungerOnes continue to ask for currently unavailable information. "Just bring the questions along."

◇

My apartment is full of rocks. I have round stones washed by the ocean and heart-shaped rocks from the bed of the Columbia river. I hold them in my hand when I'm doing something I've never done before. I take a special rock to my writing class and another to doctor's appointments. Often I'll hold a crystal or a bloodstone before I see a client, letting my breath bring calm to my body, stilling my hands until I feel the slow earth pulse of the stone that I'm holding.

I have a beautiful polished slab of obsidian I bought at a rock shop. When I looked into it I could see my face held within its black volcanic glass.

I thought it would inspire me if I could see it while I was writing music, so I propped it up on a table. When I struck the first chord, the obsidian mirror fell backwards, breaking into four pieces. I cried because the stone was precious to me and I knew it would never be the unblemished looking glass that it had been. I glued it together. I looked mournfully at the long cracks until I understood that the mirror is a reflection of me:

scarred from the fall and joined together in a new whole. I see my self in each of its pieces, just as I've come to know the many sides to my self.

I wanted to display the mended mirror on a window ledge but I was afraid the mirror would fall again. I rattled the ledge, slammed the door to my apartment and shook the window, just as I search within my self for balance and security while stretching past my old limits. I placed the obsidian mirror on the window ledge. When I see it there now, I remember that growth involves breaking and healing. And risking a new vision.

LOUISE M. WISECHILD is a writer, musician, bodyworker, teacher and lecturer specializing in work with adult survivors of childhood abuse. She is the editor of the anthology *She Who Was Lost Is Remembered: Healing From Incest Through Creativity* and author of *The Mother I Carry: A Memoir of Healing From Emotional Abuse.* In addition to her non-fiction books and articles, she is also writing a fantasy trilogy, a murder mystery and a play, each of which explores alternatives to violence based on creativity, community and cooperation. Information on her workshops and lectures for survivors and professionals may be obtained by contacting her care of Seal Press.

Selected Titles from Seal Press

THE MOTHER I CARRY: *A Memoir of Healing From Emotional Abuse* by Louise M. Wisechild. $12.95, 1-878067-38-9. Using memory, the voices of inner children and various methods of self-awareness and healing, Wisechild offers a moving testament of recovery from childhood emotional abuse.

SHE WHO WAS LOST IS REMEMBERED: *Healing From Incest Through Creativity* edited by Louise M. Wisechild. $18.95, 1-878067-09-5. This collection presents the work of more than thirty women visual artists, musicians and writers, along with essays by each contributor on how she used creativity to mend from childhood abuse.

NO MORE SECRETS by Nina Weinstein. $8.95, 1-878067-00-1. A beautifully written and sensitive novel for young adults as well as for survivors of sexual abuse of all ages, this coming-of-age story tells of sixteen-year-old Mandy's recovery from a childhood rape.

THE BLACK WOMEN'S HEALTH BOOK: *Speaking For Ourselves* edited by Evelyn C. White. $16.95, 1-878067-40-0. A pioneering anthology addressing the health issues facing today's black woman. Contributors include Faye Wattleton, Byllye Avery, Alice Walker, Audre Lorde, Angela Y. Davis and dozens more.

GETTING FREE: *You Can End Abuse and Take Back Your Life* by Ginny NiCarthy. $12.95, 0-931188-37-7. This important self-help book covers issues such as defining physically and emotionally abusive relationships; getting emergency help; deciding to leave or stay; the economics of single life; and how to be your own counselor. Also available on audiocassette, $10.95, 0-931188-84-9.

SEAL PRESS, founded in 1976 to provide a forum for women writers and feminist issues, has many other titles in stock: fiction, self-help books, anthologies and international literature. Any of the books above may be ordered from us at 3131 Western Avenue, Suite 410, Seattle, Washington, 98121 (please include 15% of total book order for shipping and handling). Write to us for a free catalog or if you would like to be on our mailing list.